South Africa

THE WORLD'S LANDSCAPES
Edited by Dr. JM. Houston

A. J. Christopher
University of Port Elizabeth, South Africa

with a Foreword by

J. M. Houston
Chancellor of Regent College, Vancouver

South Africa

Longman   London and New York

Longman Group Limited
Longman House
Burnt Mill, Harlow, Essex, UK

*Published in the United States of America
by Longman Inc., New York*

First published 1982

British Library Cataloguing in Publication Data
Christopher, A. J.
　South Africa. – (The World's landscapes)
　1. South Africa – Description and travel
　I. Title　　II. Series
　916·8　　DT779

　ISBN 0-582-49001-4

Library of Congress Cataloging in Publication Data
Christopher, A. J.
　South Africa.

　(The World's landscapes)
　Bibliography: p.
　Includes index.
　1. Landscape assessment – South Africa.
2. Man – Influence on nature – South Africa.
3. South Africa – Social conditions. 4. South Africa
– Description and travel – 1966–　　. I. Title.
II. Series: World's landscapes.
GF91.S6C48　　　　　333.73'0968　　　　81-8254
ISBN 0-582-49001-4　　　　　　　　　　　AACR2

Printed in Great Britain by
William Clowes (Beccles) Ltd.,
Beccles and London

For Matthew
Richard
Anne
Sally
Paula and
Sarah

To reflect upon when they are grown up

Contents

Contents

List of figures

List of tables

Foreword

by Dr J. M. Houston, Chancellor of Regent College, Vancouver, BC

Despite the multitude of geographical books that deal with differing areas of the world, no series has before attempted to explain man's role in moulding and changing its diverse landscapes. At the most there are books that study individual areas in detail, but usually in language too technical for the general reader. It is the purpose of this series to take regional geographical studies to the frontiers of contemporary research on the making of the world's landscapes. This is being done by specialists, each in his own area, yet in nontechnical language that should appeal to both the general reader and to the discerning student.

We are leaving behind us an age that has viewed Nature as an objective reality. Today we are living in a more pragmatic, less idealistic age. The nouns of previous thought forms are the verbs of a new outlook. Pure thought is being replaced by the use of knowledge for a technological society, busily engaged in changing the face of the earth. It is an age of operational thinking. The very functions of Nature are being threatened by scientific takeovers, and it is not too fanciful to predict that the daily weather, the biological cycles of life processes, as well as the energy of the atom will become harnessed to human corporations. Thus it becomes imperative that all thoughtful citizens of our world today should know something of the changes man has already wrought in his physical habitat, and which he is now modifying with accelerating power.

Studies of man's impact on the landscapes of the earth are expanding rapidly. They involve diverse disciplines such as quanternary sciences, archaeology, history and anthropology, with subjects that range from pollen analysis, to plant domestication, field systems, settlement patterns and industrial land use. But with his sense of place, and his sympathy for synthesis, the geographer is well placed to handle this diversity of data in a meaningful manner. The appraisal of landscape changes, how and when man has altered and remoulded the surface of the earth, is both pragmatic and interesting to a wide range of readers.

The concept of 'landscape' is of course both concrete and elusive. In its

Anglo-Saxon origin, *Landskift* referred to some unit of area that was a natural entity, such as the lands of a tribe or of a feudal lord. It was only at the end of the sixteenth century that, through the influence of Dutch landscape painters, the work also acquired the idea of a unit of visual perceptions, of a view. In the German *landschaft*, both definitions have been maintained, a source of confusion and uncertainty in the use of the term. However, despite scholarly analysis of its ambiguity, the concept of landscape has increasing currency precisely because of its ambiguity. It refers to the total man–land complex in place and time, suggesting spatial interactions, and indicative of visual features that we can select, such as field and settlement patterns, set in the mosaics of relief, soils and vegetation. Thus the 'landscape' is the point of reference in the selection of widely ranging data. It is the tangible context of man's association with the earth. It is the documentary evidence of the power of human perception to mould the resources of nature into human usage, a perception as varied as his cultures. Today, the ideological attitudes of man are being more dramatically imprinted on the earth than ever before, owing to technological capabilities.

South Africa has special interest because of the political perception it should be a 'White Man's Country' on the southern tip of Black Africa. The measures needed to fulfil this aspiration are discussed factually. The demographic consequences of the Bantu Laws Act of 1964 and the previous acts to channel Black labour into defined areas have not prevented the rates of Black to White population from increasing in favour of the Blacks between 1960 and 1980, because of the White flow of immigrants to the towns. The towns while viewed as White Man's Land, have also eluded this policy of 'White South Africa'. Nevertheless, the political imprint upon the landscape is profound, with a high degree of government regulation in its modifications and controls. The redetermination of boundaries between the Blacks and the Whites has resulted in many previous landscapes being erased and new areas created.

Dr Christopher concludes with the question: Is there a symbolic and distinctive South African landscape? In one sense, yes, each racial group has introduced its own symbolic features. From other perspectives, the landscapes may be contentious of political influences. Throughout his fascinating study of the evolution and character of South African landscapes, Dr Christopher has presented an objective and scholarly review of all the material available in lucid and descriptive language. It is a book all those interested in South Africa will find substantial and challenging to reflect upon.

J. M. Houston

Preface

South Africa presents a unique challenge to the study of landscape in its variety, both physically and culturally. Two approaches appear suitable for its interpretation. The first, drawing upon Whittlesey's paper, 'The Impress of Effective Central Authority upon the Landscape' (1935) in the realm of political geography, seems particularly apt for South Africa. Significantly it is the areas of recent settlement, where the implementation of government decisions may be traced through to their imprint upon the landscape, that offer most scope for this approach. Much of the work in this field has emphasised the colonial situation of settlement involving the layout of towns and the distribution of farms. Johnson's *Order upon the Land* (1976) and William's *Making of the South Australian Landscape* (1974) are contributions of this genre.

Planning legislation of the present century, largely devoted to the urban areas, has produced an even greater body of research as government decisions are implemented to establish new towns and industries. National plans and planning objectives have profoundly affected modern South Africa. Yet planning policies in South Africa have had one facet of a very different nature from those elsewhere. The ethnic complexity of the country has been such that successive governments have viewed the population as made up of separate national entities, to be segregated from one another as far as possible. The segregationist policies developed into the more elaborate, and constantly changing system of apartheid and separate development. The landscape implications of this policy have been far reaching. At the present time some 13 per cent of the country is allocated to the Black (African) states. These contain over one-third of the total population, yet they are predominantly rural and economically dependent upon the major urban areas in the White part of the country. Even within the White areas, towns have been planned for segregation, with separate suburbs for each racial group, separated from one another by waste land buffers. As Smith (1976) stated: 'Apartheid is a distinctively spatial planning strategy . . . a remarkably bold exercise in the spatial reorganisation of society.' Owing to the very inhibiting moral and political overtones of this policy, geographers have not devoted the amount of attention to the spatial aspects that might have been expected. Consequently the impress of central authority is one of the main strands of this work.

The second approach follows the school of cultural landscape history developed by writers such as Sauer in the United States and Hoskins in England. Such studies have recognised that it is in the ordinary yet often highly complex landscapes that the cultural wealth and history of peoples are expressed. South Africa as a 'New Land' of European colonial settlement and an 'Old Land' of established indigenous settlement, offers considerable scope for this approach to the study of its landscape. The evolutionary view pioneered by Hoskins in *The Making of the English Landscape* (1955) seeks to disentangle the historical impress, and so opens up major possibilities for South Africa as the changes in the landscape over the last 500, indeed 100, years have been profound. This is forcibly borne out when it is remembered that Johannesburg–Soweto and the adjacent towns originated with the gold discoveries of the 1880s. Today they are the major wealth generators of the subcontinent and the hub of the South African space economy. The landscape evolutionary school would appear to offer one of the most satisfactory frameworks for the study of South Africa. Inevitably the themes offered and the arguments used are personal. In part this is due to the highly selective and patchy spread of geographical and relevant research and writing available to the author. South African geography has suffered from serious areas of neglect as a result of a lack of manpower and frequent external indifference (Rogerson and Franke, 1976; Stander, 1970). Thus the picture presented of South Africa, as in the case of Hoskins's study of England, *One Man's England* (1978), might be subtitled, 'One Man's South Africa'.

In any work on South Africa certain definitions are necessary. South Africa is taken to include the area designated at the Union in 1910, of the four British colonies of the Cape of Good Hope, Natal, Transvaal, and Orange Free State. It thus includes all the Black states, which have come into being as a result of the South African Government's policy of Separate Development, whether self-governing or independent. The definition of people is rather more problematical. The South African Government has, for census and legislative purposes, divided and subdivided the population into various ethnic groups. The politically dominant group of settlers and descendants of settlers from Europe are now named Whites. The indigenous peoples, except the San (Bushmen) and Khoikhoi (Hottentots), are classed as Blacks, although the terms 'Kaffir', 'Native', 'Bantu', and 'African' have been used as various times. As the newspaper editor P. Quobusa commented, 'My grand-father was a Kaffir, my father was a Bantu, I am a Plural, what will my son be?' Similarly the government department which has responsibility for the affairs of the indigenous population has undergone constant renaming from the Department of Native Affairs, to Bantu Administration and Development, to Plural Relations and Development, and most recently to Cooperation and Development, as established terms took on a derogatory connotation. The indigenous peoples have further been divided on a linguistic basis into 10 'national units'. The two remaining groups are the Asians, descended from nineteenth- and early twentieth-century immigrants from Asia, mainly India, and the Coloureds, who are probably the most diverse group of all including indigenous groups such as the San and Khoikhoi, Asian immigrants of the Dutch period, and those of mixed ancestry. Terminology has been the subject of much political argument, and possibly one of the most controversial questions is state nomenclature. South Africa has granted independence to three of the Black states. They are internationally unrecognised, although they have the external trappings of independent statehood. Should 'independent' be put in inverted commas each time the term is used? This would be tedious and of little consequence. Similarly when the Black states are referred to on the one hand, the rump South African state is, in official terminology 'White South Africa,' while 'The Common Area' is more fashionable in other circles. In general, official terminology will be used throughout, except where it may be confusing.

A. J. Christopher
Port Elizabeth
September 1980

Postscript

In January 1981 the town of Laingsburg was the scene of one of the major natural disasters to occur in South Africa in the present century. The normally dry Buffels River, which flows through the town, came down in full flood, with devastating consequences. The combination of heavy rainfall and soil erosion after sustained drought in the catchment area above the town, resulted in a high rate of run off and deposition of silt. Two-thirds of the original town was destroyed, leaving only the public buildings such as the church and school, and most of the commercial premises, but few of the houses, reasonably intact. Damage to the extent of R12.3 million was caused and over 150 people lost their lives. Although the upper section of the old town is capable of rehabilitation, there are doubts concerning the practicability of rebuilding the remainder of the town on the present site. The disaster, however, does not detract from the value of the examination of the town in Chapter 8, and serves as a reminder of the vagaries of the environment. Ironically Laingsburg was selected as typical of the small South African town simply because of its unexceptional features.

Acknowledgements

Many persons and organisations have rendered valuable assistance in the preparation of this book. It is not possible to acknowledge and thank everyone individually, but I am nevertheless indebted to all of them. I wish to make particular mention of Maré van Renen, Dorothy Mandy and Anna Gamble for cheerfully typing the manuscript. Finally I wish to express my gratitude to my wife, Anne, for encouragement and invaluable assistance during the field work, research, writing and editing of this study. The resultant work is a token of my appreciation.

1
The land

The geomorphological features of the South African landscape represent the present stage in the long history of earth movements and igneous activity responsible for building up the land, and the agents of weathering and erosion whereby it has been worn down. Geologically the history of the subcontinent has resulted in the evolution of a structure which in generalised form is relatively simple, yet on closer inspection reveals a high degree of complexity (Mountain, 1968). Indeed the structural history is still subject to re-evaluation and interpretation (Pretorius, 1979). The geological timescale in South Africa is lengthy, with the oldest rocks of the Basement Complex dating back approximately 1500 million years. The Archaean era Old Granite and highly metamorphosed sediments of the Primitive Systems underly the subcontinent and are at present exposed in an irregular belt from Namaqualand to the eastern Transvaal. These rocks contain a wide variety of minerals including gold, and indeed it is from these rocks that many of the minerals found in later formations are believed to have originated.

Upon the Basement Complex a series of major rock formations were laid down, each separated from the next by lengthy periods of erosion and igneous activity. The pre-Cambrian, Palaeozoic, and pre-Karroo were each periods of extensive sedimentation and outpourings of igneous rocks. Vast igneous intrusions such as the Bushveld Igneous Complex were accompanied by extensive mineralisations and minor volcanic activity. Economically the pre-Cambrian Witwatersrand system with its rich gold-bearing rocks has been the most significant in South Africa's development.

The activity associated with the Karroo period is particularly noteworthy as the sediments laid down in that era have been uplifted and in places virtually horizontal extents of these rocks cover approximately half the country. These deposits include the most valuable coal measures, with individual seams of as much as 8 m average on the Witbank field. During the Karroo period the Cape Mountain building era occurred, when the extensive pre-Karroo sediments on the margins of the subcontinent were folded into a series of mountain ranges trending north-north-west to south-south-east and

1

east to west. The junction area of the two sets of folds in the south-western Cape is one of the most complex relief areas in the country. Towards the end of the Karroo period the interior plateau was covered by extensive lava flows of the Stormberg series which erupted from a series of fissures and vents.

At the close of the Karroo era a long period of relative stability ensued, during which slight warping in the interior plateaux occurred, tilting the Karroo rocks by 12° in places. On the eastern and southern margins monoclinal flexuring and faulting associated with the break-up of the Gondwanaland super-continent produced an outline for the subcontinent more akin to that of today. The faulting and flexuring to the north in the Limpopo Valley and the Lebombo Range was associated with the development of the great East African Rift Valley system. It was in this period that the highly significant kimberlite pipes were erupted, from which diamonds have been mined. The break-up of Gondwanaland was of such a form, that with the exception of the Aghulas Bank, there is little continental shelf off the South African coast.

Since Jurassic times South Africa has been subjected to several cycles of erosion separated by periods of uplift and warping. During these eras deposition on the fringes of the subcontinent took place and in early Pleistocene times extensive sand deposits were built up in the Kalahari basin, the southernmost of which extends into the northern Cape. Finally the most recent continental uplift has produced a series of raised beaches, which are particularly well developed on the southern and eastern margins of the subcontinent.

In terms of landscape formation the post-Karroo erosion cycles have substantially removed vast thicknesses of the more recent deposits, particularly the Karroo system, to reveal the rocks of previous ages around the margins of the country especially in the north. The extensive Stormberg lava flows have been reduced to a limited area in Lesotho and adjacent areas, where they form the highest land surfaces and exhibit the remains of the earliest of the recognisable planation sequences. The present movements are slight and little noticeable earth movement takes place, while vulcanism is extinct.

In terms of minerals the country is remarkably richly endowed (Table 1.1). In addition to the gold and diamond deposits most other minerals and metals occur somewhere within the country, with the significant exception of petroleum. This has provided the country with an industrial and financial base with which to pursue policies which have been condemned by the rest of the world, yet face the prospect of sanctions with relative equanamity. The foundation of this is gold, of which South Africa accounts for close to 60 per cent of world production, and in 1980 paid for two-thirds of all South African imports. Coal and iron have supplied the basis of an iron and steel industry and the energy required to fuel industrialisation, as well as providing export commodities. Despite the wide range of minerals, their occurrence is essentially concentrated within the Transvaal, which has one of the major mineral assemblages of the world; although this was only realised less than 100 years ago.

Table 1.1 South African mineral production 1980

	Value 1980 (R million)	% of world production 1979	Rank as producer
Gold	10 370	53	1
Coal	1 495	3	7
Diamonds	553	18	3
Copper	300	3	11
Iron ore	296	4	9
Manganese	145	22	2
Asbestos	101	5	3
Chrome	90	36	1
Vanadium	★	45	1
Platinum	★	51	1

Source: Department of Mineral and Energy Affairs.
★ Figures are not made public.

Physiographic features

The Great Escarpment

The dominant relief feature of South Africa is the Great Escarpment which divides the country into two distinct physiographic regions – the interior plateaux and the marginal lands (Fig. 1.1). The Great Escarpment itself is formed by the headward erosion of streams cutting back into the plateau, and is most pronounced where the streams have encountered resistant rocks and where it separates erosion surfaces of different ages. The most spectacular section is the Natal and Cape Drakensberg Ranges between Natal and the eastern Cape, where the Stormberg lava series is most complete and the plateau surface levels most elevated. Thus at Mont-aux-Sources the escarpment face is over 2000 m in height, and on either side relative reliefs of 1000 m are not uncommon (Fig. 1.2). The highest parts of the subcontinent are to be found in this area including Thabana–Ntlenyana just inside Lesotho, with an elevation of 3482 m. Indeed this section of the escarpment is so formidable that in a section of 350 km only three roads traverse it.

On either side of this central portion of the Great Escarpment it is less spectacular, and far less formidable a barrier to transportation, but still well marked. To the north of the Lesotho Highlands the Escarpment is in places only a minor feature and is much dissected, with remnants of the plateau isolated to the east of the main feature. In the eastern Transvaal two escarpments appear as steps from the plateau to the margins. In places the relief features are striking as for example Mount Anderson near the Swaziland border, which rises to 2285 m with a 1000 m escarpment. But this is a rare occurrence and the Transvaal Drakensberg tends to disappear towards the north. In the southern and western Cape the relative height of the Great Escarpment is related to the presence of intrusive dolerite sills within the Karroo rocks.

3

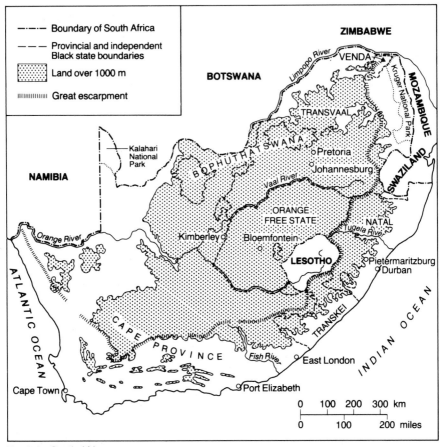

Fig. 1.1   South Africa.

Thus a series of mountain ranges extend from the vicinity of Calvinia to the eastern Cape. Two major breaks occur, in the vicinity of Beaufort West and where the Great Fish River breaks through from the interior. On the western margin the escarpment is a poorly defined feature south of the Orange River.

The plateaux

The interior plateaux form the major physiographic province of the country, covering approximately two-thirds of South Africa. In broad terms the plateaux rise from the west at elevations of 1000 m in Namaqualand and Bushmanland, to 2500 m in the Highveld region of the northern Orange Free State and southern Transvaal. Most of the plateaux are drained by the Orange–Vaal River system which flows into the Atlantic Ocean. The margin of the drainage basin coincides with the Great Escarpment for most of its length on the southern and eastern margins. It is only in the northern Trans-

Fig. 1.2 Mont-aux-Sources, Drakensberg, Natal. The escarpment forms one of the major physiographic barriers in South Africa. It is an area of spectacular scenery which attracts tourists and mountaineers. (Satour)

vaal that drainage flows into the Indian Ocean, either through the Limpopo system or directly by breaching the Great Escarpment.

The plateaux rise in steps, with the marked relief features frequently in the form of flat-topped dolerite-capped hills in the south where the Karroo system is exposed. In the north the more complex older rock systems interrupt the plateaux with ranges of hills such as the Waterberg Range of the western Transvaal, which rise approximately 700 m above the general plateau levels. In the main the relief features are subdued and few present any problems for transportation. The generally level nature of the landscape and low gradients for the rivers introduce a certain degree of monotony, yet have their own particular appeal.

On the outer margins of the plateaux the levels tend to rise towards the Great Escarpment, as remnants of the Stormberg series remain in the eastern Cape and the eastern Orange Free State or where other more resistant rocks in the Karroo series form marked relief features (Fig. 1.3). Most of the features appear to be structural, although the successive pediplanations of the subcontinent have been propounded by King (1963) as an explanation for the interior plateau surfaces. The chronology of denudation appears to be highly complex and related to a long timescale from the breaking up of the supercontinent, Gondwanaland. Within most of the interior the agents of weathering of arid and semi-arid climates have been dominant, and hence the detailed features range from the barchan dune fields of Gordonia to the extensive pediplains of the western Orange Free State.

The marginal lands

The marginal lands below the Great Escarpment may be divided, in landscape terms, into three broad regions: the southern Cape folded mountain belt, and the eastern and western margins on either side of the mountains. The marginal lands vary in width from 200 to 300 km on the southern and eastern extremities but are less than 80 km wide in the west.

The Cape folded mountain belt is a distinctive landscape region of South Africa consisting of a highly complex folded structure with parallel ridges separated by long valleys, where the less resistant rocks have been removed (Fig. 1.4). Thus some valleys are anticlinal and others synclinal. The two sets of folds are basically simple so that the valleys are long, extending for up to 400 km along the south coast and 200 km along the west coast. The greatest complication occurs where the two folding trends meet in the Drakenstein region and it is here that the highest elevations occur such as the Matroosberg (2251 m) in the Hex River mountains; although the Swartberg between the Great and Little Karroo achieves the peak elevation of 2326 m. Within the overall structure a number of major and minor basins occur such as the Great

Fig. 1.3   Mesas, eastern Orange Free State. The almost horizontal bedding of the rock formations over large parts of the South African interior has resulted in distinctive hard rock capped hills with extensive scree slopes. (Satour)

Fig. 1.4 Folded mountains, south-western Cape. The folded mountain belt is a highly distinctive physiographic province with a complex set of valleys and mountain ridges. Marked contrasts in climate are reflected in abrupt changes in vegetation composition. (Anne Christopher)

and Little Karroo, and the Elgin and Ceres basins. The contrast between the highly resistant Table Mountain sandstone forming the mountains and the weaker shales forming the lowlands is most marked, with the result that the Cape folded mountain belt is scenically a most spectacular landscape.

The Namaqualand coastal belt is narrow and consists essentially of the lands below the Great Escarpment, which are generally not a spectacular feature in this region. However, the coastal belt is arid with the result that a distinctively desert form of landscape has developed. The marginal lands to the east of the Cape fold belt are more spectacular, being formed on the approximately horizontal beds of Karroo and earlier age rocks. This simple structure is complicated by a monocline through eastern Natal which results in an oceanward tilt to the rocks in the coastal belt. Thus the oldest basement rocks are exposed in the centre of the monocline. The eastern marginal lands have been subject to massive erosion by a series of eastward flowing streams which through headward erosion have caused the Great Escarpment to retreat. The land is thus more broken and dissected than the other regions of the country. It is only in the north of Natal that a true coastal plain has developed and a flat low level surface has been formed.

The coastal belt possesses few natural harbours. In the main the shores appeared to be inhospitable to navigators during the Age of Exploration and the Portuguese thus settled in Angola and Moçambique rather than South Africa. The southern Cape coast backed by the folded mountains has a number of bays, but few that are sheltered, and generally cliff coastlines and bars across the valley mouths deterred landing. On the eastern coast a number of major lagoons such as Durban, Richards Bay and Lake St Lucia were blocked by sand bars.

Also lacking are navigable rivers. The interior is drained by the Orange–Vaal system, which loses much of its volume to evaporation. Navigation is further hampered by rapids and the Augrabies Falls. The other rivers are relatively short and lack volume because of small catchment areas and limited rainfall. The rivers also suffer from steep gradients in the better watered eastern side of the country and because of the recent history of uplift have irregular long profiles with rapids and waterfalls. Thus movement within the coastal margins was limited and often difficult, in contrast to the ease of transport experienced in the interior.

Climatic constraints

South Africa, because of its latitudinal and altitudinal extremes, experiences a wide range of climatic types (Jackson and Tyson, 1971). Broadly its location between 22° and 35° south of the Equator places it within the zone of the tropical anticyclones. These, because of the comparatively narrow extent of the continent compared with those of the northern hemisphere, are more stable and exercise a continuing influence throughout the year. However, in summer some weakening of the anticyclone over the land allows for the develop-

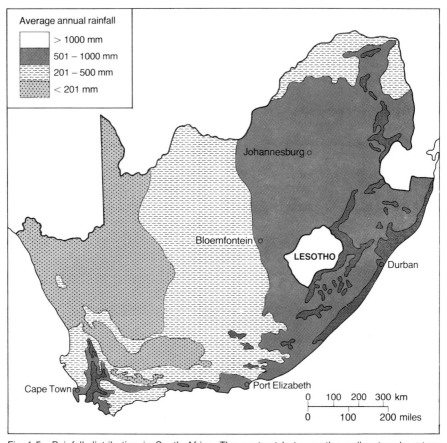

Average annual rainfall

> 1000 mm

501 – 1000 mm

201 – 500 mm

< 201 mm

Johannesburg o

Bloemfontein o

LESOTHO

Durban

Cape Town o

Port Elizabeth

| 0 | 100 | 200 | 300 km |

| 0 | 100 | 200 miles |

Fig. 1.5   Rainfall distribution in South Africa. The contrast between the well-watered eastern and southern regions and the dry interior is most apparent. Lack of water is one of South Africa's most pressing problems. (After South Africa, 1970)

ment of weak troughs of low pressure over the eastern interior, resulting in an inflow of moist air. In winter the northward shift of a few degrees of latitude in the paths of the westerly winds of the southern oceans, results in an influx of moist air associated with a series of depressions affecting the extreme south of the subcontinent.

The atmospheric circulation pattern gives rise to a marked seasonality in precipitation patterns, which are the most important elements within the overall climate of South Africa. In terms of the annual average rainfall there is a noticeable increase from west to east (Fig. 1.5). If the rainfall figures along the line of latitude of approximately 29 °S are taken from Alexander Bay on the Atlantic coast (41 mm), Upington in the western interior (156 mm), Bloemfontein in the eastern interior (504 mm) and Durban on the Indian Ocean coast (1008 mm), the gradation is well illustrated. A second area of higher than average rainfall occurs in the extreme south of the country, but this is limited inland by the mountain ranges, which block the progress of the moist air. Here the pattern of relief is particularly important with high rainfall totals on the mountains and lower precipitation on the lowlands. Thus Cape Town receives 600 mm but the nearby mountains receive up to 3000 mm. A similar phenomenon is noticeable in the eastern marginal areas where the major river valleys exhibit some degree of aridity, compared with the interfluves between them.

Rainfall totals are low, as over half the country receives under 400 mm. Added to this are the high evaporation rates. Potential evaporation losses vary from over 3000 mm a year in the north-west of the country to under 1500 mm in the midlands of Natal. Continuous and heavy evaporation losses restrict agricultural potential, so that only one-third of the country is climatically capable of sustained crop raising, without irrigation. The aridity of South Africa is most marked, as the mountains of the south-western Cape block rain-bearing winds into the interior, creating an extensive rain shadow effect. Thus parts of the south-western interior of the Cape Province receive only 100 mm (e.g. Laingsburg), while stations on the windward side may receive several hundred millimetres. The contrasts in precipitation over short distances characterise this area.

Apart from a small zone on the southern coast the rainfall regime is highly seasonal in character. North of the Cape fold mountain belt rainfall is predominately a summer phenomenon, with a pronounced lack of winter rainfall except on the east coast. Only in the south-western Cape is there a marked winter rainfall regime, but this peters out rapidly to the north as increasingly arid conditions are met. On the southern coast this merges into the summer rainfall area more gradually, with an all-the-year round regime in the vicinity of Port Elizabeth at the eastern end of the folded mountain belt.

The other marked feature of the rainfall regime is the degree of variability. Relative variability of annual rainfall in the eastern interior and the eastern and southern coastal belts is less than 25 per cent, but it increases westwards to reach 50 per cent in the lower Orange River Valley and higher figures are encountered on the arid coast. As a result drought is a recurrent problem over large areas of South Africa, but it is not a concept to which the agricultural industry has adjusted. Investigations have suggested that a 20-year cycle with other shorter-term cyclical fluctuations are normal, with the result that although droughts may not be accurately predicted, they may be expected as an integral part of the South African climate (Tyson *et al.*, 1975). Hence the warnings of another drought period for the 1980s (Tyson and Dyer, 1978).

The temperatures experienced at South African meteorological stations range from annual averages of 11 °C to 23 °C. These averages hide substantial variations resulting from the effects of continentality and altitude as well as latitude. There is a greater range of temperature in the centre of the country namely the northern Karroo, and least variation on the west coast. Thus Alexander Bay has an equitable temperature range but interior stations may

11

experience a difference of 20 °C between the average for the warmest and coldest months. Temperatures in mid-latitudes present few difficulties of human adaptation, although the same may not be true of domesticated plants and animals.

Probably the incidence of frost is the single most significant factor for agriculture. At the coast frost is absent, but inland, even a few kilometres, it becomes a possibility. The average number of frost days reaches over 100 in the Drakensberg Range, but is approximately 60 days over a large area extending from the interior portion of the south-western Cape to the eastern Transvaal. The period during which frosts may occur is similarly longest in the Drakensberg where frost may be experienced for over half the year, while extensive areas of the high plateau may experience frost over a period of 120 days. Only the coastal belt and the northern half of the Transvaal have frost-free periods exceeding nine months of the year. In the interior frost may take the form of black frosts where no ice crystals are formed, but the vegetation wilts and turns black as a result of the cold.

At the other end of the scale high temperatures are experienced in the northern and north-western areas of the country, together with basins within the coastal belt such as the Great Karroo. In general high temperatures in the interior are fairly constant in the summer months, although locally conditioned by cloud cover. On the coastal margins rapid increases in temperature may occur when the circulation is such as to draw air off the plateau so that it heats adiabatically to form the hot *Föhn* or '*berg*' winds. High temperatures, often allied with high humidity, have adverse effects upon the human occupation of parts of the Natal coastal belt and the lowlands of the eastern and northern Transvaal. In the past it was often the diseases associated with these conditions which made them hazardous, rather than the temperatures themselves.

South Africa is relatively poorly endowed with water resources, with two-thirds of the country receiving an average precipitation of under 500 mm per annum. Half of this area receives under 250 mm per year. Moreover, the eastern margins which receive the highest rainfall also experience the greatest tempo of runoff, with only a limited area suitable for irrigation. Furthermore with high evapo–transpiration rates it has been estimated that only 8.9 per cent of the average rainfall flows away in the rivers. An added problem is the decline in runoff in recent years. Figures produced in the 1960s suggested that the average runoff had fallen by 20 per cent in 20 years in the country as a whole, while in certain areas the decline had been as much as 80 per cent (South Africa, 1970: 58). It is important to emphasise that this decline has occurred without a reduction in rainfall. At the same time runoff has become more rapid with the problem of periodic floods, requiring flood control measures, especially on the Vaal River. A measure of the variability of runoff may be illustrated from Kenhardt, where the Hartbees River recorded over half its runoff for 30 years in a six-month period in 1961. While the Molopo River, on the northern border of the Cape Province, with a catchment area of 250 000 km^2 has not flowed into the Orange River for over 100 years.

Clearly the provision of an adequate water supply has been one of the limiting factors in the development of South Africa. The agricultural industry is much dependent upon irrigation and water supply. Industrially the siting of the major metropolitan region on the main watershed has presented grave problems as water has had to be obtained from increasingly greater distances, including the transfer of water from the Tugela River system of Natal into the Vaal River. Similarly diversion of water northwards from the Lesotho mountains is in the planning stage. Water, or rather the lack of it, has been a powerful influence on the attempts to decentralise the South African economy.

South Africa lacks the major artesian basins found in countries such as Australia. Small ground water resources are tapped in suitable formations such as the dolomite areas of the south-western Transvaal, but less than 10 per cent of the country's requirements come from underground supplies. Most water comes from the collection of surface supplies in dams, but this is problematic owing to the high evaporation losses. Thus as much as two-thirds of the inflow into dams in the central Karroo is lost by evaporation, compared with less than one-tenth in the high rainfall regions.

The ecosystems

The vegetative covering has provided one of the best indicators of agricultural and pastoral potential, and so was carefully noted and its changes investigated, as a measure of the agricultural and pastoral misuse of the land (Acocks, 1975) (Fig. 1.6). The dynamic nature of the vegetation in the face of man's activities has increasingly been recognised. There is no evidence to suggest that the climate has changed significantly in historic times, yet the vegetative pattern has altered markedly (Kokot, 1948). This reflects active clearance of land for agriculture and the introduction of intensive and selective grazing activities in the drier parts of the country. As a result the ecological balances have been upset and deterioration and change have resulted.

The broad vegetation zones reflect the climatic and altitudinal zones, although the foregoing comments must be borne in mind. In general terms the western plateau core of South Africa is covered with a sclerophyllous desert and semi-desert scrub (the Karroo) (Fig. 1.7). This merges eastward into grasslands and at high altitudes in the Drakensberg into tundra conditions. Around this core to the north and in the lower altitudes a savanna bush vegetation is dominant. This vegetation grouping exhibits a considerable range of forms merging into the Karroo, the grasslands and the remnants of the east coast tropical forests. In the southern and western Cape the Mediterranean climatic macchia (fynbos) is limited in extent to the better watered areas. Remnants of the temperate evergreen forests survive where

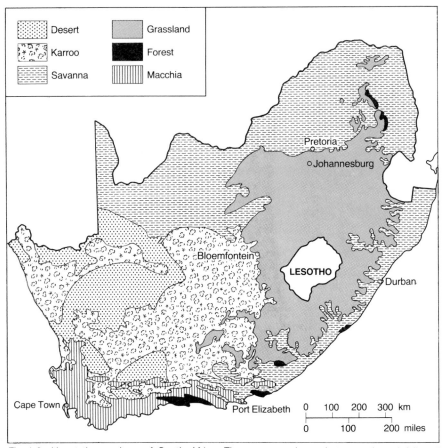

Fig. 1.6 Vegetation regions of South Africa. The correspondence between the rainfall and vegetation maps is most marked, but owing to the dynamic nature of the vegetation systems, substantial advances of Karroo (semi-desert plants) have taken place since the map was compiled. (Adapted from Acocks, 1975)

rainfall totals are particularly favourable and where felling has not been too devastating.

The subtropical and temperate forests today occupy scattered patches along the line of the northern Drakensberg and in the Natal coastal belt, but are most extensive in the southern Cape in the vicinities of George, Knysna, Alexandria and King Williams Town. The subtropical forest of the coastal plain has largely been destroyed and secondary jungles with wild dates, wild banana and lianes now merge into the grassland and thornbush savanna lands. The temperate forests cover some extensive areas, with the tallest trees achieving heights of 50 m, but usually they are far less impressive. Species of yellowwood, stinkwood, ironwood, etc. were originally much sought after for constructional timber for houses, or machinery. Today the main demand comes from furniture makers, and felling is tightly controlled as most of the remaining forests fall into government reserves.

14

Fig. 1.7 Karroo vegetation, Prince Albert district. The semi-desert and arid regions of South Africa are covered with a variety of plants of which the salt bush is the most common. Overgrazing has reduced the plant cover and increased erosion, particularly sheet erosion, thereby removing the top soil and exposing the rock fragments below. (Anne Christopher)

The Cape macchia or sclerophyllous bush occupies the southern and western Cape. Owing to the long dry summers, plants have had to adapt to either going though their life cycles in the winter under cool wet conditions, and then survive the summer heat in a dormant state, or go through their entire life cycle within a few weeks in spring. Low bushes of 1–2 m are the commonest form with plants possessing extensive underground bulb systems and small leaves. Probably the best known types are the proteas, which are the South African national flower. It is noticeable that grasses are almost completely absent. Some trees such as the cedars of the Cedarberg survive, while other evergreen trees occur in clumps in sheltered ravines.

The savanna lands occupy an extensive area of South Africa occupying much of the northern and eastern lands below an altitude of approximately 1500 m. Frost controls the upper limit, while increasing summer aridity restricts its coastal extent. The savanna bushlands include a wide range of vegetation species with an upper stratum of umbrella-type trees and an undergrowth of grasses. Most trees have drought resistant qualities where the leaves are reduced to thorns, hence the common appearance of thorn trees. Also marked water storage facilities are needed so that extensive underground root systems support life in the dry season, and incidentally bind the soil, making it more resistant to erosion. The water-storing baobab tree, together with the fever trees lining the water courses of the northern Transvaal are noticeable variations (Fig. 1.8). In the drier Kalahari the trees become more widely spaced and the grasses cease to provide cover but break up into clumps which again become sparser as aridity increases. Similar transition zones are present elsewhere (Fig. 1.9).

The true grasslands are of limited geographical extent, as they grow where drought, severe night frosts and winter temperatures hinder the growth of the indigenous trees. Significantly, imported Australian and European trees are able to survive in such a climate. Two main types of grassland are distinguished; the short, sweet, varieties, which are limited to the drier margins of the grassland zone, and the tall (3 m+) sour, varieties of the eastern and northern parts of the grasslands. In between is an extensive area of mixed grasslands. The seasonal nature of the sour varieties used for grazing purposes had a marked effect upon the seasonal farming practices of early pastoral herdsmen and farmers in the Orange Free State and Transvaal, who practised a form of transhumance. The grasses tend to grow in clumps, with extensive root or rhizome systems, which if disturbed can severely weaken soil cohesion. At high altitudes the grasses become lower and a short alpine grassland appears, merging into a true tundra vegetation in the higher portions of the Drakensberg.

Fig. 1.8 (*Above*) Baobab tree, northern Transvaal. The savanna or bushveld regions include a wide variety of plants. In addition to the thornbushes and mopane trees, the baobab's water storage capacity enables it to survive in the dry and hot northern areas of the country. (Satour)

Fig. 1.9 (*Below*) Aloes, northern Transvaal. Another aspect of the savanna regions with mixed aloes and euphorbia bushes. (South African Railways)

The core of South Africa is covered with Karroo bush and scrub. Within this area low rainfall of under 400 mm per annum, together with high annual and diurnal ranges of temperature limit the possibilities for plant growth. As a result the vegetation consists of stunted woody scrub and succulent plants, which are widely spaced in the soil. The degree of coverage decreases westward. In the eastern areas grasslands appear but the grass content also diminishes westward and in years of low rainfall. On the western coastal margins virtual desert conditions prevail with characteristic desert succulents. Although a considerable range of vegetation exists within the Karroo, probably more than any other vegetation type it is subject to varying appearance according to the season or the longer-term fluctuations in rainfall. Thus with a high degree of rainfall variability the Karroo lands present different vistas in different years; and hence owing to selective grazing practices the carrying capacity varies accordingly, and assessments of the potential of these lands have been widely divergent.

Changes in the ecosystems

The impact of man has been particularly devastating upon the vegetation, as the process of desertification has been marked on the critical Karroo–grassland border, and deterioration of the vegetation in other sensitive ecosystems such as the forest lands has led to a major retreat of both forest and grasslands. Although unsuitable grazing practices have probably been the most important cause of deterioration, the ever increasing demands placed upon the tree and shrub cover for building material and for fuel have been disastrous, particularly in the Black areas, where population pressures have built up. Wood remains one of the major sources of fuel in the Black areas and among the Black population on White-owned farms. The cumulative effects of timber cutting have effectively changed the character of the vegetation over large areas, and this process shows little sign of abating (Feely, 1980).

One of the problems of the physical environment of South Africa has been its sheer size. It has always been regarded as a large extensive country with plenty of land for agricultural purposes. As a result little attention was paid to such aspects as soil conservation while both Black and White farmers considered that the solution to their problems lay in moving on to fresh lands. In addition, for the pastoralist there is the belief that the grazing ground is only brought to full value and productivity after it has been 'tamed' by trampling. This may have been true of isolated areas but has in the main been conducive to the destruction of delicate vegetation communities and wholesale soil erosion. Thus soil erosion has been one of the major themes of South African agriculture since the spectacular drought of the 1930s, if not before (Fig. 1.10).

The results of overgrazing in particular have been far reaching. The vegetative cover has been weakened in large parts of the country with the result that droughts have become more serious in terms of damage done.

Fig. 1.10 Soil erosion, near Vryheid, Natal. The ploughing of environmentally marginal lands has led to large-scale soil destruction. Once the binding force of the top soil has been removed there is often little resistance to the removal of the lower horizons to expose the bedrock, producing gulleys (dongas) 10 m or more deep. (South African Railways)

Vegetation loses its regenerative capacity so that successive rains become more damaging to the top soil and a vicious cycle of decline continues. As a result desert and semi-desert vegetation has extended eastwards and northwards, although in terms of climatic statistics there has been no change. The grasses in particular have been subject to retreat and replacement by Karroo shrubs and thornbushes. These in turn have weakened the soil to erosion and allowed in new pests, which did not flourish in the grasslands. In the northern Cape virtually impenetrable thorn trees have invaded approximately 2 000 000 ha, making it impossible for use as grazing. It is the advance of the Karroo plants which has excited most notice. Karroo pioneer plants have spread over all but the easternmost fifth of the country, but the advance of the continuous cover of Karroo plants at the expense of the grasslands has been noted from ERTS (Earth Resources Technology Satellite) photographs to have been as much as 70 km in the most exposed parts of the Orange Free State in the period 1953–72. Unfortunately it is often the palatable species which are selectively grazed leaving the poorer ones behind, whether it is grass species or Karroo bushes. This is in contrast to the previous state of affairs when the indigenous animals grazed a wider range of plants. Thus grazing capacities have been reduced and the possibilities of reclamation diminished. Projected patterns indicate that by the middle of the next century the desert will have advanced 300–400 km eastwards. The steppe-type Karroo vegetation will have advanced at a similar rate towards the east and towards the north, resulting in the permanent loss of grasslands in the northern and eastern Cape and the central Orange Free State.

2

The people

The archaeological background

The archaeological and anthropological evidence for the occupation of South Africa by man covers the last two million years (Inskeep, 1978). Sites inhabited by Stone Age man are widely scattered throughout the subcontinent, although concentrations may be noted in the southern Cape and in the Transvaal. This in all probability is a reflection of the present limited state of knowledge of the distribution of early man, dependent as it is upon the degree to which artefacts and remains have survived and the areas in which a limited number of archaeologists have worked. The Late Stone Age is of some concern so far as landscape evolution is concerned as it would appear that from about 6000 B.C. to the beginning of the present era, the societies present in the subcontinent achieved a high degree of mastery over their environment. The economy of hunting and gathering was taken to an advanced stage with the invention of the poison arrow and the light bow. The plentiful animal population of South Africa and the ease of hunting allowed a degree of leisure to be enjoyed by these societies. As a result art forms such as bead and pendant manufacture were developed. In addition rock painting and engraving assumed importance, and indicate a society with symbols and a mythology. This society developed in relative isolation, but about 2000 years ago changes began to occur and populations became less stable and settled.

The introduction of domesticated sheep and a knowledge of pottery manufacture marked a major break in the social evolution of South Africa. It is uncertain whether these changes were introduced by new groups of herders from the north. The links between the hunter–gatherers and the herders were strong and the physical differences noted by later European travellers may have been due to dietary factors. Alternatively, innovation may have been introduced by the coastal traders as a part of the east coast trade system. Trading links between the Mediterranean and China and East Africa were significant, and may have influenced cultural changes in South Africa. Whatever the explanation, the succession of peoples and cultural influences which were to result in the highly heterogeneous ethnic and cultural composition of South Africa, began 2000 years ago.

The next major interruption came in the period A.D. 300–500 when communities of cultivators and livestock keepers established themselves in the northern Transvaal. The groups, variously described as early Bantu speakers or Sudanic speakers, possessed a knowledge of mining, smelting and iron working. Links with the east coast trade, and more especially the gold trade of Zimbabwe were well established through the Indian Ocean trade system. Although the origin of the first cultivators is open to doubt, that of the next wave of invaders is not. About A.D. 1000 the ancestors of the present Bantu-speaking peoples spread rapidly from Central and East Africa through Zambia, Zimbabwe, Moçambique and the eastern half of South Africa. The numbers involved were not large, but through superior organisation and technical ability they were able to incorporate the pre-existing peoples into their social structures. By the fourteenth or fifteenth centuries A.D. they had effectively occupied most of the lands associated with them. This interpretation of the archaeological record is in marked contrast to much of the earlier, and indeed current, South African historiography which suggested that the Whites and Bantu speakers entered the country at approximately the same time and eventually met along the line of the Fish River in the eastern Cape (South Africa, 1980).

The indigenous peoples

The Khoisan peoples

The oldest surviving groups in South Africa are descended from the hunter–gatherers (San) and herders (Khoikhoi), who were designated the Bushmen and Hottentots by the early White settlers (Wilson and Thompson, 1969). These peoples occupied much of South Africa prior to the advent of the Bantu speakers and the Whites. They appear to be closely related and the divisions perceived by the immigrants were largely arbitrary, representing the two extremes of a continuum. Their comparatively basic, but well ordered Late Stone Age economy was subjected to overwhelming pressures by both invading groups. The hunter–gatherers retreated before the herders and were pushed into progressively more remote areas such as the Kalahari Desert and the Drakensberg Mountains, from where they were eliminated in the course of the nineteenth century (Wright, 1971). Only in Botswana and Namibia have they survived with their traditional social structures. Within South Africa this group is evidenced by a rich heritage of rock art, which is widespread and has received extensive study in modern times. As an art form, paintings appear to have been drawn until well into the nineteenth century as scenes depicting White wagons and British soldiers testify.

The herders developed along somewhat different lines. Pressures from the Bantu-speaking groups had caused them to be displaced into the drier, western half of the country by the beginning of historic times. The question of their assimilation into the Bantu-speaking peoples remains to be conclusively studied, but there appear to have been few hard and fast lines and the frontiers between the various indigenous groups do not appear to have been mutually exclusive. The herding economy appears to have become well organised with marked seasonal migrations according to the availability of grazing and other foodstuffs.

The arrival of the Whites, as a result of the establishment of the Dutch colony, was disastrous. The sheep and cattle herding economy was at first complementary to that of the agriculturally based White settlers. However, competition for grazing grounds, once the colonists had acquired sheep and cattle, resulted in conflict which could only be one sided. The Khoikhoi population was largely decimated as a result of exposure to European-borne diseases, particularly smallpox, for which they possessed no immunity. The epidemic of 1713, although only one of a series, was particularly devastating as it broke the clan organisation and hence the ability to resist. Thus in the course of the eighteenth century, their numbers were reduced and their traditional grazing grounds were appropriated by White graziers.

Two options were open for those who remained. Either they could stay and become the servants of the White farmers, or they could retreat before them. Usually this choice was not clear-cut as many who stayed later retreated, once they had acquired White skills, animals (particularly horses) and most notably firearms. These groups, of whom the Griquas were the most significant, occupied frontier lands between the Whites and Blacks, acting as a buffer between the two until well into the second half of the nineteenth century. At times they held the frontier against both Black and White invaders, but ultimately they were overwhelmed as independent entities (Ross, 1976). Reserves were established for some, and individual farms were granted to others, but in the main they became labourers for the White settlers. It is highly doubtful if many pure blood Khoisan people exist today, as the inter-marriage between them and their Black and White neighbours has been considerable and spread over a long time. Thus in 1911 only 27 000 Hottentots were enumerated in the Cape of Good Hope compared with 99 000 some 36 years before. Nevertheless, their blood probably flows in the veins of some members of all the other groups now living in South Africa.

The landscape heritage of the Khoisan peoples has been little investigated. The hunters and gatherers who operated in small groups of one or two dozen persons left little imprint, beyond their decorated caves. They used the existing herds and do not appear to have overhunted. Name references to Bushman features such as 'Bushman's Rock' or Bushmanland, etc. are all that remain. The Khoikhoi (Hottentot) herders contributed more, through their herding of sheep and cattle and their construction of semi-permanent settlements. This provided points of reference for later groups and there are frequent references to 'Hottentots Kraal' and other such appellations, suggesting White and Black inheritance of earlier settlement sites such as Pofadder, named after the Korana leader, Klaas Pofadder. The full extent of this continuity between Khoikhoi settlement and White settlement needs to be investigated. Other features including the initial routes between settlements were in all probability used by the early White and Black explorers. The Khoikhoi languages have survived in the names given by early explorers to landscape features, thus 'Kragga Kamma' (clear water), and 'Okiep' (very brack) abound in the Cape Province. Even such apparent English names as Goodhouse owe their origin to the Nama, 'Gudaos' (sheep drift) (South Africa, 1978).

The Bantu-speaking peoples

The Black Bantu-speaking peoples appear to have been settled in South Africa for at least 1500 years, during which time considerable diversification has occurred. These people may be distinguished both physically and linguistically from the Khoisan peoples whom they displaced or incorporated. They also possessed a more advanced economy based on a knowledge of agriculture and metallurgy, more especially the development of mining and smelting techniques for iron and gold. Diversification existed in the economy, depending upon the physical environment, but the emphasis was upon animal husbandry with a varying degree of sedentary agriculture. The tribal and clan groupings were more settled with semi-permanent villages or farmsteads surviving for long periods of time, in contrast with the comparatively nomadic existence of the Khoisan peoples.

Migrations before the historic period are at present open to considerable dispute, but it would appear that the Bantu-speaking peoples broke up into a series of comparatively isolated groupings separated by mountain ranges, and disease-ridden areas. Four broad divisions have been distinguished, the Nguni, the Sotho, the Venda and the Tsonga, each with a markedly different speech, culture and history. Within each of these groupings tribal and sub-tribal distinctions have been recognised, but each speaks a mutually intelligible language, although even this is breaking down at the present time.

The largest group are the Nguni, accounting for two-fifths of the population of South Africa, who occupy the lands to the east of the Great Escarpment from the eastern Transvaal to the vicinity of Algoa Bay. Their economy was originally based on cattle grazing and on settled agriculture. Settlements were small, consisting in the main of extended family units surrounded by their own fields and grazing grounds (De Jager, 1964). Although such an economy was essentially sedentary, movement was possible as people sought additional land, and groups split to establish new colonies. Thus there was a steady outward colonisation movement resulting in conflict with neighbours, whether Khoisan, other Black groups or Whites. Political control was loose, with each tribal grouping linked through chiefs and paramount chiefs, who exercised, in the main, only limited powers.

Changes in historic times have been particularly profound for the Nguni peoples. Most significantly the Nguni areas of modern Natal were transformed by the reorganisation of the traditional clan and tribal structures by two paramount chiefs, Dingiswayo (1808–18) and Shaka (1818–28). The reorganisation involved the ruthless suppression of rivals and the emergence of a military kingdom named after one of the tribal groups in the area, the Zulu. The emergence of this organised, military state had widespread repercussions over the southern half of Africa. The period of warfare and movement which followed is referred to as the Mfecane in the Nguni languages, meaning the time of crushing, giving an idea of the disaster which overtook many of the subcontinent's peoples. In Natal the various Nguni tribes were welded into the Zulu nation. Beyond this zone a series of refugee tribes and groupings fled before the raids of the Zulu armies, and they in turn came into conflict with others, who were either strong enough to resist or were in turn forced to flee. Consequently those Nguni to the north of the Zulu hearth, through a measure of resistance and diplomacy, were able to survive as the Swazi nation. The Swazis, although in other respects closely related to the Zulu, have developed politically on very different lines in the last 150 years. The Zulu nation in resisting White advances was able to build a solid history of achievement, including in 1879 a severe defeat of the British army. No other grouping or nation in South Africa was able to resist colonisation to the same extent.

In the area between the Zulu kingdom and the western boundary of Nguni settlement, no such centralising power emerged. Individual tribes and tribal confederations were thrown into turmoil by the Mfecane, but failed to achieve a central authority. As a result the chieftaincies were annexed piecemeal to the Cape Colony in the course of the second half of the nineteenth century. It is significant that the language was standardised on Xhosa, one of the most westerly of the dialects, and therefore most distinct from Zulu, based on usage in northern Natal. Thus differences have been emphasised rather than lessened in the historic period as the Xhosa and Zulu languages have evolved under the pressures of a modern technological age and a nationalist ideology. A further group of Nguni to the north of Natal were welded into the Swazi nation, most of whose members live in Swaziland, but which overlaps into the neighbouring districts of South Africa.

On the Highveld above the Great Escarpment, the Sotho-speaking peoples occupied the lands from the vicinity of the Orange River to the borders of Zimbabwe. Owing to the drier environment than the Nguni homelands, the Sotho rated animal husbandary more highly in their economy. Sheep and cattle were significant and traditional settlement appears to have been more migratory, although often only on a seasonal basis. Many of the Sotho settlements were large and built of stone. As such they provided permanent sites to which the seasonal migrations returned. The villages were usually large and the term 'town' was often applied to them by early European travellers.

The period of the Mfecane and the subsequent period of White colonisation, extending over the 1820s and 1830s, was particularly disastrous for the

Sotho peoples. Several Nguni groups fleeing from the Zulu armies, as well as the Zulu armies themselves raided the Sotho lands. On the open plateau where movement was relatively easy, armies, tribes and marauding bands plundered at will and large tracts were laid waste. The Sotho heartland in the western Transvaal was occupied for a while by the Matabele, fleeing from the Zulu, before they in turn fled north to Zimbabwe. The Sotho tribes sought safety in the mountains of Lesotho or in the more arid lands to the west or in the bush country to the north. The break-up of the Sotho societies occurred immediately before the White colonisation of their lands. Thus large tracts of the modern Orange Free State and Transvaal were occupied by Whites in the 1830s under the impression that the lands were open and unoccupied.

With few exceptions the Sotho were unable to resist White encroachments and the chieftaincies were destroyed one by one within the area of South Africa. In Lesotho, as a result of the diplomatic skill of Moshoeshoe 1, the modern Basotho nation was able to avoid direct subjugation to settler rule and Botswana, where the chiefs were under Khama of the northern Bamangwato, was able to do the same. The scattering of the Sotho peoples was formalised by the distinction of North, South and West Sotho (Pedi, Basotho and Tswana) languages, which were developed from the dialects of the more remote parts of the Sotho lands. The intrusion of other groups such as the North and South Ndebele with mixed Nguni and Sotho traits added further confusion to the linguistic pattern. These diverse Sotho groups account for one-quarter of the population of South Africa.

In the north and north-east of the Transvaal the Venda people appear to have been comparatively late arrivals from the north. They were skilled miners and stone workers, who had strong links with the Shona of Zimbabwe. Owing to the relative inaccessibility of their lands they were able to survive the Mfecane, and until the 1870s, the penetration of White settlers, thereby retaining comparatively large tribal lands and a distinctive culture. In numerical terms however they are small, with only half a million enumerated in 1980, but with the highest proportion of any South African Black group living on their traditional lands. The fourth distinct linguistic group is the Tsonga, who occupied the area of southern Moçambique and overlapped into the eastern Transvaal and the north of Natal. Their cultural differences were emphasised by early contact at Delagoa Bay, with Portuguese traders, with whom they built up the first trade links in eastern South Africa. The major South African subgroup of the Tsonga, the Shangaan, were restricted by the tsetse fly areas and so based their grazing economy on goats rather than cattle.

The Bantu-speaking peoples' broad groupings and traditional economies were adversely affected by the Mfecane and subsequent White occupation, yet their major outlines remained. The political fragmentation and the emergence of modern groupings occurred as the traditional economies were disrupted and finally destroyed. Yet these peoples, because of their numbers relative to the immigrant populations, were able to maintain sufficient of their cultures to resist assimilation or extermination.

Population estimates are notoriously poor, but in 1904 when the first census was taken in all the South African territories there were 3.1 million Bantu speakers in South Africa, of whom two-thirds resided in the Cape and Natal. Estimates before that date are often no more than conjecture and even more recent figures are open to question (Hattingh, 1973). In general the Black peoples did not suffer the decimation which overtook the San and Khoikhoi peoples. Numbers appear to have increased steadily once the internecine wars had been ended, with the advent of White control. Even the major upheaval of the cattle killing of 1856 in the Xhosa lands (which was a reaction to White pressures) did not result in irreparable losses, owing to the relief works which were instituted by the Colonial Government and the basic resilience of the Xhosa economy. Thus in the face of White settlement the Blacks did not mortally succumb as did the Indians of North America or Argentina, the Aborigines of Australia, and to a lesser extent the Maoris of New Zealand. They increased in numbers and have always outnumbered the immigrant groups, although they have been politically subject to them.

As a result of increasing urbanisation, people from the various Black nations have had to live together. The old divisions have in some cases been lessened as the urban Black population has been caught up in the South African economic system, if not its political system. Recent official recognition that not all Blacks are to become citizens of other states has opened up the possibility of recognising Black South Africans as a part of an overall South African nation. Thus the major Black townships, such as Soweto, which are unattached to Black states, have given rise to a Pan-African nationalism, which views the ethnic based Black nationalisms as White engendered. It is worth noting that even within Soweto, segregation in housing allocation is pursued between the various Black groups (Mashile and Pirie, 1977). At the other end of the scale the fragmentation of Black national groups such as the Xhosa is an interesting development. In an effort to create nations the Ciskei and Transkei Governments, after a period of dispute, have emphasised separate identities, and are intent on establishing recognisably different national identities. However, in 1980, the Ciskei Commission rejected independence in favour of continued South African citizenship (Ciskei, 1980). Thus accidents of administrative history in the late nineteenth century have resulted in the perpetuation of differences across linguistic and tribal groupings. Whether the Swazis, Basothos and Tswanas of the South African states are separate from their neigbours in Swaziland, Lesotho and Botswana is more a political question than a social or anthropological one. Nations can come into being as a result of concerted legislative pressures, but the answers in South Africa are still not recognisable. The confusion on this issue is well illustrated by the problems of nomenclature. The Bantu-speaking peoples have been officially classified as Kaffirs, Natives, Africans, Bantus and now Blacks, while each national group name has been applied to its members.

27

The impact of the Bantu-speaking peoples upon the landscape is far more pervasive than that of the Khoisan peoples, as the former group retained some of their traditional lands and have influenced the development of a large part of South Africa. The traditional areas are examined in Chapter 4 and the Black contribution to other landscapes is outlined in subsequent chapters. Certain general points may be made. Traditional costume and architecture have survived in parts of South Africa. Thus the rural people and their landscapes have retained stronger links with their past than have those who have migrated to the towns. Studies of traditional dress and costume illustrate the range of distinctive styles still associated with each grouping (Tyrrell, 1968). The influence of European, Western styles, and more recently Black African, especially West African, have overlain these. In architecture, traditional building styles have remained much in evidence, ranging from the stone circular huts of the Sotho areas to the wattle and daub of the Nguni areas. Modifications such as the introduction of square, instead of round, houses reflect a Western, particularly missionary influence, where angularity was a sign of Christianity (Bundy, 1979). Corrugated iron has now largely replaced thatch as a roofing material. Some styles such as the Zulu reed and the highly decorated Ndebele houses have very largely disappeared except as tourist attractions. More recently imported styles from Black Africa have begun to influence government and other architects in the search for an African identity (Fig. 2.1).

The immigrant peoples

South Africa has attracted immigrants from other continents in greater numbers than any other part of Africa. Although too far south to induce the Arabs, and apparently too inhospitable for the Portuguese, it proved to be one of the key supply points for Dutch and English ships passing between Europe and India and the East Indies (Indonesia). Under the control of these two powers settlers emigrated from Europe and from Asia, but the influx was small compared with those destined for other continents.

The Europeans (Whites)

The Dutch East India Company established a refreshment station at Cape Town in 1652, as an alternative to the impoverished colony on St Helena. To this station small numbers of immigrants came from the Netherlands, Germany and France, as well as the more transitory officials of the Company. The colony which developed on the southern tip of Africa was not regarded as particularly important to the Netherlands, and it remained subordinate to Dutch interests in the East Indies. As a result of the upheavals of the Na-

Fig. 2.1 The University of the North, near Pietersburg. The University was established in 1960 as a separate institution for Black students. As such it looked to indigenous cultures for building styles and is representative of many such edifices. (University of the North)

poleonic Wars, the Cape Colony was finally occupied by Great Britain in 1806, and the Dutch connection was ended.

Despite the low official priority accorded to the settlement at the Cape, the Dutch heritage has been of the utmost significance for the later development of South Africa. In 1806 there were only 25 000 Whites in the Cape Colony, who by 1980 had become the ancestors of the present Afrikaner nation of approximately three million souls (Elphick and Giliomee, 1979; Adam and Giliomee, 1979). The evolution of the Afrikaner nation is unique in the annals of European overseas settlement with regard to the development of their own language, Afrikaans, from its original Dutch roots; and also regarding the strong cultural and political identity, separate from their colonial origins.

The Afrikaner nation as it grew developed a number of distinctive traits which have had a direct bearing upon the evolution of the South African landscape. The strong frontier heritage, where for 200 years the frontiersman fashioned a new way of life very different from his settled agricultural background in Europe, is the most significant of these traits. The extensive pastoral economy of the Cape Colony, and later other areas of South Africa, as practised by the pioneers, left an indelible imprint upon man and land. The search for new grazing lands in a continent of apparently unlimited land, resulted in the migration of Afrikaner graziers across South Africa and into countries as far away as Angola, Zambia and Kenya. This restlessness (trek fever) was evident until the 1930s, although by then the migration had become a rural–urban migration, as free land had run out.

The frontier heritage is reinforced by the Afrikaner desire for independence, as re-written in Afrikaner historiography (Van Jaarsveld, 1975). Often this desire was for independence from any government, whether Dutch, British or local. Separate republican states were often ephemeral, but two, the Orange Free State and the South African Republic (Transvaal), survived for sufficient length of time to establish marked state-ideas. These two republics were conquered by Great Britain in 1900 during the Second Anglo-Boer War (1899–1902), or to use the terminology of Afrikaner historiography the 'Second War of Freedom'. The republican ideal, together with a binding sense of nationalism was re-established in 1961 when South Africa cut its links with the British Commonwealth and assumed republican status. The Afrikaner nation by this time was politically dominant in South Africa and its leaders were free to organise the country as they wished, along lines significantly different from other countries of European settlement. It was the frontier rather than the settled historic core which had become the seat of power (see Pirie *et al.*, 1980).

In 1806 the British administration was securely established and in 1820 the first substantial group of British settlers arrived. Subsequent migrations resulted in the emergence of a large British population with, until recently, strong political and cultural links with Great Britain. Much of the immigration was urban based and only limited rural areas in the eastern Cape and

Fig. 2.2 Dutch Reformed Church, Cradock. The church is a replica of St Martin-in-the-Fields, London, and was built when British cultural influence was having a major impact upon the Afrikaners. Similarly the Dutch Reformed Church in Graaff Reinet is a modified reproduction of Salisbury Cathedral. (South African Railways)

Natal were settled by the British. However, British ideas in administration, architecture and industry were pervasive, and resulted in a strong dichotomy between the two major groups within the White population. Owing to the influence of British administrative control over much of South Africa during the formative period of the nineteenth and early twentieth centuries, the British imprint upon the landscape was greater than their numbers would have suggested (Fig. 2.2). Furthermore the British colonists' access to the capital markets and technical knowledge of Great Britain and the English-speaking world, resulted in the linking of South Africa to the industralised and com-

31

mercial world economy which developed in the nineteenth and twentieth centuries. It also provided a degree of uniformity between South Africa and other such frontier regions. It is worth noting that the British administration sought to create a British dominion in South Africa after the Second Anglo–Boer War through a massive immigration drive, in order to achieve numerical superiority (Streak, 1970). The plan failed, so that the numerical, and therefore political dominance of the Afrikaner within the White group has not been seriously challenged (Schoeman, 1977). However, the business and industrial sectors of the economy have, until recently, been dominated by the English-speaking group.

Significant numbers of other European nations came to South Africa, of which the German contingent was probably the most numerous. During the Dutch period they virtually outnumbered the Dutch, but were open to cultural assimilation and so were absorbed into the Afrikaner nation. However, German group settlement under the British, in the eastern Cape and Natal, defeated the objects of assimilation and the Germans remained a culturally if not necessarily a linguistically separate entity for a long period of time. Scandinavian settlements in Natal also added to the cultural diversity. Few Frenchmen came, apart from the Huguenots in the Dutch period, who were also assimilated into the Afrikaner nation. During the present century, in addition to immigration from the traditional countries, large numbers of Portuguese have settled in the Transvaal, although South Africa took in few of the Portuguese nationals who fled from Angola and Moçambique at the time of independence in 1975. The Portuguese introduced the first sizeable southern European and Roman Catholic element into the White population, and as a result have tended to remain culturally more distinct than the northern European, Protestant immigrants have done. Other small, but significant groups of Jews, Greeks and Italians have made a contribution in particular spheres of activity such as the retailing and catering trades.

Thus the White South African nation, which has exercised political control over the country since 1910, has highly diverse origins and even today is linguistically and culturally divided, with 56 per cent Afrikaans speaking and 39 per cent English speaking. In terms of political power the Afrikaner group has held the reins of government firmly. All South Africa's prime ministers since 1910 have been Afrikaners. Politics have been viewed as the degree to which the Afrikaner politicians were willing to include the English-speaking group in the machinery of government. In terms of internal policies probably little difference was apparent, as for example legislation passed by the United Party Government of General J. Smuts (1939–48) may be viewed as the preliminaries to the National Party Government of Dr F. Malan (1948–54). The majority of both groups held similar views on racial politics concerning South Africa's Black population. The organised National Party Government has left a highly significant imprint upon the landscape of South Africa, through a legislative programme of remarkable continuity since 1948, which has deep geographical implications.

The Asians

The other significant source of immigrants in the colonial eras was Asia. The supply of European labour was insufficient, and from 1657 onwards slaves were imported by the Dutch from their East Indian possessions, India and Madagascar. This group was predominantly Muslim in religion and Malay in speech (Bradlow and Cairns, 1978). The Malayo–Portuguese language acted as a lingua franca from East Africa to the East Indies in the seventeenth and eighteenth centuries. Thus the group, together with those whom they assimilated, became known as the Cape Malays or Cape Muslims, even though only a small proportion came from Malaya. The Muslim artisans exerted a considerable influence over the early Cape settlement as they provided a major part of the skilled manpower needed to establish the initial colony. Their influence upon architecture, as the main builders, was particularly noticeable. Despite some slaves being taken on to the frontier the majority remained, together with their descendants within the western Cape. Although culturally a distinct group, they are merged for statistical purposes with the Khoisan peoples and a much larger group of racially mixed parentage, as the Coloured people. This heterogeneous group numbered 2.6 million in 1980, of whom 6 per cent were Cape Muslims.

The second group of immigrants were Indians introduced as indentured labourers into Natal in the period 1860–1914, to work in the sugar cane fields. Later they were joined by free Indians who paid their own passages and who introduced business capital and acumen. The Indian community is diverse with Hindu, Muslim and Christian elements, although the Hindus constitute two-thirds of the total. In addition although most, particularly the younger generations, use English or Afrikaans as home languages, the array of languages, from Hindi and Urdu of northern India to Tamil from the south, has acted as a divisive force in the community. The Indians profoundly affected the development of Natal, and to a lesser extent the Transvaal. Although at first a rural community, introducing intensive market gardening, they have become a highly urbanised community in the present century with a conspicuous presence in the retail trade, particularly the cheaper products. Owing to the strong cultural links which are maintained with the Indian subcontinent, Indian areas in South Africa present highly distinctive landscapes in the African context.

Other Asian groups, noticeably the Chinese, have immigrated to South Africa. The Chinese were mainly introduced as indentured labourers to work on the gold mines in the first decade of the present century, but were almost entirely repatriated afterwards as a result of a major governmental crisis over their treatment. A few subsequently migrated permanently but there has been no development of distinctive 'Chinatowns' in South Africa. The Indian and Chinese populations are comparatively small – 0.8 million in 1980, but are almost entirely urban based, with the result that it is mainly in the urban areas that distinctive landscape enclaves are to be found with affinities to Asia

Fig. 2.3 Grey Street Mosque, Durban. The Indian immigrants utilised traditional styles to establish distinctive Indian quarters. Thus the complex of Mosque, madressa and shops, on two levels, stands in marked contrast to the office blocks behind. (Anne Christopher)

(Fig. 2.3). It is the Asian communities which have been most severely regulated by the racial legislation of the past 100 years.

The various immigrant groups whether they came to South Africa as master, servant or slave have tended to maintain many of their distinctive cultural traits. Possibly the feeling of isolation or the feeling of a threat posed by large numbers of indigenous peoples resulted in established patterns of European and Asian civilisations being maintained. Assimilations did take place as the Afrikaner nation evolved from many diverse linguistic areas, yet in terms of religion the Church could act as a binding force. Similarly the Cape Muslims who came from even more diverse backgrounds, were able to take solace in religion and bind themselves into a distinct cultural entity. Small immigrant groups tended to be absorbed by larger ones, but South Africa did not become a melting pot for immigrants, let alone one including the indigenous population. Instead segregation, differentiation and the development of distinctive cultural traits have been encouraged. Divisive linguistic and cultural politics and histories have tended to accentuate differences, just as differences within the indigenous groups have been accentuated. These in turn have been reflected in a highly differentiated cultural landscape, which has often resulted in the appearance of landscapes closer to those of Europe or Asia than those traditionally identified with Africa.

Population profile

The population of South Africa is far from static both in terms of numbers and in distribution. Substantial increases in the present century, together with a large-scale migration to the towns has changed large parts of the country. In terms of size the population of South Africa has increased from 5.2 million in 1904 to 12.7 million in 1951 and 28.7 million in 1980 (Table 2.1). These figures mask very considerable shifts within the population composition as a result of differential growth rates between the various ethnic groups. Thus the White and Asian growth rates are substantially lower than the Black and Coloured growth rates. This has significant implications for the future as Sadie (1973: 38) has suggested:

> If the White population is not going to be strengthened by immigration it will be exceeded in size by the Coloured population after the year 2010. At the moment (1972) it is still some 80 per cent bigger than the latter. From the point of view of economic development the relative size of the White population – which provides the major portion of entrepreneurial initiative – and the Asian population – which is assuming an increasing role in this regard – is very important. These two groups together constituted 20 per cent of the aggregate population in 1970. If demographic tendencies continue on their course these two will have a 16 per cent share in 2000 and a 13 per cent share in the year 2020. This way lies relative impoverishment of the Bantu and Coloureds even while their per caput incomes could rise. They have, for practical purposes, only their labour to offer whose employment is dependent upon the enterprise and capital supplied by the other two groups.

Such a bleak forecast has in part been borne out by the economic depression of the 1970s, when large-scale Black and Coloured unemployment constituted serious social and political problems. It should be pointed out that major advances in medical care have reduced infant mortality rates dramatically, thereby contributing to this state of affairs. In Port Elizabeth, for example, in the decade 1969–79, Black infant mortality rates fell from 322‰

Table 2.1 Population* of South Africa 1904–2020

	Millions				
	Total	*White*	*Coloured*	*Asian*	*Black*
1904	5.2	1.1	0.4	0.1	3.5
1921	6.9	1.5	0.5	0.2	4.7
1951	12.7	2.6	1.1	0.4	8.6
1970	21.4	3.7	2.0	0.6	15.1
1980	28.7	4.5	2.8	0.8	20.6
2000	49.1	5.7	4.9	1.2	37.3
2020	79.1	7.0	7.7	1.6	62.8

* Population based on estimates by Sadie (1973), without assumed 30 000 net White immigrants per annum.

Table 2.2   Relative *per capita* Gross National Product of various groups in South Africa 1946–76

| | Per capita Gross National Product (English White South Africans = 100) | | |
	1946	1960	1976
White			
English	100	100	100
Afrikaners	41	64	71
Coloured	11	13	17
Asians	14	14	20
Blacks	6	7	8

to 52‰. White rates in the same period fell from 22‰ to 13‰ and for Asians from 47‰ to 31‰. That this may not be an insuperable problem is suggested by examining the rise in the economic position of the Afrikaner nation since 1945 (Table 2.2) (Adam and Giliomee, 1979). However, the Afrikaners' position with regard to Anglophone White South Africans is not strictly comparable owing to the lower economic base level of the Black population and the lack of political control of state resources so important to the Afrikaners' rise.

If the size and growth of the population constitutes one of the major planning problems facing South African administrations now and in the future, its distribution is also likely to require attention. In 1904 only 23 per cent (1.2 million) of the population were town dwellers. By 1980 the percentage had doubled, constituting 14 million persons. The speed with which this occurred is remarkable, with the numbers living in the urban areas doubling in 20 years. Furthermore, whereas in 1904 the towns were still ethnically White (half of the total urban population was White), this has now changed with heavy flows of Coloureds and more recently Blacks into the urban areas. Thus in 1980 Whites constituted little more than one-quarter of the urban population. The proportion is likely to continue to fall as an increasing proportion of the Black population moves to the urban areas. This has implications for town planning, as between 1980 and 2000 urban populations are likely to double as they doubled in the previous 20 years. Rural–urban migration has resulted in an ethnically differentiated rural depopulation of parts of the country. The rural White population reached a peak in 1931, since when it has been in decline, although this has been most marked in the drier parts of the country where decline had set in by the turn of the century. The Asians reached a rural peak in 1951, but only declined markedly after 1970, while the rural Coloured population has continued to rise. It is the Black population which still exhibits a high rural growth rate, especially in the Black states.

The complex history of the growth and migration of population has resulted in one of the most diverse ethnic make-ups of any country in the

Table 2.3   Percentage distribution of national income by racial groups in South Africa 1936–77

Year	*Blacks*	*Coloureds*	*Asians*	*Whites*	*Total*
1936	19.7	4.1	1.7	74.5	100.0
1946	20.1	4.2	1.9	73.8	100.0
1956	20.6	4.8	2.0	72.5	99.9
1967	18.8	5.4	2.4	73.4	100.0
1977	25.5	7.3	3.2	64.0	100.0

Source: Smith (1973: 95) and South African Institute of Race Relations (1979: 102).

world. The political and legislative machinery established by the White dominated government of South Africa since its inception in 1910 has added to the intricacy of the pattern which has emerged. The cultural landscapes of South Africa can only be explained in terms of the ethnic groupings occupying them and the complex network of legislative enactments passed to administer and rule the country.

Another significant aspect of the population profile is the disparity in income between the various groups. Surveys in the early 1970s showed that Whites earned two to three times the Coloured or Asian earnings in the same industry and over five times the Black earnings. Thus the Whites received approximately three-quarters of the total income in employment and the Blacks only one-fifth of the national income (Smith, 1973). Investigations suggest that the proportions had changed little between the 1930s and the 1960s (Table 2.3). However, the wage levels of Black labour on the mines and in manufacturing have been increased markedly in the 1970s and similarly Asian and Coloured incomes have also risen more rapidly than those of Whites. Thus between 1967 and 1977 the index of inequality of incomes has been reduced from 0.63 to 0.56. Nevertheless, it is the White population with a high disposable income which has and still does determine patterns of consumption and economic development within the country. This results in a marked relationship between Black areas and poverty, which allied to the peripheral nature of most of the Black regions, has significant spatial implications for South Africa.

3

Perceptions and politics — a White man's country?

European settlement, opportunity and reality

The major drive for change over the last century or more has been the view of South Africa as a 'White Man's Country' on the southern tip of Africa. In one way this followed the vision of the French in North Africa, where a portion of France was established in Algeria. Yet the southern African experience was on a very different scale and with very different participants. Comparison is closer to the experience of North America, Australasia and parts of South America, than with the rest of Africa. The same attractions of agricultural land, minerals and trade opportunities enticed people from Europe to southern Africa as to other temperate parts of the world. Thus the first perception influencing South Africa in the modern period is of a land of White settlement opportunity.

How realistic was this perception? The initial Dutch settlement in 1652 was designed to establish a refreshment station for ships sailing between the Netherlands and the Dutch East Indies. The supposed fertility of the soil around Cape Town led the first commander at the Cape, Jan van Riebeeck, to envisage close settlement and intensive cultivation along the lines of the Dutch or East Indian countryside which he knew. Thus in 1652 he wrote of the eastern part of the Cape peninsula 'It is moreover so fertile and rich that neither Formosa, which I have seen, nor New Netherland (New York), which I have heard of, can be compared with it'. (Thom, 1952: 36) Thousands of cultivators were anticipated, but 10 years later with only 15 settlers on the tract of land, he realised no further grain land could be given out; and grazing was all much of the land was fit for. Each of the seventeenth-century settlements opened by the Dutch East India Company at the Cape was capable only of extensive cultivation and large-scale animal grazing. In 1712 after only a small number of agricultural immigrants had arrived, the colony was closed to further agricultural settlement. The later colonisation history of the Dutch East India Company's rule at the Cape is one of economic retrenchment and attempts at restricting the outward movement of its subjects into the areas occupied by the indigenous peoples.

The British administration after 1806 regarded South Africa as a part of the temperate Empire capable of absorbing considerable numbers of British immigrants. This statement must be qualified by the comment that interest in South Africa was, with rare exceptions, minor compared with the effort which went into the colonisation of the British North American and Australasian colonies. South Africa elicited its own crop of promotional literature, stressing the fertility of the soil, the mildness of the climate, and the similarity to the most advantageous features of northern Europe, whence it was hoped to obtain settlers (Christopher, 1973a). The vision of a new England or a new Germany was fostered by government officials and the principals of the settlement schemes, and reinforced by the immigrants who sought to re-create a new and better Europe on the southern tip of Africa. The picture of Arcadia could scarcely fail to attract intending immigrants as the following descriptions of the Albany District in the eastern Cape of Good hope in the 1840s illustrates:

> The scenery of this Arcadian country has called forth the unqualified praise of every inhabitant and sojourner. Towards the sea, well grassed and gently undulating meadows are interspersed with park like scenery. Natural shrubberies variegated by flowers of a thousand hues, everywhere arrest the attention of the delighted beholder. These elegant prairies are covered with numerous flocks of sheep and healthy cattle and sprinkled with the cottages of farmers. . . . (Chase, 1843: 33)

Such pictorial eulogies were commonplace on the frontiers of European colonisation of the nineteenth century and the extravagances became particularly excessive when the promoters of settlement schemes eloquently described the areas which concerned them. Thus Joseph Byrne, engaged in attracting colonists to Natal in 1848 for his own personal profit, could write:

> The author of these pages has visited many climes, has dwelt beneath the burning sun of India, has traversed Australia, visited New Zealand and many other lands, but never have his eyes rested upon a land blessed by a bounteous Providence with a more fertile soil than Natal. (Byrne, 1848: 48)

Furthermore the picture of a healthy climate was promoted and indeed members of the British Indian establishment made use of the Cape Colony as a recuperation centre. It is significant that others were attracted as settlers to a country which offered a cure for consumption. Cecil Rhodes, who was to have such an impact upon the development of the subcontinent, originally came to South Africa because of his poor health in England. Official accounts noted the healthy, dry and bracing climates of the interior and the almost universal 'salubrity' of the climate.

Reality was somewhat different, as the flow of settlers from Europe suggests. Each reception area for European colonists was in competition with others, more particularly with the United States. Clearly South Africa was not highly regarded by intending emigrants, as in the period from 1815 to 1914 over 22 million people emigrated from the United Kingdom, but under one million went to South Africa. Even then most migrants came late in the century to exploit the growing industrial economy, not the agricultural potential.

Two factors militated against large-scale migration from Europe into South Africa. The first was the reality of the comparative poverty of the physical environment, and the second was the presence of a large indigenous population, both of which were usually misrepresented in the emigration literature and even in the official reports.

Warnings to intending settlers in southern Africa were indeed more common in the literature circulating in Great Britain than those extolling the attractions. The extensive tablelands and plateaux of the Karroo, devoid of trees and often of grass, were viewed as deserts, while the vagaries of the climate and the virulence of the plant and animal diseases were distinct threats to the agricultural community. The most emphatic official statement on the subject was produced by the Commission on Land Settlement in South Africa after the Anglo–Boer War, when the problems of agricultural settlers were summed up:

> . . . would have great difficulties to contend with . . . the conditions under which agriculture and stock raising are conducted in South Africa are very peculiar. The seasons are uncertain, the recurrence of drought often causes serious disasters and the injury inflicted by locusts and by the various pests and diseases which, in South Africa, affect almost everything in the animal and vegetable world, make the occupation of farming an exceedingly precarious one. (Great Britain, 1901: 14)

The presence of European settlers in South Africa was itself a drawback, as the trials and tribulations were widely reported, and this did little to make the country seem attractive to potential agricultural settlers. Even the constant comment that those who came out to the agricultural schemes often did better in the towns, could hardly encourage rural settlement.

The presence of a large indigenous population, although often stated to be an advantage for colonists, had severe drawbacks for the progress of European settlement. First, the almost continous warfare of the nineteenth century and the political problems of the twentieth century undoubtedly inhibited the flow of settlers, who preferred more secure havens. Second, the indigenous population provided a source of unskilled labour, at a price at which White immigrants could not compete. Thus recurrent warnings that unskilled and often unmoneyed immigrants were unwanted were frequent, as a British Government Report (1888) explained:

> For ordinary labour in towns or on farms throughout the Colony there is also a large supply of natives who are generally preferred to white men, not only because they are cheaper, but because they are better suited to rough work. Englishmen can not work so well in hot climates (Great Britain, 1888: 20)

Most land disposal regulations framed by the colonial governments assumed the intending colonist possessed considerable capital. At one stage the amount of land a man might purchase in Natal was determined by the amount of capital he had available. Moreover, model budgets suggested that more capital was required than most immigrants were likely to possess. Sums of several hundred pounds were usually suggested as necessary to establish the agricultural colonist. Thus the rural areas attracted only a small portion of European immigration in the nineteenth and twentieth centuries, and most major rural extensions to farming were occupied by established rural dwellers, mainly the Afrikaner, whose approach to this type of settlement differed markedly from that of the British.

At least since the 1880s large-scale European immigration has not been thought desirable by the Afrikaner inhabitants. The need for White farmers was not viewed favourably by Afrikaner political groups, such as the Afrikaner Bond, either in the last century or the present:

> We do not want agricultural emigrants for the Colony. We have to hand the best material for that line of industry . . . It will be impossible to get a class anywhere who could contend with the vicissitudes of this country as the Boers have done. (*Cape Times*, 1887)

The demand for some form of control over immigration became ever more vociferous. After 1948 a fairly restrictive policy was pursued, with careful selection of skilled workers and an official eye to make sure that immigration should present no political problems. Since it is now apparent that immigration poses no political threat to the Government or economic threat to the existing White population, a more liberal approach has been pursued in recent years with an increased intake, noticeably from southern European countries.

Thus South Africa did not achieve the racial make-up of other temperate lands of White settlement. The Whites remained a minority and had to live together with a numerically superior indigenous population and the Asian immigrants. This situation prompted the search for 'political whiteness' as opposed to sheer 'numerical whiteness'.

A White Man's Land in the rural areas?

The idea of White supremacy and the converse idea of the inferiority of the Coloured races of the world were probably part of the cultural make-up of the first White settlers to come to South Africa in the seventeenth century. Certainly it developed in the eighteenth and nineteenth centuries in the interior districts of the Cape Colony, which were isolated from the more liberal concepts becoming fashionable in Europe. Thus in the 1830s when a series of republics were established by Afrikaner emigrants from the Cape Colony, racial attitudes had become fixed and the inequality of White and non-White was written into the constitutions of the fledging states. That of the South African Republic, drawn up in 1858, probably expressed the point most clearly with a statement that 'the people desire to permit no equality between

Coloured people and the White inhabitants, either in Church or State'. Coloured people were further defined as 'half-castes down to a tenth degree'. Distinctions between civilised and uncivilised, Christian and heathen, were drawn up in the republics of the nineteenth century, and indeed in the British colony of Natal, whose colonists similarly attempted to bar Blacks from any exercise of political or economic power. Only in the Cape Colony in the nineteenth century were liberal ideas pursued with a colourblind franchise and at least the ideal of equal rights for all civilised men, whether Black or White.

Until the 1830s the Cape Colony possessed a balance between Black and White in terms of numbers and hence the Blacks presented no political problems for the Whites, who were firmly in control. It was only with the incorporation of large Black populations into the White state system that any 'policy' was deemed necessary. The various governments then attempted to solve the problem of administering large numbers of people with a different cultural background, either with the aim of assimilating them into the European culture, or segregating them from the Whites or sometimes a combination of the two. The result was the emergence of the rural location or reserve, set aside for exclusive Black use under traditional rule and tenure. Here it was expected that those Blacks not required to work on White-owned farms or in the towns would live permanently. Although early colonial reserve policies contained the idea of upliftment, and eventual cultural assimilation as applied to the Ciskei and Natal, sheer expense resulted in their being forgotten, and the reserves were left to stagnate, only being officially 'rediscovered' fairly recently.

If White rule was to continue it was recognised by 1910 that South Africa had to be a White Man's Land, with a substantial White population on the land set aside for White occupation. The opportunity to settle Whites upon the land in large numbers was lost in the nineteenth and early twentieth centuries, when immigration was a proposition. In the present century rural development schemes for the indigenous White population sought to maintain a large White rural population. The agrarian ideal persisted for a long time in South Africa, with the demand to keep as many Whites on the land as possible, if only as managers of Black labour. The 1960 Commission of Inquiry into European Occupancy of the Rural Areas concluded that 'an economically independent, morally strong and vocation conscious farming community is a prerequisite to the continued existence of Christian civilisation in our country'. It further commented that if the African numerical preponderance in the White rural areas was allowed to continue and become more pronounced then 'this state of affairs will in the end hold out a serious threat to White civilisation in this country'. Thus in the rural areas Whites felt threatened and the idea of a 'White Man's Land' was under serious pressure by the middle of the twentieth century.

Official measures to change this state of affairs included substantial aid to the White farming community through financial and other means. The establishment of the Land Bank in 1912 provided a means whereby farmers could borrow money at low rates of interest against the security of their land. In the 1970s approximately one-fifth of all farm borrowing was from this source. Other assistance was offered through agricultural research and training, whereby experimental farms undertook programmes of breeding, planting and raising to test new crops and stock, before the farming community undertook investment in innovation. Training programmes at State Agricultural Colleges attempted to raise the standard of agricultural education in the present century. This remains one of the major problems of the rural community, as in 1970 under 10 per cent of White farmers had completed a high school education. A programme of agricultural extension aimed at assisting farmers to adopt more profitable methods and products has been provided by Extension Officers. In addition the State has supplied farming planning and conservation works and has played a major part in the programme of keeping a healthy agricultural industry in the White areas.

A major feature of the White agricultural industry has been the official introduction of control and marketing boards, and the encouragement of cooperatives. Control and marketing boards have been established for most products, with the aim of encouraging efficient production and controlling the volume of production, so that oversupply does not harm the producer. Stabilisation funds to even out price fluctuations have added to the range of aids available to farmers. Many of the agricultural organisations are of some considerable size with several hundred employees. However, despite these aids the level of farm incomes has not risen at the same rate as in the urban areas, and the economic position of many farming enterprises hardly warrants their survival other than for political and social reasons.

The Commission of Enquiry into Agriculture (1970) came to the conclusion that one-third of the White-owned farms in South Africa were uneconomic, and that they needed to be phased out as rapidly as possible. Agriculture was now viewed as an economic proposition and not as a way of life or as a political activity. Whether such a policy of recognising a declining farm population and planning for it will be politically acceptable is debatable. Renewed pressure to maintain a White presence in the rural areas is likely to build up as the military benefits of such a presence are evident in an era when guerilla warfare is prevalent. Thus it was noted in 1979 that in the northern Transvaal it was possible to travel for over 150 km without crossing a White occupied farm. Hence claims for increased subsidies and benefits to retain or re-establish White occupation of some of the 'White' rural areas appear likely in the 1980s. However, the decline in the rural White population is likely to continue as a result of the economic rationalisation of agriculture.

Parallel with the decline in the White rural population and the official attempts to stem it, have been a series of measures to prevent the imbalance between the races becoming more marked. In the period 1921 to 1960 the ratio of Black to White rural inhabitants in the White-owned areas changed from 3:1 to 8.5:1. Measures had been introduced in the nineteenth century to remove Blacks from White farms, but in the main they had had little effect as the majority of White farmers always considered that they were faced with an imminent labour shortage. The system of labour tenancy, particularly in Natal and the Transvaal, resulted in a large number of Blacks renting, and therefore living on, White-owned farms, in return for six months' labour. In this manner at least twice as many Black labourers lived on the farms as were actually working at any given time. Usually the margin was much higher to overcome the fear of a labour shortage. In addition some companies and individuals held farm land to draw rentals from the Black tenants, or as labour reserves to ensure a supply of labour for the urban areas, mines, or other commercial farms.

After 1948 a more effective system of control in the rural areas was introduced through the Prevention of Illegal Squatting Act of 1951 and the Native Laws Amendment Act of the following year. These measures aimed at 'channelling' Black labour into defined areas and ensuring that the farming areas did not loose necessary labour. Taken in conjunction with the introduction of new and more effective pass laws, and the Population Registration Act, the movement of Blacks within the country was controlled, both by restricting entry to the labour market and exit from the rural areas. The pass laws remain one of the most significant and controversial elements in the legislation preventing Black rural–urban migration, and hence contribute to the continued rapid growth of Black population in the rural areas.

In addition measures were taken to remove 'excess' labour from the White rural areas, and the transformation of the rural Black population in the White areas into a stable labour force. The abolition of labour tenancy constituted one of the major prongs of attack. This was understandably a slow business. Many farmers wished to retain the system as they possessed sufficient land to offer tracts to their Black tenants. A further report by a Commission of Inquiry resulted in the passing of the Bantu Laws Act of 1964. As a result large numbers of Black rural workers and their families were declared redundant to the needs of White farmers, and were resettled in the Black states, if they could find no alternative employment. Between 1960 and 1970 some 340 000 labour tenants, together with 750 000 squatters on White and privately owned Black farms were estimated to have been removed and resettled in the Black states. In addition a further 400 000 labour tenants were removed between 1971 and 1974, when the labour tenancy system might be said to have come to an end. Resettlement upon such a scale had a profound effect upon rural areas of South Africa.

Despite these enormous shifts of population the Black to White ratio in White-owned rural areas continued to change in favour of the Black population between 1960 and 1980, as the White flow into the towns continued unabated. In the latter year the ratio stood at 10.6 : 1. However, a change in the nature of Black agricultural labour appeared, as increasingly contract workers from the Black states were introduced to White-owned farms. Thus permanent Black labourers with their families have been replaced by temporary workers without families. In landscape terms the results have been profound: it has not resulted in a White rural area as envisaged in the past.

Parallel with this movement was the drawing of the Eiselen line in 1955 which reserved the central and western Cape as a preference area for Coloured labour by restricting the number of Black workers in the western areas. The policy became operative in 1962 and the line was pushed eastwards to include Port Elizabeth in 1971. Thus Black workers from the western half of the country have been moved eastwards to create a White–Coloured area, where even if the population is not White as originally envisaged, it will become 'non-Black'.

A White Man's Land in the urban areas?

A further strand in the complex mixture of racial attitude was added as a result of Indian immigration to Natal. In 1859 arrangements were made for the introduction of indentured Indian labourers to work on the sugar plantations of Natal. The period of indentured service was five years, but if a further five years' service was given, the immigrants were entitled to a free return passage to India. However, at the discretion of the Governor a grant of land could be given instead, to the value of the fare (approximately £10). Many chose to stay and sold their labour on the free market or engaged in market gardening, thus coming into competition with White farmers. However, it was the arrival of the free Indian, or 'Arab' as he came to be known, which radically changed the situation. The free Indian, paid his own fare, and was financially independent, and so usually entered commerce, as a general storekeeper or trader. This development was in direct competition with the White commercial community. As a result of the Indian trader's hard work, acceptance of small profit margins, and often better assessment of his customers' (especially Blacks) needs, he prospered and White storekeepers were unable to compete in some areas. Whereas in 1880 there were only 7 Indian shopkeepers in Natal, by 1891 there were 770 Indian storekeepers and traders.

After the introduction of responsible government in 1893, the Natal Government attempted to exclude all free Indians from the Colony. This was much in line with the general rise in White settler feeling against Asian immigrants throughout the British Empire in the second half of the nineteenth century (Huttenback, 1976). Natal, indeed, had the doubtful distinction in 1897 of devising the model legislation for keeping Asians out of the Colony in a non-racial manner. The 'Natal Formula' of a simple education test for intending immigrants was widely copied throughout the British Empire. The Natal legislature continued to pass discriminatory laws restricting Indian rights to the franchise, to trading licences, and even attempting in the early years of the present century to abolish Indian rights to trade at all in the hope, repeated by the Union Government after 1910, that the Indian population might be repatriated to India. In 1911 the Government of India, finally tired of the continual friction with the Natal authorities over the position of its nationals, terminated the original agreement on indentured emigration and Indian immigration virtually ceased. Indeed in 1927 the Union Indian Relief Act sought to reverse the movement by offering Indians in South Africa free passages to India and cash bonuses of £40 for adults and £20 for children. This was only repealed in 1975, when the South African Government finally recognised that the Indian population was permanently settled in the country (Pachai, 1979). Under 20 000 had made use of the provisions of the Act.

Elsewhere in South Africa, Indians fared badly as they were seen as a danger to established White urban interests. In the Transvaal, Indians entered as traders at the time of the first British administration (1877–81), and were the subject of controversy between the succeeding republican administration (1881–1900) and the British Imperial Government. In 1885 Asians were debarred from citizenship and from owning land, although bazaars were assigned for Asian occupation in the main towns. In the Orange Free State restrictions were imposed in the same year (1885) preventing the acquisition of land by Asians, while in 1890 Asians were denied the right to even enter the State without a permit. This legislation has been enforced ever since, with the result that at any given time only a handful of Asians have lived in the Orange Free State. In the Cape of Good Hope restrictions were imposed by the East London Municipality in 1894, when a bazaar was set aside for Indians. Later, Asians were only allowed to enter Transkei or indeed travel from one province to another under permit. Restrictions on the movements of Indians, except to the Orange Free State, were only lifted in 1975. Similarly the introduction of Chinese indentured labourers to work on the gold mines of the Transvaal in the first decade of the present century aroused so much White opposition that the scheme was discontinued and the Chinese were repatriated.

The moves by the White population against the Asian immigrants were largely based on the idea of keeping the towns and the business sector of the economy firmly in White hands. It is scarcely surprising that given the twin strands of republican and colonial discrimination, the Union period witnessed a consolidation of the White determination to keep the urban areas as a 'White Man's Land'. An inquiry into Black living conditions in the early 1920s resulted in the acceptance of Colonel C. F. Stallard's doctrine that 'the town is a European area in which there is no place for the redundant native'. The towns were therefore to house, on a temporary basis, Blacks who were employed in the urban areas, but once that period of service had ended they were to return to the rural areas. Under the Natives (Urban Areas) Act of 1923, separate areas were to be set aside by all towns throughout the country to house their Black populations (Davenport, 1971).

In the main this Act confirmed the intent of many previous enactments, but laid down the distinctive basis of segregation in South Africa. Refinements of the Act were passed at intervals as greater restrictions were placed on the movement and residence of urban Blacks, particularly through the operation of influx control and the pass system.

However, it was the continued anti-Indian feelings of the Whites in Natal which prompted the build-up of a series of enactments which were to be the foundation of much of the segregation practice in South African towns, and lead to their transformation. Indian purchases of residential and commercial land from Whites in the towns of Natal, particularly Durban, and to a lesser extent the Transvaal, led to an outcry against 'penetration'. In consequence the Trading and Occupation of Land (Transvaal and Natal) Restriction Act (the Pegging Act) was passed in 1943, which froze the transfer of land between Asians and Whites for 10 years. Continued legislative action culminated in the passing of the Group Areas Act of 1950 (Davies, 1971).

The Group Areas Act is one of the key pieces of racial legislation with a strong geographical basis (Van Reenen, 1962). The idea behind the Act was to segregate each of the racial groups in the country into separate residential and commercial areas. Thus every person in South Africa was assigned to a racial group, and each group was to occupy a specific area in the towns – the group area. Each group area was designed to be physically separate with a buffer strip, or no-man's-land, between it and the next. As the Blacks had been partially segregated under the Act of 1923 and other earlier items of legislation, the Group Areas Act largely aimed at sorting out the White, Coloured and Asian groups, and indeed subgroupings within them to create Malay, Chinese and other group areas. This legislation had a profound effect upon the towns throughout the country, resulting in the creation of vast new residential areas to rehouse those displaced, as a result of living in an area proclaimed for another group. In general all city centres, business districts and industrial areas were proclaimed White. Indeed residential areas close to the city centre, even if predominantly Black, Asian or Coloured, were proclaimed White. Thus the towns were viewed as 'White Man's Land', with other racial groups living out of sight of the White community. Some towns were able to achieve numerical White majorities by attaching the Black group areas to a Black state (Pretoria) or making the Black group areas a separate municipality (Johannesburg).

Separate development

Even when the urban areas were proclaimed White, few were to achieve a majority of White inhabitants. The idea of a White Man's Land continued to elude the descendants of the White settlers, even though they held firm control of the South African Parliament and took steps to strengthen that control by removing Black representatives and the Coloured voters from the electoral process. In the rural areas large numbers of Blacks were settled in the exclusively Black areas and the remainder became the 'White South Africa' of current terminology. However, the rural parts of White South Africa, have become progressively blacker in the present century, as White rural depopulation took place. In the towns, the urbanisation of Blacks, Asians and Coloureds undermined the vision of them as exclusively White, and indeed the idea that White enterprise controlled them.

Against the background of threats to a White South Africa the policy of separate development unfolded. At first this was purely local segregationist, but out of it came the concept of national segregation, with the idea of creating a White majority of *citizens* within 'White South Africa.' In 1959 the Promotion of Bantu Self-Government Act provided for the creation of separate sovereign states in the place of the existing Black rural areas. A series of nation-states were to arise from the reserves, to which all Blacks in South Africa would owe allegience and possess citizenship. Politically South Africa would then become the White Man's Land, with a series of Black-controlled states on the periphery, which would be economically but not politically linked to South Africa. Then the White Government could achieve a political accommodation with the Asian and Coloured peoples, while retaining an overall majority.

The plan was far reaching, involving the erection of a series of new national governments and the restructuring of the political economy of the subcontinent. In practical terms three states have already achieved independence, namely Transkei in 1976, Bophuthatswana in 1977 and Venda in 1979. The remainder are now internally self-governing, and may achieve independence in the future. The area involved in the present independent states is small (6.1 million ha), but in 1980 it contained approximately one-fifth of the Black population of South Africa, and approximately one-third of the Black citizens of the country. Thus the resulting rump South Africa has become a 'Whiter' country, as the White politicians had hoped.

The policy of apartheid (separateness) or separate development as it has emerged, has resulted in two basic areas of geographical segregation: the rural division between Blacks and non-Blacks, and an urban division between all the groups. The policy has been worked out in detail since 1950, but many of the attitudes and even physical cornerstones of the policy have been inherited from earlier ages.

The initial White settlement over much of the subcontinent was based on the assumption that the indigenous population was numerically small and could be largely ignored politically. Only occasionally were Black indigenous groups sufficiently strong to deflect the course of settlement and prevent the loss of their own lands to the White settlers. In the period 1830–1913 a series of blocks of land were set aside by the various colonial and republican governments, for the more significant Black groups to live under their traditional form of economy. In places these reserves were fairly extensive, particularly in the areas annexed by the Cape of Good Hope and Natal. In others they were virtually non-existent particularly where republican governments saw no reason to provide any land for the indigenous population. Farms for White settlers were granted on an enormous scale in the nineteenth and early twentieth centuries, so that little remained in Black possession. Even what did remain was under pressure, as for example the White settler demand in 1904 to throw all Zululand open to White settlers. When the Commission appointed to delimit reserves for the Zulu population examined the country, it reported that Whites 'appear to be labouring under the impression that all the Commission was required to do was to indiscriminately throw open the whole of the lands suitable for European occupation, irrespective of the interests of the Natives occupying these lands, who in fact, had hardly been considered as a factor in the settlement' (Natal, 1904). It is hardly surprising that in states under the control of White settlers, little land was set aside for the Black population, and therefore extensive tracts of White-owned land were occupied by Blacks, usually designated 'squatters'. In 1913 the Natives Land Act formalised the situation by delimiting the Black reserves, and prevented any further Black purchases of land in the 'White' area.

In was only in 1936 that effective occupation and legal status of Black-occupied lands were brought closer into line. The Natives Trust and Land Act released an area of 6.6 million ha for permanent Black occupation, thereby increasing the legal Black area to 16.9 million ha. The released areas, defined in the schedule of the Act could be purchased for the Black inhabitants by the South African Native Trust (now the South African Development Trust), when capital was made available by Parliament. The cost estimated at £10 million in 1936 has since escalated: by 1978, five times that figure had already been spent. Much of the released area was in the Transvaal where inadequate provision had been made for the Black inhabitants. Purchase was slow and in 1978 some 0.8 million ha were still outstanding. The Act did little more than recognise the position existing at the time of Union. Clearly the fragmented nature of the original reserves and the additional released areas provided *ad hoc* solutions to individual problems of land provision for the rural Black population. No grand design was evident in the 1936 Act as the Black areas were viewed as integral parts of the South African State, which still hoped to incorporate the Protectorates (the present states of Botswana, Lesotho and Swaziland) into its territory.

Since 1948 a grand design has been apparent, particularly after the appointment of Dr H. F. Verwoerd as Minister of Native Affairs in 1950. The policy of separate development was pursued on territorial and organisational bases. The consolidation of the Black areas became a matter of importance, first by the removal of 'black spots' and second by the grouping of the lands belonging to the various ethnic groups. The removal of 'black spots' involved the expropriation of Black-owned areas in predominently White-owned areas. Most such areas originated in the period prior to 1913, when Blacks could purchase land individually in Natal and the Cape. In 1955 it was estimated that there were approximately 162 000 ha of such areas. In addition some of the scheduled reserves and released areas were regarded as 'poorly situated black areas', in that they were also in predominantly White rural areas. All told approximately 0.3 million ha were so regarded. The majority of these have been expropriated and by the end of 1976 some 250 000 Blacks

Table 3.1   Land apportionment of the South African Black states

Black state	Position before consolidation(1973)		Position after proposed consolidation (1975)	
	Area (000 ha)	No. of blocks	Area (000 ha)	No. of blocks
Transkei	3871	2	4501	3
Ciskei	942	15	770	1
KwaZulu	3273	48	3239	10
QwaQwa	48	1	62	1
Bophuthatswana	3799	19	4043	6
Lebowa	2248	14	2518	6
Venda	618	3	668	2
Gazankulu	633	4	741	3
Kangwane	208	3	391	1
KwaNdebele	20	3	73	2
Total	15 662	112	17 006	35

had been removed from the 'black spots' and resettled in designated Black areas.

Such movements become insignificant when the proposals associated with the independence of the Black areas are examined. The concept of independent Black states in South Africa was set forth in the Promotion of Bantu Self-Government Act of 1959, which provided for the establishment of a series of homelands for the various Black nations within South Africa. As the policy has unfolded in the following 20 years, some 10 states came into being for the Zulu, Xhosa (divided into two states), Venda, Shangaan, Swazi, Tswana, South Sotho (Basuto), North Sotho (Pedi), and South Ndebele peoples. The regrouping of territory associated with the establishment of these states is substantial, and the exchanges involved required a major redrawing of boundaries and shifts of population. Even under the most recent (1975) consolidation proposals the then existing 112 blocks were to be consolidated into 35 blocks (Table 3.1) (Lemon, 1976). Only three states were to be consolidated into single units. KwaZulu was to be consolidated to 10 blocks, from the existing 48 with over 150 'black spots' – still a far cry from the theoretical single state (Best and Young, 1972b). Even the three independent states of Transkei, Bophuthatswana and Venda will consist of three, six and two portions apiece respectively, after consolidation (Fig. 3.1).

Significantly no further territory was to be made available, other than that released under the 1936 legislation, which was passed with no view of viable Black political states. This has remained a major stumbling block as only half the Black population lived within the Black states at the time of the 1980 Census. If individual national groups are considered, the proportions living within their own homelands varied from 63 per cent of the Venda people to only 13 per cent of the South Sotho people. Additional land has been claimed

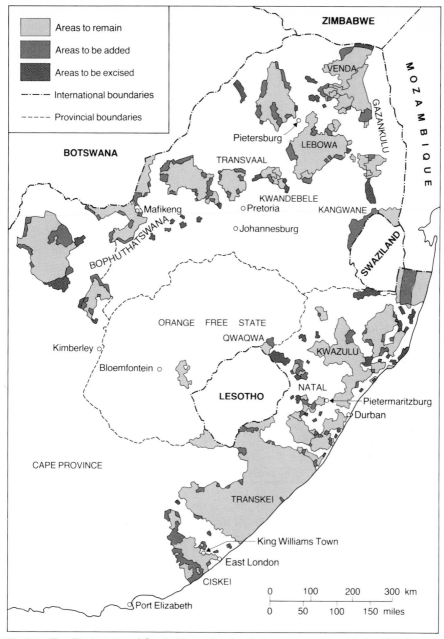

Fig. 3.1   The Black states of South Africa, showing their proposed consolidation (1975). New plans are being formulated which may change this map appreciably.

on economic or historic grounds by virtually all the national governments concerned. Indeed the land issue has been the one which has clouded inter-governmental relations, resulting in the breaking of diplomatic relations between South Africa and Transkei. The problem was aptly expressed by President Lucas Mangope of Bophuthatswana at his country's independence celebrations in December 1977:

> Independence and consolidation are only the two sides of one and the same coin. If any one side of this coin lacks integrity and credibility, the coin will be regarded as faked, and it will be rejected. It is quite self-evident, that the Achilles' heel of Bophuthatswana's credibility is the present state of consolidation, or rather non-consolidation. (*Eastern Province Herald*, 7.12.1977)

South African Government statements made in 1979 suggest that a reconsideration of the whole basis of land division may be in the offing to establish more territorially viable states. The 1975 consolidation proposals have been modified for Kangwane in 1978, to retain the main areas with industrial and agricultural potential. The 1936 Natives Trust and Land Act is about to be superseded, but the outlines of the new division of land at the time of writing were unclear. Whether the more revolutionary schemes of partition will be implemented is open to doubt (Blenk and Von der Ropp, 1977).

The establishment of separate Black states within South Africa has had a host of geographical implications, both for rump South Africa and the emergent Black states. In the main these have been directed towards the development of the Black states as economic and political units. Two prongs are evident: first, the South African Government has encouraged the growth of 'border' industrial areas, where industrialists may establish factories close to the border of one of the independent or self-governing states, and the workers commute from the Black state to the factory and back again each day. In this manner the permanent flow of Black workers to the towns in the White areas may be slowed. Direct investment by Whites in the Black areas was at first prevented, although now it is allowed under controls, so that industrial areas may be established within the borders of the Black states. Second, the Black governments have embarked upon national development planning to attract industry and improve agriculture within their own state areas. This is done without regard to what may lie on the other side of the new states' boundary. White South Africa has adopted the same policy. Thus South Africa is no longer a planning suit. The South African National Physical Development Plan (South Africa, 1976) ignored the Black states, while national plans for independent (e.g. Potgieter, 1977) and self-governing (e.g. Thorrington-Smith *et al.*, 1978) states have shown little concern for neighbouring White areas.

The Black states have had to establish a political infrastructure in a comparatively short time. New capital cities have been planned or provisionally established, and new bureaucrasies have come into being. The scale has ranged from full national government executive, legislative, administrative and judicial complexes, to new magisterial offices, schools, and even border posts. Thus the quest by the White population of South Africa for a secure place on the continent has resulted in the development of a number of policies which have had a direct impact upon the landscape. The legislative background to the South African landscape is fundamental to any understanding of the present.

4

Landscapes of non-commercial agriculture

Any examination of the landscapes of South Africa is immediately confronted with a basic dualism between the Black states and the remainder of the country. The division of land between Black and White is of fundamental significance to the evolution of the South African landscape, as it is within the Black areas that the traditional systems of husbandry were fossilised and then decayed (Fig. 4.1). It is thus possible to talk of a distinctive agricultural landscape, even if the concept of a distinctive agriculture has been challenged (Lipton, 1977). The Black areas have acted as labour reservoirs for the White areas, and as a result commercial agriculture has been neglected until very recently. Although 'non-commercial' may be a misnomer, it indicates the fact that little of the production of the Black areas enters the market economy, and that the recurrent deficits in agricultural production are made good by purchases from the surpluses of the White areas. Consequently in the mid-1970s only between one-sixth and one-eighth of the agricultural production of the Black states entered the market economy.

The delimitation of the Black areas

It was only in the 1830s and 1840s that the foundations of the present legal division of land between Black and White were laid. White settlement in the Cape Colony had not been challenged by the presence of large numbers of indigenous peoples. The advance of the frontiers of the Cape colony until the 1770s presented a 'soft frontier', with the frontier settlers incorporating or driving away the indigenous population but not meeting any marked barriers. However, first in the eastern Cape and later in Natal and the interior, large numbers of semi-sedentary Blacks barred the advance of the White settlers. The problem of White land hunger and relatively large Black numbers was resolved in the Rural Location or Reserve Policy, which was adopted by colonial and republican administrations alike, as the reserves incorporated lands which could not be settled by White colonists. The initial proposals to create large compact reserves, or preferably a line demarcating Black from

54

Fig. 4.1 Transkei rural landscape. Nguni settlement was mainly dispersed, with separate family housing groups adjacent to the arable lands. The remaining land is used as communal grazing. (South African Railways)

White, were unsuccessful as independent Black states were increasingly viewed as threats to the colonists in the nineteenth century. Thus attempts at creating successively a large Kaffraria (Ciskei–Transkei), Basutoland (Lesotho plus the eastern Orange Free State) or Zululand (the lands north and east of the Tugela River) gave way to the small controlled locations under the supervision of colonial and republican officials.

The first important locations were established in the eastern Cape in the 1840s as territories for the Fingo tribes, who had supported the British in the frontier wars. Within these locations traditional laws and land tenures were preserved under the overall suzerainty of the British colonial administration. As such, the areas of the locations were demarcated and White settlement within those boundaries was forbidden. The process was extended by the British Government in the 1850s when British Kaffraria was divided into locations where the Black population was to continue to live without White interference, but interspersed with areas open to White farming settlement. Significantly in some of the small-scale farming areas Blacks and Whites mingled. This was viewed by the Government as desirable as a civilising influence upon the Blacks in European ways on the one hand, and introducing Black agricultural skills to White immigrants on the other hand. The current White-held myth of Black agricultural incompetence is largely a product of

55

the last 100 years. Thus the locations were designed to accommodate the large numbers of Blacks who were surplus to the labour requirements of the White farmers, and who were left to their own devices as much as possible.

Rural locations were also adopted by the republican authorities as a means of solving the problem of living with large numbers of Blacks. At first, Black chiefs were treated as independent leaders. Later they were regarded as vassals, with separate states under the sovereignty of the Republican Government, which as in the colonial areas, reserved the right to impose taxation upon their vassals. The complex histories of Orange Free State–Lesotho, and Natal–Zululand relations reflect the decline of the Black areas from independence to dependence and final partition. In the Transvaal the indigenous powers fared worst of all with few areas remaining nominally within this sphere of Black ownership by 1900.

The main outlines of the Black states had been set by 1913 in the Cape, Natal and the Orange Free State. Within the Transvaal, large areas although nominally owned by Whites and indeed partitioned into farms, were actually occupied and farmed by Blacks with probably the same degree of interference in their affairs as Blacks experienced in the demarcated locations. The 1936 Natives Trust and Land Act provided for the enlargement of the Black areas to take account of these lands and to provide security for some of those Blacks living within the regions they had long occupied. In addition a small number of farms actually occupied by Whites were to be purchased to provide for some of the growth in the Black population of the country.

It is worth noting that in the Rural Location Policy, with the exception of the Transkeian territories, the Black areas were highly fragmented. In British Kaffraria (Ciskei) this was done so that White and Black farmers could learn from one another by 'looking over the fence at their neighbours' and so improving the standard of both. Thus small locations were officially thought to be desirable. In Natal, the Black areas were fragmented to break the possibility of any federation hostile to colonial interests, and for security each location was made dependent on the surrounding White farming areas. In Zululand the land suitable for White plantations and ranches was excised from the Black areas, leaving a highly fragmented remainder, and this was in effect the experience of Black areas elsewhere. What is worth noting is that the cultural and technical assimilation policies largely failed and that these fragmented areas remained socially and technically isolated, rather than open to the diffusion of ideas and methods from outside. As a result of the differing political, and hence economic powers of the White and Black areas, the two diverged in landscape terms when after an initial period of prosperity the Black areas began a period of economic decline, which appears to be continuing. The lines drawn by nineteenth- and twentieth-century bureaucrats to demarcate Black and White areas in South Africa have thus had a profound landscape impact.

In terms of the 1913 Natives Land Act these areas were guaranteed as

Black areas. However, the area involved (9.5 million ha) was already inadequate for African needs and did not represent the effectively Black occupied areas. Consequently under the 1936 Natives Trust and Land Act provision was made for the purchase of additional land (6.6 million ha) for the Black areas. In the main this was already occupied by Black groups practising traditional agriculture, although some areas were puchased from White farmers and provided room for experimentation. However, the political pressures on the authorities were such that most of these purchased areas soon became extensions of the traditional farming areas.

Traditional Black agriculture

One of the major distinguishing features of the traditional economy of the Black states in South Africa was the land tenure system. This was an integral part of the social organisation of the people and in marked contrast to White concepts. Land was not owned by individuals but was held by the group, whether clan, tribe or larger grouping. Rights to use the land for residence or cultivation were granted to individuals according to the needs of the group and the individuals within it. Thus areas for cultivation were granted for each wife a man married, and it was she who cultivated that land and raised the crops necessary. Grazing areas remained in communal use, and grazing activity was controlled by the men in the community, who were also responsible for hunting the wild animals. Arable plots were held at the discretion of the local chief or headman and were redistributed when the plot was no longer required. The plots were not inheritable and could not be disposed of by sale or gift; they were taken back into the communal pool when the recipients died or were no longer able to cultivate them.

The traditional system provided for expansion through taking new areas into cultivation and the abandonment of worked-out areas. In the period before the fixing of rural location and reserve boundaries new land could be acquired and population increases could be accommodated, as could the movement of large groups of people to new areas. In general the population densities appear to have been comparatively low, although no reliable estimates are possible. Substantial areas of grazing lands separated communities, as did extensive areas of semi-natural vegetation, where the indigenous wild animals could be hunted. In some cases extensive no-man's-land remained between the various chieftaincies which were in conflict with one another. Thus in the nineteenth century, although population densities appeared high compared with the White areas, they were by modern standards low, probably under 25 persons per square kilometre even in Zululand and Transkei, and included extensive uninhabited regions (Daniel, 1973).

The production emphasis varied substantially within the Black groups, ranging from an almost exclusively pastoral economy in the drier western and the northern parts of the country to a mixed crop–stock economy in the south and east. However, it is virtually impossible at present to gauge the balance between the two, except to state that stock farming appears to have been the main interest, if not support, of all the Black groups. It was in cattle that the traditional economy possessed a form of movable and inheritable wealth, with an overriding religious connotation. Thus cattle raising formed the basis of most economies and substantial herds were built up, which were the attraction of a community's enemies in times of strife.

Any discussion of present-day agriculture in the Black areas presents enormous problems depending upon the view taken of the pre-White contact period. There are few facts upon which to base any meaningful discussion and what follows must be viewed as tentative. It is perhaps worth quoting a recent study which seeks to demolish existing ideas or myths about the subject:

> The myth that Blacks are poor farmers has been convenient for their white competitors and employers, who held the political power. The myth pre-dated Tomlinson (1955), but received its final embodiment, buoyed up by a battery of largely unfounded statistical 'findings', in his massive and 'authoritative' report. The aim of this paper has been to question the certainties – the facts and statistics which provide the apparently solid and authoritative basis for this myth. It is not possible as yet, given our abysmal ignorance about black farming, to provide alternative answers. (Lipton, 1977: 85)

The concept of two agricultures in South Africa, the one efficient and White, and the other inefficient and Black, has been widely accepted. The core of this image is the nature of Black agriculture as small scale, unmechanised and burdened by traditional customs and attitudes, which preclude any move to adopt a more economic approach to agriculture. Thus in the Black areas the landscape reflects not only a different scale of farming but a different era. This assumption has been questioned by work in other parts of Africa including Lesotho, which has shown that Black small-scale farmers have produced yields, comparable in terms of net value added, to the capital-intensive White sector. It is therefore largely a measure of what is put into the Black areas which distinguishes them from the White farming areas in an economic sense. In landscape terms it is a matter of scale and cultural background which distinguishes Black areas from the neighbouring White farms. That this continues to be the case after such a long period of contact between Black and White has been cause for concern. An investigation of the dual nature of agriculture in 1975 commented:

> It is also clear that Bantu who have for years given excellent service on White farms revert to their traditional ways of life as soon as they return to the homelands and, contrary to what is expected, take with them very little of what they have learnt about management from White farmers. (Du Preez, 1975: 9)

Thus the diffusion theory so often applied to the adoption of agricultural techniques has a powerful barrier along the lines separating Black and White, which has tended to reinforce and accentuate differences rather than minimise them.

The White impact

The traditional economies of all the Black areas were severely affected by White occupation. Large numbers, probably the majority of the Black population, were dispossessed and were reduced to the status of tenants on White-owned farms. Even within the areas which remained in Black possession considerable movement and disruption took place as groups were transferred to new reserves, when government policy was decided upon. Furthermore the opportunities to move and to extend the grazing areas were lost through the demarcation of boundaries and the imposition of intertribal peace. Peace and medical attention resulted in a dramatic decline in death rates and hence population expansion, which aggravated the situation.

However, the initial response to colonisation of the land by White settlers was the rise in Black agricultural and pastoral production to supply the colonists' needs (Bundy, 1979). Early White farmers found cultivation problematical, even with Black labour, and it was consequently easier to purchase their requirements from the local Black population. There appears to have been a period of Black prosperity following the initial shock of occupation. The spur to production was the need for currency as a result of the imposition of taxation in the form of hut and poll taxes by governments and private landowners. Nevertheless increasingly the traditional economy was undermined as the trading stores and pedlars made industrial goods available, which could only be acquired through the introduction of a money economy. Of the goods available, firearms were particularly disastrous as wild animals were rapidly eliminated, and hunting ceased to be a support for the economy. In general though, the response to the need for currency was to increase agricultural production rather than seek work in the White areas.

The increase in production benefited certain classes in Black society as the more adventurous farmers were able to achieve a moderate income. However, capital was converted into livestock, particularly cattle, as there was little else that could be done with the unspent profits. In the Ciskei and Transkei efforts were made from the 1850s onwards to establish peasant agriculture through the introduction of individual inheritable title for crop land, so that private improvements could be encouraged and could be retained by the farmer and his heirs. In 1894 the Glen Grey Act provided for careful planning and the establishment of an individual tenure in the Ciskeian and Transkeian territories. One of the features of the programme was that plots could not be subdivided and so, as land for colonisation was not available, a landless labouring class would come into being, at the same time as those with land would be obtaining some degree of prosperity.

The rise in prosperity was short lived. Animal diseases, particularly the rinderpest outbreak of 1895–96 and later east coast fever outbreaks were disastrous as cattle numbers were decimated in some districts. Parallel with this was an increased efficiency on the part of the White traders, who through virtual monopoly conditions were able to hold down prices, while maintaining high prices for imported goods (Palmer and Parsons, 1977). Thus in the period 1890–1910 the signs of impoverishment became apparent. Unlike the White farming sector, little state assistance was given to enable the Black farming areas to recover from the crises. The result was a greater movement by young males to paid employment in the White sector of the economy and the abandonment of agricultural planning and practice to the women and the aged. As each area reached crisis point so the flow of labour increased markedly, often fluctuating according to the years of surplus and deficit production. The general indebtedness of the population resulted in this flow of labour becoming permanent as the need for cash increased. Thus one of the dominant features of the rural areas, the absence of the able-bodied males, assumed major proportions. This feature has had the result of decreasing pressure on the land, yet equally it has had the effect of draining the Black areas of their most energetic workers.

A number of general comments on land, labour and capital are necessary when examining the agriculture of the Black areas. These cover some 15.5 million ha or 13.7 per cent of the area of South Africa. Of this apparently 14.7 million ha are classified as agricultural and approximately 1.6 million ha are cultivated. Thus if the 1951 figure of 600 000 farming families is taken, this would provide 24 ha of land per family, including their share of the communal grazing area, or 2.7 ha of cultivated land per family. These figures appear to be approximately correct from later studies, but must be regarded with extreme caution as no reliable agricultural census is undertaken in the Black areas and no comprehensive study has been undertaken since the 1950s.

In terms of capital in the period between the formation of the Union and the Second World War little state expenditure on Black farming took place, whereas large sums were expended on the White sector. Since then increased expenditure on Black agriculture has narrowed the gap to approximately 2 : 1, White : Black state expenditure. Credit facilities are negligible in Black areas, and farmers do not have access to the Land Bank, which requires security for loans in the form of mortgages on land, or indeed to most forms of normal agricultural credit, which in 1978 amounted to nearly R30 000 per White farm. It is through the provision of credit that agricultural risks may be taken and crises overcome. Thus with the normal forms of finance unavailable, surpluses have been converted into livestock, which have shown greater investment potential than the alternatives. Credit in the White sector was also used to invest in new seeds, fertilisers and machinery. Only one-tenth of the crop land in the African areas receives any chemical fertiliser and there is little prospect of this proportion increasing markedly. Even in the sphere of state investment in irrigation, only 24 000 of 900 000 ha of irrigated land lies in the Black areas, although this position is now changing. Marketing, transport and other facilities are largely lacking or are only at a rudimentary stage and thus little incentive for improvement is present. As a result, although the agricultural potential of the Black states amounts to 23 per cent of the country's total, actual production is estimated at 2 per cent.

Possibly it is in the provision of labour in the Black agricultural sector that most disagreement and lack of information occurs. According to 1970 estimates there were nearly one million Blacks engaged in agriculture in the Black areas, a figure disputed as being too high. Thus approximately 2.2 ha of cultivated land was worked per person. Estimates of as much as 6 ha per person have been produced and give a measure of the sheer lack of information available. However, to cultivate even 1 ha without mechanised equipment is about the limit of physical capability. It therefore would appear that the areas are underfarmed, with extensive rather than intensive cultivation. Thus the paradox of extensive and underutilised land appears, with insufficient men to work it productively using the available technology. Here the basis of agriculture becomes apparent. In most cases it is not worth the while of the landholder to cultivate and take the risks and expenses of attempting to cultivate, when products from the White sector can be purchased reasonably cheaply. Migratory labour is likely to provide a more profitable outlet for the rural landholder, without subsidies or credit for seed, fertiliser and machinery, and without a marketing system at the end of the process. Thus even on the Taung Irrigation Scheme, approximately half the settlers at any given time are absent, working in the White areas (de Villiers, 1978).

Reform of traditional agriculture

After a long period of assuming that the larger the scheme and the larger the farm the more viable it is, agricultural thinking in various parts of the Third World has concluded that small family farms are able to raise yields above those on large-scale farms using hired labour. The incentive of working for oneself, so that additional profits are retained by the individual and his family, is a major driving force in smallholding agriculture under the free enterprise economy. It is in the provision of services and in marketing that economies of scale are beneficial. With the rapid growth in rural population greater attention to the agricultural potential of the Black areas is clearly necessary, and in the main this needs to be labour intensive, so that resources can be diverted to capital works such as irrigation, extension services, research and training and an efficient marketing system. Small-scale farming does not need to be unscientific, only intensive.

Official neglect of Black agriculture has been such that it was only in 1955 with the Report of the Commission for the Socio-Economic Development of the Bantu Areas (Tomlinson Report) (South Africa, 1955) that Blacks were considered as anything other than labour reserves. The main economic recommendations of the Report were rejected by the Government and only a few structural changes were introduced. These had a marked effect upon the landscape of parts of South Africa, particularly the Nguni areas, but little economic reform has been evident. The same agricultural systems operated if within a slightly different geographical pattern. Within the Black areas the population was grouped into agricultural villages, usually with large plots of

0.2 ha. The arable lands were then regrouped, and those which had previously been on steep or eroded slopes were abandoned. The village and the arable lands were then fenced from the remainder of the land which became common grazing (Fig. 4.2). This redistribution fixed the area of arable land and in theory the number of cultivators, but this has not always been so, and new distributions and extensions have sometimes resulted in the need for a second replanning. Moves to reduce stock numbers have also been unsuccessful and with the experience of the Zimbabwean Land Husbandry Act of 1951 in mind, few attempts have been made to interfere with the private ownership of livestock.

Economic changes in the Black areas became imperative as political changes occurred. Self-government and independence resulted in the emergence of a Black political elite, who, as elsewhere in Africa, viewed the rural areas as the major source of potential wealth if only a means could be devised to revive them. The result has been a series of plans designed to raise agricultural production and overcome the disabilities under which Black agriculture has been pursued. The landholding systems, credit facilities, education and research facilities, cultivation practices and marketing systems have all come under scrutiny. Inevitably the new governments have found the whole inheritance from the past overwhelming, and no moves have been made to introduce revolutionary changes, either for economic or political reasons. Thus, so far, the concepts of African Socialism have not been involved.

The main tendency has been to introduce special schemes for particular crops and to slowly change the agricultural system, through the influence of the success of these special schemes. The various governments have tended to focus upon irrigation projects as a means of growing specialised crops. In Transkei at Quamata, in the Ciskei at Keiskammahoek and in the future in KwaZulu on the Makatini Flats, significant schemes have been planned or are in operation. Cash crops such as sugar cane have been developed in KwaZulu where in 1976 some 17 000 ha were under cultivation (Lenta, 1978). In order to expand this production the South African Sugar Association established the 'Small Cane-Growers Financial Aid Fund' to assist small growers develop their efficiency and productivity. A sum of R5 million was set aside for credit and for farmers' centres for training and demonstration. Provision for small settlement schemes is planned for a later stage of the programme of development, once the necessary infrastructure has been created.

Other approaches to development have been through the provision of improvements such as irrigation water, which has necessitated a complete reorganisation of the existing agricultural pattern. An illustration may be found in the Ciskei, where in 1976 at the Tyefus Location on the Fish River, the community agreed to change the existing system (Ciskei, 1976). The traditional land rights to approximately 4 ha of arable land, were surrendered by the landholders in exchange for 0.25 ha of irrigated subsistence plots. The remaining land surrendered was pooled to provide new irrigation farms of 4 ha for selected members of the community, who were considered to have the

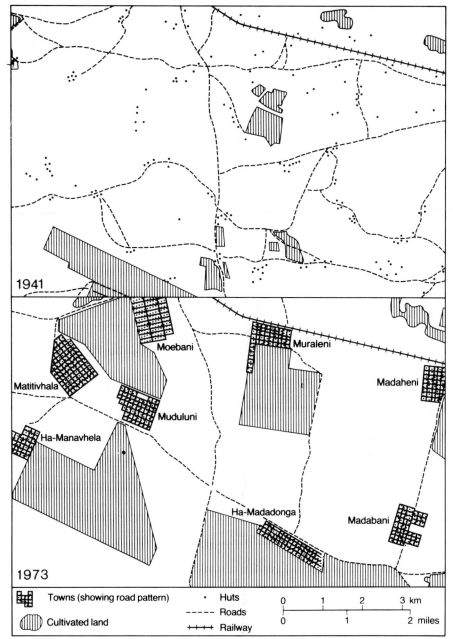

Fig. 4.2   Village regrouping in Lebowa (northern Transvaal). The complete replanning of the landscape is evident between 1941 and 1973.

ability to work such farms, and a community farm, which occupied approximately half the area involved. The commercial farms and the community farm have been engaged in raising cash crops such as tobacco and cotton for sale, and thus earning the capital to buy foodstuffs, which have not been successfully cultivated. Community supervision through centralised marketing, technical facilities and fund raising has been essential to ensure the success of the scheme. It is interesting to note that the grouped village has partially broken down as the commercial farmers have chosen to live on their arable farms, while the remainder of the community lives in the village. Inevitably other communities are watching the progress of this pilot scheme before committing themselves to such a radical change.

On similar lines the Ditsobotha Pilot Rural Development Project was begun in 1975 by the Bophuthatswana Government using a private firm of consultants. Approximately 3800 ha were divided into 200 lots, and virtually the whole area was cultivated, but under dry land farming conditions. Although the results were encouraging it was realised that the plots of 19 ha each were too small and that 45 ha would be necessary to achieve the target of a net income of R1500–R2000 per annum. However, as an example for other farmers the project has been highly successful and other schemes have followed, both in this district and elsewhere in Bophuthatswana. Most have emulated the Ditsobotha Project, but others such as the Molopo Scheme on 30 000 ha have developed a communal cattle ranching project (Bophuthatswana, 1977).

Significantly over 100 irrigation schemes have been undertaken in the Black areas, but in general they have not been successful as they have been run as subsistence farms, with levels of cultivation similar to the traditional areas, and with high rates of absenteeism when the plot-holders have taken work in the White areas. Success with the Vuvulane Irrigated Farms in Swaziland has however indicated that without traditional constraints and with a high degree of supervision, success is possible.

Colonisation schemes

One of the significant aspects of change in the Black areas of South Africa has been the large-scale exchanges of land and population between the White and Black areas. As a result of the 1936 Natives Trust and Land Act approximately six million ha have been purchased by the South African Development Trust to be added to the Black areas. Although part of this has been for resettling Blacks displaced from private Black-owned farms purchased as 'black spots', and others displaced from the White farming areas, a substantial tract remained which was open and free from any traditional farming system. The presence of this land has presented a major challenge and opportunity to the various South African and Black state government departments which had to plan its future.

Two approaches have been apparent: either to regard such areas as land available for the extension of traditional farming activity, or as land available for experimentation and the introduction of commercial farming. The former has been politically the most acceptable, and it was the approach adopted by the South African Department of Cooperation and Development, and indeed by the governments of most of the Black states. The large and growing numbers of landless Blacks have exerted pressures on the administration to obtain land, and they were the first priority in the period from 1936 to 1960. A study undertaken in the Ciskei (Mills and Wilson, 1952), suggested that the policy of the administration was to settle as many people as possible on the land. As a result the arable plots of farmers settled on Trust land were only two-thirds the size of those on communal tenure land and under half that of those with freehold tenure. Even this understated the position, as Trust land farmers were not permitted to obtain additional land if it became available.

Many of the Trust purchases did little more than recognise the existing situation, where the Black population had previously been the tenants of White landowners, and particularly in the Transvaal, tenants of the major land development companies. In the main, in such areas the traditional land-holding system had been comparatively little disturbed, as White landowners had interfered sparingly, so long as the rentals had continued to be paid and the supply of labour had not been interrupted. The experiments in farming methods and tenure were only possible where White occupiers were displaced, and this was mainly in the Ciskei and KwaZulu. In these cases the result has been a major transformation of the landscape, as in general the pre-existing White farmsteads and buildings have been largely demolished and traditional Black structures erected in their places, so that virtually all traces of White occupation have been removed.

Pressure to continue this policy of smallholder settlement would effectively have extended the problem areas of Black traditional farming. The massive resettlement programme from the 'black spots' and the White farming areas resulted in additional demands for land, much of which had to be satisfied by providing land in areas purchased from White farmers. Black state governments have frequently been faced with crises which have required instant solutions, rather than ideal solutions (Fig. 4.3). The Ciskei, which has had to receive large numbers of refugees from all parts of the Cape Province, holds half its land area in repurchased White farms. Pressure to throw all of these open to the refugees and existing residents has been considerable, as this is politically by far the most popular course for a government to take.

The impact of the refugee problem is well illustrated by the Ntabethemba resettlement scheme in the northern Ciskei. In 1975–76 after the transfer of the Herchel and Glen Grey districts from the Ciskei to Transkei, approximately 25 000 people arrived as refugees in the Ciskei. The refugee camp at Thornhill, a Development Trust farm, mushroomed and the Ciskei was faced with a crisis. Further farms were purchased and in all 31 000 ha were made available for the resettlement of the refugees. Dry land farming was

recognised as being impractical and the Ciskeian Department of Agriculture and Forestry followed the Tyefus scheme. Thus those farmers with land rights received 0.25 ha arable plots and irrigation water, which could provide subsistence and a small food surplus. In addition every family received a town plot in a series of agro-villages which have been laid out throughout the area. Grazing was allowed on the remainder of the land, but in places four times as many animals were grazed as the estimated carrying capacity, with the result that in a matter of four years the pasturage has been virtually depleted. When the basic scheme is functioning some refinements are to be introduced. First, commercial 4 ha plots will be provided with the same object as at Tyefus. Second, tribal farms for cash crops will provide community incomes. Third, a game-ranching operation is planned in the drier and more rugged part of the area, together with stock grazing ground where animals destined for sale may be fattened. The three refinements may prove to be politically problematical as refugees continue to arrive and demand land, thereby depleting the supplies of irrigation water and land and available grazing.

Alternatives to subsistence style colonisation have been attempted in several Black states, where the opportunity exists to modernise agriculture. The areas are unencumbered with traditional landholding customs, and hence present fewer problems for establishing commercial enterprises. Three basic approaches are possible: either the taking over of the existing farms by Black farmers and their continuance as before, or the establishment of a new settlement of commercial farmers, or the development of a state farm.

The first approach has been rare and generally limited to only a few farms where the Black farmers have the know-how and capital to work the establishment, and it might sometimes be added, the political influence to acquire the land. In some cases the land acquired is of sufficient significance for the pre-existing economic structure to be maintained. This has generally been true of specialised horticultural enterprises. Thus the Zebedelia Citrus Estate, incorporated into Lebowa, has continued to be run as it was before incorporation. Specialised areas such as the pineapple farms of the Peddie district, incorporated into the Ciskei, have similarly changed little. The White farmers have either been retained as managers or the Department of Agriculture and Forestry supervises production, while training Ciskeians to take over the farms.

The second approach has been either to subdivide existing units or to establish a completely new system of small farms, which can be organised to take account of the limited capital and farming experience of most of the settlers. Irrigation settlements have proved to be the most popular means of developing the resources of the newly acquired Black areas. It is here that the

Fig. 4.3 Glenmore resettlement township. In 1979 so-called 'redundent' Blacks in the eastern Cape were resettled in the Ciskei at Glenmore on the Fish River. A White-owned farm was purchased for the purpose as part of the Ciskei consolidation programme. (*Eastern Province Herald*)

Fig. 4.4   Keiskammahoek Irrigation Scheme, Ciskei. Intensive dairy farming based on irrigated pastures and crops provides support for a new middle class of Black farmers. (*Eastern Province Herald*)

relatively abundant water supplies of the Black states can be put to good use. One example is at Keiskammahoek, on the site of one of the British–German Legion schemes of the 1850s. In 1975 the Ciskeian Government undertook a study of suitable irrigation sites in the territory and identified Keiskammahoek as having the best prospects for development as an irrigation scheme. However, little of the land was sufficiently level for annual crops and the decision was taken to develop superior quality pastures as the basis of a dairying enterprise. The scheme is dependent upon a high degree of organisational control and supervision, which is provided by an international development company, most of whose officials have had experience of similar schemes elsewhere in Africa. A total of 175 settler families were allocated 4 ha plots upon which the grasses and crops are grown (Fig. 4.4). Capital, technical assistance and marketing facilities are all provided by the development company, which runs a home farm of 200 ha. Under the scheme it is expected that each family will be able to earn a net income of approximately R3000 per annum, thus leading to the creation of an agricultural middle class, something which has been lacking in the Black areas so far. This is an interesting concept illustrating the ideology of the Ciskei Government, which views the future in terms of Western capitalism rather than African Socialism.

Fig. 4.5   Tea plantations, Transkei. Estate farming within the Black states has been comparatively rare. (Information Services of South Africa)

Similar, but less controlled schemes have been established elsewhere. Thus
the Taung Irrigation Scheme was laid out with 1.7 ha plots for individuals
and 3.5–6.5 ha plots for partnerships. This is in marked contrast to the adjacent Vaal–Hartz Scheme in the White area where individual plots of 15–
25 ha were laid out. Similar variations were noted in Natal where irrigated
plots dating from the early part of the present century averaged under 1 ha in
the Black areas, yet generally exceeded 20 ha in the White areas.

The third alternative is to use the acquired areas as state farms. This
approach has been acceptable in order to provide a cash income and employment. Thus at Quamata in Transkei the tea estates have been organized as a
commercial plantation by a private company working under state control,
rather than as a supervised smallholders scheme (Fig. 4.5). The KwaZulu Government is similarly opening up the Makatini Flats in the north of the territory as a series of large sugar estates. Other specialised crops needing careful
attention, such as coffee, have been developed in Venda and Lebowa. State
farms however remain poorly developed in the Black states, owing to a lack
of suitable land and a marked resistance to the political implications of state
farming. However, the tribal or communal farms operated on many of the
resettlement schemes have obvious implications for the future, as a balance is
struck between private initiative and state intervention.

69

The present landscape

The present Black landscapes are a complex inheritance from the pre-colonial, colonial and modern periods. The delimitation of the Black areas over a long period of time, their entry into the market economy and then impoverishment, have had a major impact upon the landscape, as indeed have the large-scale intrusions of modern development planning. The picture is one of relative stability in areas such as cultivation; but one of instability in terms of settlement patterns as village grouping and resettlement programmes are undertaken with increasing urgency.

Change is probably the most significant feature of the Black rural areas at the present time, after a long period of stagnation. Population pressures are such that traditional areas have been replanned to cater for the increased numbers of landholders and indeed for the swelling numbers of the landless. Regrettably accessible detailed investigations of these changes are comparatively rare.

Studies by Hattingh (1973 and unpublished) of one of the most heavily populated rural areas of Lebowa in the northern Transvaal come to some interesting conclusions. The Modjadji Location in 1977 possessed a population density of 218 persons per square kilometre. The population appears to have risen rapidly in the present century, yet the agricultural systems employed are markedly traditional and few commercial methods have been adopted. Comparative work indicated that between 1938 and 1977 the cultivated area had declined slightly, yet the number of hut groups had doubled and the population had increased by 160 per cent. Thus each family cultivated only 2 ha on average in 1977, whereas this figure had been 4.7 ha 40 years before. Indications of a decline in yields are also evident and the Location has ceased to be self-supporting in basic foodstuffs. Again the problems of the Location appear to be structural ones related to the essential unprofitability of agriculture.

Reorganisation of the Modjadji Location was planned in 1966, and these plans were only put into operation in the 1970s, so that the patterns of settlement in 1977 still reflected the highly scattered and fragmented inheritance from the past (Fig. 4.6). This is not to suggest a significant degree of continuity. It was found that between 1938 and 1968 only 14.4 per cent of hut groups remained in the same position. Further, settlement has shown a marked shift towards the boundary of the Location, with the White areas (Fig. 4.7). This concentration raises the question as to the relationship of much of the population to the White area, from which a large measure of support comes. Within the new villages an increasing proportion of the population is without land rights, and so dependent almost entirely upon the White areas.

Similar changes in settlement patterns are to be found elsewhere, with markedly increased rural or semi-rural populations in areas adjacent to the White areas, especially the metropolitan regions such as Pretoria and Durban. In the more remote districts the rates of increase are lower, but Black rural

Fig. 4.6   Settlement in the Modjadji Location. The hut group with adjacent arable field is the basic unit of the rural landscape. (P. S. Hattingh)

depopulation appears to be extremely rare. Thus in Bophuthatswana a shift of population has been discerned towards the districts close to Pretoria, such as Winterveld (Smit, 1977). As a result high density rural settlements and slums have emerged where residence, rather than farming, has been the object of the settlement. Consequently new style rural–urban fringes have appeared in the Black areas of South Africa, akin to developments in the Third World city.

One of the major problems for all the Black states has been the influx of refugees from the White areas and from other Black states. The smaller states in particular have lacked resources to cope with the numbers involved and severe rural crises have arisen. Thus the State of QwaQwa in the Drakensberg on the Lesotho border had, between 1970 and 1980, increased its population from 25 000 to 232 000. Many of those arriving were displaced from White farms, bringing their livestock with them. Consequently in the same period cattle numbers doubled, with the result that the land was then stocked at three and a half times the estimated carrying capacity of the natural grazing. The immigrants were not provided with land rights, and so were denied access to arable land. At approximately an average density of 400 persons per square kilometre in 1980 in a mountainous area, portions of the State took on the appearance of extensive shanty towns rather than a rural landscape, where two-thirds of local income was generated by migratory workers outside the State's borders. Clearly the rural areas of QwaQwa serve functions other than those of an agricultural production zone, especially when it is con-

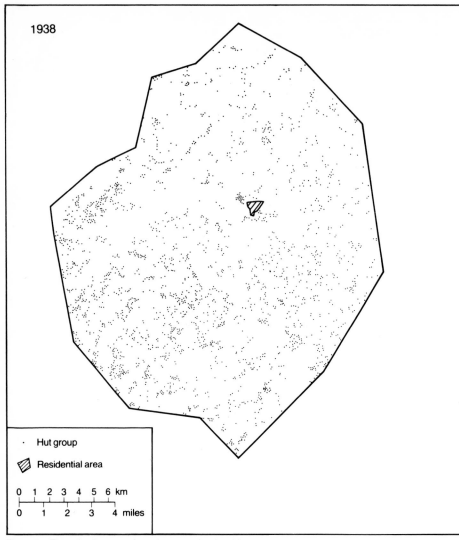

1938

- · Hut group
- ▨ Residential area

0 1 2 3 4 5 6 km
0 1 2 3 4 miles

Fig. 4.7 The distribution of settlements in the Modjadji Location, 1938–77. (Adapted after P. S. Hattingh)

sidered that the value of such production in 1976 amounted to under R5 per person. It is scarcely surprising that resettlement schemes have been unpopular with the governments of the Black states, on economic as well as political grounds. Similar problems have arisen in other Black states where extensive resettlement in a rural context has taken place, but rarely with the degree of planning noted in the Ciskei.

The major feature of the Black rural areas is their poverty, where traditional agricultural systems have been undermined through competition with a highly organised, and often highly subsidised White agricultural sector.

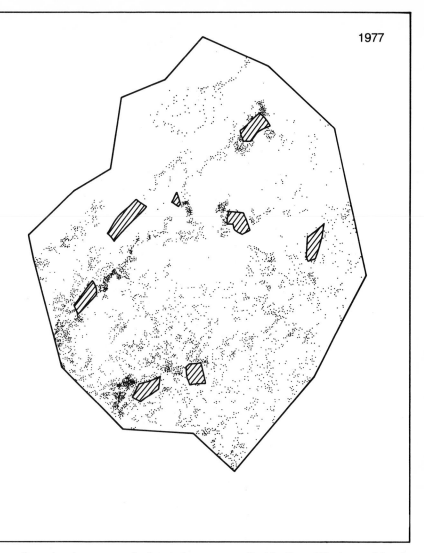

1977

Costs of production are such that it is more profitable for a Black rural land-holder to work in the White economic sector and retain his land as security, than to attempt to make his living from the land. Thus the Black rural areas are maintained by the remittances of the migrant workers, and this dependency appears to be increasing as wages improve in the White industrial sector and Black agriculture shows only either a slow expansion or stagnation. Consequently even in the most agriculturally advantageous Black state, KwaZulu, the value of agricultural production showed little increase in real terms in the 1960s, and in terms of contribution to the Gross Domestic Product declined significantly. The 1970s have shown little improvement in the situation.

73

Fig. 4.8   Traditional Black rural housing in the 'White' farming area. (Anne Christopher)

The National Accounts of the various Black states are depressing, particularly when attention is directed towards the agricultural sector. Whether these figures, as with most statistics for the Black states, may be credited is open to doubt. The agricultural contribution to the national economy has declined in all the Black states, reflecting a greater degree of state spending. Agricultural production per head of population in 1976 averaged approximately R23. Even if the total Gross Domestic Product is considered, the range of *per capita* incomes of the Black states in the mid-1970s was low, averaging R91 in 1976. These figures could be increased to R320 if the estimated remittances of the migrant workers and the daily commuters were included. With levels of production as low as this, even with the income derived from migrant workers and other sources, such as direct aid from the central government, poverty is very real. Yet the escape route to the White areas has meant that starvation can be averted and the worst effects of poverty avoided, an extreme version of the core–periphery syndrome.

Black influences on White agricultural landscapes

Except for portions of the Cape Province most White farms employ substantial numbers of Black labourers and servants. In 1976 the number amounted to 1.1 million regular and casual employees. Many of the labourers and their families live on the White farms and have been given portions of land to cultivate. The result is frequently a dual landscape superimposed on each White farm, with the Black-occupied area the scene of traditional housing types, cultivated areas and livestock (Fig. 4.8). At one time the agricultural censuses distinguished between the two. Thus in 1960 over one million ha on White farms were farmed by Blacks, who possessed one-seventh of the livestock and cultivated one-tenth of the maize on the farms. Such a contribution is a significant element throughout South Africa. Its impact however is declining as the number of farm workers is reduced and as more regular housing is provided by the farmer and the Government.

5

Landscapes of commercial pastoralism

The White areas of South Africa exhibit a very different form of rural settlement from those examined in the Black areas. Most of South Africa (63.2 per cent) is apportioned into farms owned by Whites and to a lesser degree Coloureds and Indians. Owing to the poverty of the physical environment, many farms are devoted to stock raising, and few areas are without a livestock component in their income (Fig. 5.1). Even the regions which are presently the most highly cultivated, such as the eastern Orange Free State or the Natal

Table 5.1   Gross value of agricultural production (R million)

Year	Crops	Livestock products	Total
1919/20	48	63	111
1929/30	56	68	124
1939/40	75	61	136
1949/50	231	216	447
1959/60	439	376	815
1969/70	725	548	1323
1978/79	2675	1573	4248

Source: Division of Agricultural Marketing Research.

Table 5.2   Land use in the White rural areas 1960–76 (000 ha)

Land use	1960	1965	1976
Cultivated land	9563	10 028	10 212
Permanent crops	461	821	
Artificial pasture	209	897	
Natural pasture	78 977	71 342	
Wood and forest	1081	1071	1125
Other	1499	3636	
Total	91 790	87 795	85 719

Source: Agricultural censuses.

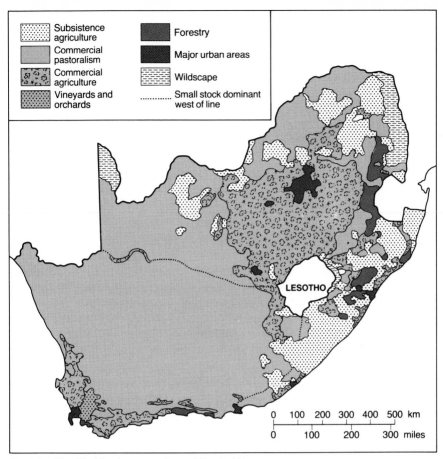

Fig. 5.1   Simplified landscape regions of South Africa.

north coast, were first colonised by settlers pursuing pastoral activities. Pastoralism is therefore a basic element in most South African rural landscapes,
although pastoral products have ceased to be the most important prop to the
rural economy (Table 5.1). Furthermore, although between 1949/50 and
1978/79 the volume of crop production tripled, pastoral production only
doubled. The area devoted to various land uses in the White areas therefore
shows the overwhelming dominance of natural pasture (Table 5.2).

Land grant systems

Although the initial European settlement at the Cape of Good Hope was not
designed to undertake pastoral farming, this soon became the major activity
of the colonists. The Dutch East India Company directors in Amsterdam envisaged a trading and bartering system, whereby the indigenous population
would exchange their cattle and sheep for Dutch-manufactured goods.

However, this scheme proved to be unworkable as the livestock supply was erratic and conflict between herdsman and colonist interrupted even that trade. The early colonists thus engaged in mixed farming, with cattle and sheep grazing as part of their economy, but at first only supplementary to crop farming. In the early eighteenth century the seasonal movement of cattle and sheep was such that some colonists pastured their stock over the mountains at some distance from the established settlements around Cape Town and Stellenbosch. As the eighteenth century progressed so the flocks and herds were pushed further into the interior and along the coastal belts, until the seasonal return to the settled areas was abandoned (Guelke, 1976). The links between the pastoralist and the settled areas became increasingly tenuous, although the stock farmers never degenerated to a state of pure subsistence. The interior pastoralist was always able to sell sufficient hides, skins or tallow to purchase essential supplies, such as guns and gunpowder, and luxuries, such as coffee and fabrics, to retain his links with the settled areas (Harris and Guelke, 1977).

As stock farming ceased to be a subsidiary to crop farming, so regulation of its extent and organisation was thought to be desirable by the officials of the Dutch East India Company. Between 1708 and 1720 a series of regulations were issued providing for the organisation and taxation of the pastoral farmers. A mutually exclusive grazing area was to be demarcated for each grazier, and upon this he was to pay a small rental. Each grazier was entitled to mark out an area for himself by selecting the mid-point (ordonnantie) of his intended land, usually a spring or noticeable feature, and then riding at walking pace, for half an hour in several directions to mark the boundaries of an approximately circular farm. The area enclosed, if the selector did not gallop, was approximately 2500 ha (Christopher, 1976a). This size became the accepted area of a pastoral farm until late in the nineteenth century, and its influence upon land grants may be traced to neighbouring countries where Afrikaner settlement took place (Fig. 5.2). The system had its disadvantages, as later farmers had to establish the mid-points of their farms at least one hour's ride from those of their neighbours, in order that no overlap should occur. Frequently the distances were even greater, so that large areas of government ground were effectively used but not paid for.

This informal system worked well while unlimited land was available and the numbers involved were small (Van der Merwe, 1938). Owing to its informality and the lack of effective government control under the Dutch administration, farmers on the margins of settlement hesitated to apply for their lands, so as to avoid payment of the licence fees, and to test out the land to consider whether it was worth paying for. The British colonial administration in the early nineteenth century sought to overcome what was regarded as the major drawback to the system, namely the lack of security of tenure, which was seen as being detrimental to the permanent improvement of land and livestock. In 1814 the Government introduced the concept of perpetual leases, with surveyed boundaries, in the hope of tying the grazier to his lands

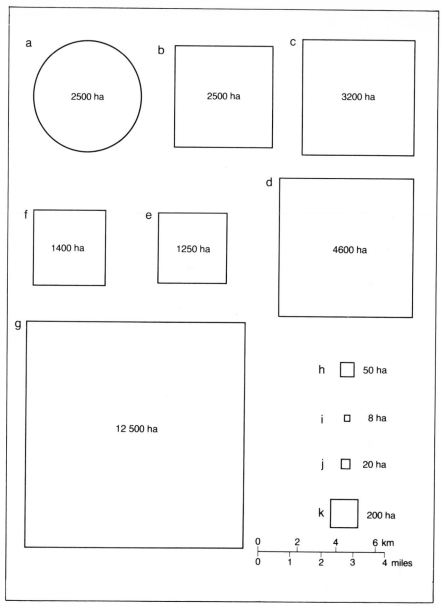

Fig. 5.2 Standard farm sizes in South Africa: (a) circular farm (half hour's walk radius); (b) square 2500 ha surveyed farm; (c) square farm (one hour's ride across); (d) square farm with horse's speed increased by 20 per cent; (e) 'half farms' of the eastern Orange Free State, northern Transvaal and eastern Cape; (f) New Republic (Zululand) farms; (g) increased grants for the Kalahari Desert State (two hours' ride across); (h) Dutch agricultural grants; (i) Natal colonisation plots for single men; (j) Natal, plots for families; (k) eastern Cape agricultural farm. (After Christopher, 1974)

and thus ending his nomadic habits, which were regarded as detrimental to his civilisation. Thus the standard 2500 ha farm was established widely over the southern Cape of Good Hope. However, its impracticality in the drier interior was recognised by the Cape Colonial Government in 1829 and no further attempts at standardisation were made in that province, as each area was surveyed into farms according to its estimated carrying capacity.

The concept of a standard farm unit survived in the minds of those Whites who embarked upon the Great Trek in the 1830s and 1840s, as well as the varrious Coloured groups who preceded them. Large tracts of the Orange Free State, Transvaal and Natal were thrown open to White settlement, where there appeared to be open land. The pioneers were each granted standard farms, often two for those who had taken part in the initial occupation of the country. The traditional circular farm was abandoned in favour of square units measured out by means of one hour's ride across the farm in each direction. The resultant size was approximately 3200 ha in extent, although it is evident that some horses were ridden at considerably greater speeds than those authorised, resulting in an increase in farm area. Standardisation was possible on the relatively level lands of the Orange Free State, southern Transvaal and portions of Natal, but it proved to be more difficult to enforce in the more rugged areas of the Drakensberg and the coastal margins of Natal, where control of particular water or level land resources was more important than the actual area which the farm covered (Christopher, 1976b).

Standard farms continued to be granted until the 1890s in South Africa, although the area had to be modified according to changing circumstances. The White conquest of the periphery of the Transvaal was contested by the Black peoples living there. In all but the south-central Transvaal the indigenous peoples had not been displaced to any great extent, nor had they been evicted from the north and south of Natal. Thus after the 1850s White pastoral settlement expanded periodically as individual tribes were conquered. In the 1880s a series of conquests opened up Zululand and parts of the western Transvaal and northern Cape (the Stellaland and Goshen Republics) to White settlement. In Zululand insufficient land was available for all those entitled to it, so that the standard-sized farm had to be cut to 1400 ha. In Stellaland and Goshen larger than standard areas were appropriated. Possibly the level plains enabled horses to be ridden more rapidly than the legal limit. The final phase of standard-sized land grants was in the late 1880s, when the Government of the Kalahari Desert State in the northern Cape offered 12 500 ha farms in the tract of semi-sand dune country. Here, it was access to the limited underground water supplies which determined success rather than sheer area.

In the Cape Colony standardisation was not adhered to after 1829, and surveyors were given a wide measure of discretion in the layout of suitable farm units. It is significant that in large measure they followed the initial squatters who had occupied the dry interior with their small stock, often decades before the arrival of the surveyor and the administrator. A series of experiments was undertaken by the Cape Colonial Government in the period between the granting of representative government in 1853 and Union in 1910, providing for the granting of large pastoral farms of up to 50 000 ha apiece. In common with all the pastoral units, tenure involved the payment of an often nominal rental, without a capital outlay. Experiments in cash sales largely failed, as prior to the development of export products the pastoral farming community on the frontier was short of cash. Forfeiture of land was rare even for late payment of rental. The theme of most legislation was to encourage families to settle on the land. The Cape Government did not encourage large commercial ranching companies such as those attracted by the Germans to Namibia and by the British South Africa Company to Zimbabwe in the early years of the twentieth century. This has been of considerable significance in landscape terms, resulting in a far closer settlement pattern than company farming would have done.

In the eastern Cape Province and in Natal small land grants, less than the 2500 ha standard, were made either to attract graziers to the better pastures, conserve the depleted resources of Crown Lands, or establish a dense White population to act as a military shield to the established areas of the colonies (Christopher, 1971). Grazing farms of as little as 400 ha were offered in Natal in the 1850s and an upper limit of 800 ha remained in force until the Crown Lands were exhausted at the end of the nineteenth century. The higher rainfall on the eastern side of the country, with the associated higher carrying capacity for stock, mainly cattle, was viewed favourably by the colonial governments for the expanding frontier. Thus the greater opportunities for cultivation resulted in the areas being viewed as suitable for mixed farming enterprises rather than for purely pastoral undertakings.

It is significant that although South Africa was not thrown open to large ranching companies, land speculation was such as to establish large holdings. In the late nineteenth and early twentieth centuries, British land investment companies and private speculators entered the land market on a substantial scale. Thus in the Transvaal in 1900 one-third of all farms were owned by investment companies. The five largest of these companies had acquired some 3.5 million ha by the outbreak of the First World War, with one company being in possession of 1.4 million ha. Such large-scale interference with the standard pattern of White-owned family farms was reflected in extensive leasing to Blacks, and the eventual purchase of many blocks of such farms by the Government for Black settlement. In all probability many of the farms purchased by the companies were either never occupied by Whites or occupied by them for only short periods and then abandoned, either because of a lack of security or unsuitability for the settler economy. Thus official pressures on the companies resulted in the fragmentation of the large estates for individual White holdings, or direct government purchase for Black settlement or game reserves. Significantly none of the companies undertook ranching enterprises on the scale to be found to the north of the Limpopo River. Government policy acted as a corrective to tendencies towards large-scale enterprise, as the ideal of individual family holdings was dominant in official thinking.

The governments of South Africa thus played a vital role in the establishment of the White pastoral areas and their maintenance. The original survey lines, now demarcated with fences, have been constraining influences upon later development, and frequently they are visible in the present landscape where contrasting grazing and conservation practices are in operation on either side of the line.

Farms

The almost total transfer of land in the White area of South Africa, from the Government to private ownership, is possibly unique in the annals of mid-latitude White colonisation. The State has lost control over resources which in countries such as Australia or the United States were retained by the authorities because of their unsuitability for agriculture. Even the minimal control of a quit-rent was abandoned in 1934 under the Abolition of Quit Rent Act, passed as a relief measure for farmers during the drought. The Commission of Enquiry into Agriculture commented in 1970 that land ownership as opposed to leasehold had developed as a strong tradition in South Africa, with the result that four-fifths of farmers own the land they farm. Doubts as to the propriety of the large-scale alienation of lands in the north-western Cape were expressed in the 1930s, as many farms had no permanent sources of water and during periods of drought there was no longer an outlet in the traditional system of 'trekking' with livestock to other non-drought areas.

The virtual absence of a state interest in land through a leasehold system may have had the result of creating 'spiritual stability and deeply fixed roots, patriotism and all the other characteristics' (South Africa, 1960), which provided the background of solidity and resilience to the Afrikaner nation, but it has had its drawbacks. The demand for land has been such as to direct men to attempt to make a living in areas highly unsuitable for the purpose, while the legal principle of divided inheritance has resulted in excessive subdivision of holdings. Demand for land has further driven up land prices, through speculation, to levels far in excess of its value as an agricultural commodity. The result has been the temptation to sell off portions in poor years and consequently farming units have became smaller and uneconomic. These features have led to a weakening of agricultural resources through overuse, ploughing unsuitable land, or more generally overgrazing, by increasing the land's vulnerability to droughts and other setbacks.

Demands for revision of land tenures in White areas are likely to founder on the virtual unassailable position of freehold tenure and the expense of state purchase, especially as the Government is committed to a large-scale acquisition programme for the enlargement of the Black areas. Furthermore, demand for land does not appear to be abating. Farmers wishing to extend their holdings, and individuals and companies seeking an avenue of investment have forced land prices up to levels little related to their economic potential. The problem of farming as a way of life, only to be abandoned as a result of failure, has inhibited any large-scale amalgamation of holdings. An inquiry undertaken in the Karroo in the early 1970s found that sheep farming was highly regarded as a way of life, which overcame the relatively poor living many farmers made on units which were too small for them (Blignaut, 1975).

Land prices in the White farming areas of South Africa have risen rapidly since the end of the Second World War. For the country as a whole between 1948 and 1978, land prices rose approximately tenfold, with those in the maize and wheat regions rising to eight to nine times the level of 30 years before. However, in the cattle grazing regions the increase is of the order of eighteenfold, but in the sheep grazing regions only fivefold. In 1979 land and fixed improvements were valued at R17.8 milliard and constituted over three-quarters of farming assets.

Good land is in short supply and after a long period of horizontal extensive frontier expansion, production can only be improved by more intensive use of existing farmland. This process involves substantial inputs. Parallel with this has been the tendency to counter declining relative profits per unit area by the purchase of adjoining land, which because of the competition for available land, tends to rise rapidly in price. This in turn results in the form of increased debt per unit area and may have the effect of turning an economic unit into an uneconomic proposition. Increases are particularly noticeable adjacent to the large cities, where even in a period of depression, small plots of 1–4 ha more than doubled in value in the five years 1973–78.

The number of farms in the White area continued to increase until the 1950 Census, by which time nearly 117 000 were enumerated. Thereafter decline set in and the number was reduced to 76 000 in 1976. This decline is in part the reflection of the smaller units being reclassified as urban (possibly 6000), and a decline in the number of medium-sized (100–2000 ha) farms. Small farms of under 100 ha and larger farms of over 2000 ha have increased in numbers, reflecting the trends towards smallholdings either in the rural–urban fringe or in irrigation areas at the one extreme, and the enlargement of stock and extensive grain farms at the other. In addition it appears that large tracts have been withdrawn from farming and are now abandoned. These trends have not eliminated the many farms which are too small and uneconomic. The Report of the Commission of Enquiry into Agriculture in 1970 considered that one-third of holdings were uneconomic, providing in 1963 a gross income of under R2000 per annum. Furthermore many farmers are in debt far beyond their ability to pay. Thus after allowing for costs, including debts repayments, a high proportion (30–40%) of White South African farms are uneconomic. A survey of the north-western Transvaal in 1965 revealed the fact that only one-quarter of farms were economic propositions, while up to one-half the farms in the other grazing areas were uneconomic units. The situation is however substantially better in the crop growing areas.

The progressive cutting up of economic farms into smaller units either on the death of the proprietor, or for speculative purposes, resulted in many of the small and oddly shaped farms on the landscape. Access to the available water resources on the original farm was often crucial to the successor farms, resulting in elongated units with excessive boundaries for the area. Ratios of 10 : 1 length to breadth were not uncommon where access to river frontages and available land was at stake. Speculative subdivision tended to be far more rectangular in form with little attention to the productive capacity of the land, whereas family subdivision sometimes resulted in the total farm being held in undivided shares, rather than being physically partitioned. In this manner small hamlets came into being as the members of the growing family built their own farmsteads close to the parent house. This form of holding has been easier to consolidate as physical division did not take place. In order to prevent further fragmentation the Subdivision of Agricultural Land Act of 1970 made all subdivision of land in the rural areas subject to strict government approval. The Act appears to have been successful in preventing further uneconomic subdivision and encouraging progress towards consolidation of holdings.

Livestock regions

The emergence of livestock regions within southern Africa was largely the result of commercial endeavours in the 60 years before the First World War. The first White settlers to adopt pastoralism relied upon cattle and the fat-tailed, non-woolled sheep. Ownership of these animals provided a means of livelihood, as a capital investment in an economy with little or no money and no means of disposing of an income. They provided the means of exchange with the Black tribes and with itinerant pedlars, to obtain products which the White grazier could not produce himself. In general the eighteenth- and early nineteenth-century White grazier was self-sufficient to a high degree. Pastoral farming became more a way of life than a commercial enterprise to many who had ventured far from Cape Town. Some graziers amassed considerable herds and flocks, while others could do little more than eke out a bare living from their animals and the land.

The nineteenth-century expansion of the world economy, more especially that of the United Kingdom to which South Africa was politically attached, was revolutionary in its effects upon the grazing farmers of the subcontinent. The demand for wool, goat hair, ostrich feathers, hides, pelts and skins increased, while the improvement in the transportation system enabled the demand to be satisfied from increasingly remote areas. As the demand, particularly for wool, grew so pastoral farming adjusted from the semi-subsistence state to a highly commercial set of undertakings. This was not effected rapidly. Semi-subsistence pastoral farms survived well into the twentieth century, and many of the attitudes evolved over long periods of isolation have also persisted.

Small stock farming

The first major demand upon the pastoral industry was for wool. Small quantities of wool were exported until the 1830s when an explosion of production occurred. Between 1830 and 1850 exports increased almost 200-fold as wool became South Africa's staple product. Merino sheep had been introduced into the Cape Colony at the end of the eighteenth century. They had succeeded in both the western and eastern Cape, but it was the eastern Cape which proved to be climatically most suited to them (Christopher, 1976c). Numbers increased rapidly from two million to six million between 1845 and 1855. By 1911 there were 21.8 million woolled sheep in South Africa, and this number after reaching a peak in the early 1930s then declined to pre-First World War levels. Decline in woolled sheep numbers was evident in some parts of the Cape as early as the 1890s when a combination of drought, overgrazing, economic depression and disease badly affected the pastoral areas. Further recession in the 1930s resulted in a marked decline. Thus the numbers of woolled sheep have been held in check for nearly a century, and the woolled sheep regions are as well defined and established as some of the better established crop regions.

The other small stock regions have been more variable and subject to marked fluctuations in demand. The Karakul sheep industry began shortly before the First World War in Namibia, when the German Government introduced the first animals. The number of Karakul sheep has risen rapidly to reach 2.4 million in 1976, mainly in the areas adjacent to the Namibian border. The industry is highly dependent on the vagaries of fashion, and the current boom might well subside with a disastrous effect upon numbers. The remaining, approximately six million sheep, are non-woolled and largely raised for mutton. Dorper (a cross of Dorset and Persian) sheep have largely replaced other breeds. They are confined to the most arid parts of South Africa where overall densities may be as little as one head of small stock per 10 to 20 ha.

Goats are mainly confined to the Black areas but approximately two million are kept on White farms largely for meat and milk supply. They have declined in numbers in the present century as other animals have replaced them. Nevertheless one commercial production is significant, namely the Angora goat for mohair. Successful importations began in the 1850s, and a relatively frost-free portion of the southern Karroo proved to be particularly favourable for their raising. Thus a comparatively restricted Angora goat region evolved in which the majority of South Africa's 4.4 million Angora goats were to be found by 1912. Drought, competition and conservation measures resulted in a marked decline thereafter, with approximately one million Angora goats left in the 1970s.

One other type of dry land stock is of significance – the ostrich. Wild ostriches were domesticated in the course of the second half of the nineteenth century. The demand for feathers fluctuated, but during the booms large

Fig. 5.3 Sheep farm in the Karroo. Farmers sought out available water supplies, aided in the late nineteenth century by the importation of the light windmill. The result is a small oasis of cultivation, trees and habitation. (South African Railways)

numbers of birds were raised on irrigated pastures for first quality plumes. The specialised ostrich area is limited, and numbers have declined from the peak of 776 000 in 1913 to 90 000 in 1976. Changes in fashion have made ostrich rearing particularly precarious, although demand for skins and dried ostrich meat has supplemented the income of the small number of farmers who have retained ostriches as a part of their farming activity – not as prior to 1914 their sole activity. The ostrich boom gave rise to the development of extensive irrigation works, as it was found that superior feathers which fetched the highest prices were only produced by birds in perfect condition. To achieve this a concentrated diet of lucerne was necessary, instead of allowing the birds to roam freely across the open land. Thus small irrigated lots became the accepted form of landscape, which with the collapse of ostrich farming were converted to other uses such as intensive dairying or sheep fattening.

The extensive small stock regions suffer from common problems within the third of the country they occupy. Low rainfall, high evaporation rates,

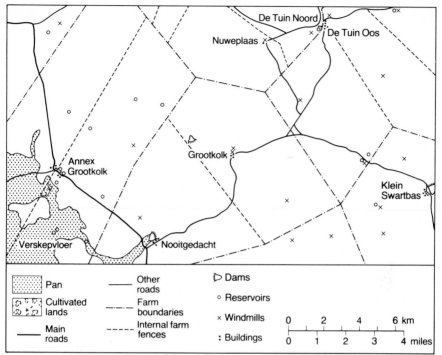

Fig. 5.4 Landscape of pastoralism, central Cape Province. The extensive farms are broken into separate fields (camps) of 2000 ha or more apiece by barbed wire fences. Each is served by a windmill and reservoirs for watering the stock (sheep in this case).

strong winds, considerable diurnal temperature ranges, all contribute to a hazardous climate. In addition are the recurring droughts with estimated drought distress factors as high as 86. Grazing land occupies 99 per cent of the region's total area of approximately 27.5 million ha, with a carrying capacity of approximately one small stock unit per 3 to 6 ha (Fig. 5.3). Cultivation is only possible under irrigation, where streams issue from mountain areas (Fig. 5.4). More extensive cultivation has been attempted, but generally with only limited success, except in the east.

A recent report noted that:

> . . . the main shortcomings of the farming systems of the Extensive Small Stock regions are due to the fact that farming systems are in many cases not adapted to the natural environmental conditions. This is reflected in the fairly general indifferent attitude to the natural veld and the overoptimism shown in the tendency to base the carrying capacity of the veld on the exceptionally favourable years, with the result that the veld is mostly overloaded or too heavy demands made on it, thus weakening the vegetation and exposing the soil to wind and water erosion. (South Africa, 1970: 117)

This was found to be particularly true of smaller farms which had to overstock in order to obtain a living, and which consequently were unable to rest the grazing and allow for recovery. One further detrimental change was the abandonment of trekking – the procedure whereby animals were moved from drought-stricken areas to other districts, thereby allowing the grazing some measure of rest. The enclosure of virtually the whole of the arid small stock region has removed this possibility of retreat and seasonal grazing. One further attitude in the semi-arid region has been the tendency to cultivate marginal land to provide some cash income. The result has often been disastrous.

The resulting loss of grass cover and other palatable shrub species, and the tempo of soil erosion have assumed serious proportions. In the 1970s the Stock Reduction Scheme was operated, whereby farmers could be subsidised to reduce the number of stock on their land in excess of estimated carrying capacity. Participation in the scheme was voluntary and such recovery as has been evident since the scheme was introduced, has been in part the result of a sequence of wetter than average years. As a result the number of sheep stood at between 31 and 32 million during the 1970s, more or less the same as the early 1950s, before the boom which resulted in there being 37.4 million sheep in the White areas of South Africa in 1966. These changes, reflecting the fluctuations of climate and world prices for wool, pelts and hair, have meant that the land has usually been stocked to the maximum possible extent.

Cattle farming

Cattle have remained the most important element in the livestock industry, but unlike the small stock enterprises, cattle have been raised more for the internal markets of southern Africa. Cattle numbers on White farms have been liable to some fluctuation but numbers increased by 50 per cent between 1911 and 1976, as new areas have been brought into ranching; more especially the northern part of the Transvaal, the northern Cape and Natal (Fig. 5.5). The mechanisation of agriculture and transport in the present century has profoundly altered the distribution of cattle, which once provided the main motive power for both. The drier interior of the Cape has witnessed substantial declines in cattle numbers, where they were kept primarily for transport purposes. Thus in 1911 approximately 5.8 million head of cattle were enumerated on White farms in South Africa, while in 1976 there were 8.6 million. This figure marks substantial shifts in distribution towards the north and removal of cattle from small stock regions.

Increasing specialisation has taken place in the present century. Dairy and beef herds have been bred as part of the general improvement of stock. The original stock, the Afrikander, was bred for hardiness, ability to withstand drought and strength to pull wagons. Attempts to improve meat and milk production were slow. In 1780 Friesland cattle were imported but it was only later, in the early nineteenth century, that British settlers introduced a range of Herefords, Devons, Shorthorns and other cattle from the British Isles.

Fig. 5.5 Afrikander cattle ranch, Transvaal. Cattle farms occupy large areas of the better watered parts of South Africa. The vegetation has been much affected by the selective grazing of grass species and selective planting of exotic trees. (South African Railways)

More recently Charolais and Brahmans have added new strains to the local stock. The result has been the development of dairy herds, amounting to some 2.4 million dairy cattle in 1976, and the remainder primarily beef animals. The provision of both dairy products and meat as well as the various ancillary uses of hides, bones, etc. has been present from the start of the White settlement, and most closely paralleled African traditional pastoralism. Thus although initial European interest was to supply passing ships, cattle production, unlike small stock production, was not geared to an overseas market. Indeed a recent Commission of Enquiry into Agriculture (South Africa 1970: 3) could state that 'agriculture really only became fully commercialised about the middle of the present century'. This statement may be taken to be particularly applicable to the grazing areas where 'traditional ideas dating back to the earliest years of settlement at the Cape, have left a lasting imprint on the country's national life'.

The extensive cattle grazing areas of the northern Cape, and particularly the northern Transvaal have been another of the problem agricultural areas of

South Africa. Despite a general increase in the size of holding, many are still too small to produce an adequate living. However, farm enlargement has occurred in recent years as the effects of excessively small land grants and subdivision have been overcome by consolidation. Nevertheless in 1970 it was stated that 'the cutting up of the area into too small farming units has already reached such proportions that beef-cattle farming on a considerable part of the farming undertakings can no longer assume any importance and the basis on which farming stability in the area rests is severely affected thereby' (South Africa, 1970: 99). By the mid-1960s in the northern Transvaal 88 per cent of farms were regarded as uneconomic. Undoubtedly this state of affairs has changed as the more vulnerable farmers have left the land in the 1970s and consolidation has taken place. In the northern Cape the situation is different as most farms are large with extensive ranching undertakings, although one-third of holdings may be regarded as uneconomic. Economic pressure to change to small stock, particularly Karakul sheep, has been such as to affect some areas of the northern Cape, which are ecologically more suited to cattle ranching.

The carrying capacity is low, with a range of one head of cattle per 6 to 25 ha. Although these areas are regarded as most suitable for grazing, supplementary feeding is frequently needed and in the Transvaal the majority of farmers undertake some cropping. In the northern Cape, however, water supplies have to be found at depth and in some cases land can not be used at all because no water can be brought to it. In the eastern Transvaal, although large tracts are deemed suitable for cattle, much of the land is either in state or private game parks and cattle are subject to a wide variety of diseases. Indeed game ranching has proved to be one of the more successful uses to which previously unfavourable land has been placed. In 1974 approximately 500 000 ha of South Africa were entirely devoted to game ranching, and possibly over one million ha in the Transvaal alone are capable of no other use, but are lying idle at present.

In contrast new scientific methods associated with the feedlot system have radically changed beef production methods, resulting in a revival of the cattle industry in the cropping area of the southern Transvaal (Fig. 5.6). Cattle concentrated on feedlots are fed foodstuffs grown on the ranches and brought in. Thus large numbers of animals may be kept in a small area: on a 12 500 ha enterprise near Middleburg in the 10-year period 1969–79, the number of cattle kept on the farm increased from 3000 to 45 000 head, with sales of nearly 80 000 in the latter year.

The dairying regions present a rather different picture as they generally occupy the more intensively used farming areas. Owing to the fairly tight official control of the industry through the Dairy Industry Control Board, dating from the 1930s, dairying is a popular occupation for small farmers. It pro-

Fig. 5.6 Cattle feedlots, Middleburg, Transvaal. The feedlots covering 120 ha contain nearly 50 000 head of cattle at a give time. This represents a revolution over traditional feeding methods. (Kanhym Investments)

vides a steady income to more farmers than any other single branch of agriculture. In 1976 there were 51 300 dairy producers, of whom though only 2300 were fresh milk suppliers. The industry has undergone some centralisation from the period prior to the Second World War, when production was geared to local markets. The introduction in 1965–66 of an effective system of cooling and transportation of milk in bulk allowed some rationalisation of production, taking into account the range of ecological and rainfall conditions to be found in the country. The major areas of production remain in the southern Transvaal and adjacent northern and eastern Orange Free State, the metropolitan areas of the Cape and the midlands of Natal. Within these regions the mixed agricultural system necessary to support dairy cattle is possible. In general improved and even irrigated pastures have been sown to produce the best results. Thus the intensity of land use is far greater than in the traditional beef production areas. The industrial use of milk for butter, cheese and other products takes up over half total production. The first butter factory was opened in the eastern Cape in 1891, and by 1927 there were 73 such factories producing 6000 tonnes. In 1976 the number had shrunk to 20 factories producing 26 000 tonnes. Similarly cheese factories have declined in number from 150 to 33 in the same period, while annual production has risen from 3000 to 30 000 tonnes.

Poultry farming

A remarkable development in livestock production has been the rise of the commercial poultry industry. Poultry was kept on most South African farms, and in 1911 some 9.4 million head were enumerated. A gradual increase in numbers took place to reach 20.5 million in 1971. Since then there has been a spectacular increase with 45.9 million birds counted in the 1976 Census. This reflects a marked change in emphasis in the industry with a swing to broiler fowl production. In the period 1964/65–1976/77 egg production rose from 124 to 238 million dozen, but chicken production increased from 10 million to 137 million per annum. In terms of value of agricultural production poultry and eggs were equivalent to sugar or dairy products in the year 1976/77. In part this reflects a change in eating habits as red meat, particularly beef, has increased in production more gradually in the same period, while chickens have become relatively cheaper.

The massive increase in production has been achieved by the entry of a small number of important companies, which have streamlined production and cut costs. The enterprises are of an industrial nature both in organisation and landscape (Fig. 5.7). The land requirements are small with sites under 500 ha apiece. However, there are also stringent requirements of flat land for groups of chicken houses situated in such a way that the prevailing wind does not blow from one site to another. Disease is the major drawback to the industry, as the high concentrations of up to 30 000 birds per house mean that contagion is a serious problem. Demands for labour and water are heavy,

Fig. 5.7 Poultry houses, Worcester. A new complex of 10 broiler houses, containing a total of 275 000 chickens. The company concerned has recently established six such sites in the district, served by a central processing plant. (Rainbow Chicken Farms)

while the distribution within the country is such that new poultry farms tend to be widely disseminated. The result is a pattern of marked concentrations, the first of which were in Natal, between Durban and Pietermaritzburg. More recently it has been the western Cape which has experienced the main growth. In 1976 the Paarl (17.6 million birds) and Camperdown, Natal (7.5 million) districts, accounted for over half the number of chickens in the country.

In landscape terms the poultry industry exhibits an agri–business factory image, with no sign of any chickens in the fields. The birds exist in climatically controlled houses until they reach an age of approximately two months. Groups of poultry houses are isolated from one another, so that the general agricultural pattern is little interrupted. In addition processing factories serve the groups of poultry houses. As these require a considerable amount of labour some provision of housing for key employees is constructed, but in the main an attempt has been made to tap existing rural labour living in the surrounding districts – a significant location factor.

Fig. 5.8   Abandoned farmstead, Aberdeen. The farmstead is now maintained as a barn, and had deteriorated appreciably in the 30 years since it ceased to be a house. (Anne Christopher)

White rural depopulation

The White rural areas have to a greater or lesser extent suffered from White depopulation in the present century, the most serious declines being in the pastoral areas, more especially the small stock regions. Natal and the southern Transvaal have continued to exhibit either slight growth in rural White population or at least a measure of stability. The Coloured and Black populations have continued to rise, even when the White population has declined, although there are indications that they too, in the small stock regions, have reached stability or decline (Smit, 1973). Thus within the 300 000 km² core of the Cape small stock region, the rural White population in 1911 numbered 98 000, and had shrunk by 1980 to 20 000. In contrast the rural Coloured population of the same region rose from 71 000 to 107 000, although the latter figure represents a decline from the 122 000 enumerated in 1960.

These figures are but the most noticeable part of a process which has been taking place since 1900. Rural depopulation has affected most White farming areas, and farmsteads and farmworkers' houses have been largely abandoned (Fig. 5.8). Thus as many as half the farmsteads in certain districts, such as the Angora goat region, have been abandoned and are either dilapidated or used for storage. As an example, the White rural population of the Aberdeen district reached a peak (3097 persons) in 1911, whereupon it began to decline, amounting in 1980 to only 10.3 per cent of the 1911 peak. The Coloured rural population continued to expand slowly until 1960, when it reached a peak 29 per cent above the 1911 level (2300 persons), but then declined by 1980 to 0.5 per cent above the 1911 level. In the present century the number of separate farms in the Aberdeen district has declined from a peak of 255 in 1934 to only 157 in 1976, and at least 109 abandoned farmsteads may be identified in the rural landscape (Fig. 5.9).

The White depopulation of the rural areas of the Cape Province, Orange

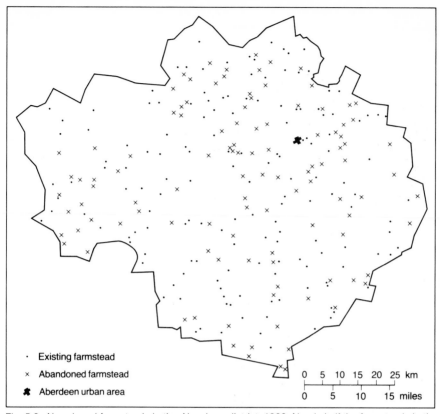

Fig. 5.9 Abandoned farmsteads in the Aberdeen district, 1980. Nearly half the farmsteads in the district have been adandoned and now exist either as ruins or storage barns.

Free State and some of the more remote northern parts of the Transvaal, has political implications which have not been lost upon the South African Government. The main reaction has been one of regret and of suggested attempts to arrest the flow of Whites from the rural areas. To a large extent this is due to the conception of the rural areas as the spiritual backbone of the nation. Thus the Commission of Inquiry into European Occupancy of the Rural Areas in 1960 concluded that 'Only a prosperous, well-established and vocation conscious farming population can make a positive and essential contribution to the continued existence and security of White civilisation' (South Africa, 1960: 47). The political dangers of both a decline in the voting strength of the rural areas in Parliament and the increasingly Black proportion of the population of the rural areas were viewed by the Government with concern. In the period between 1921 and 1980 the White proportion of the population in the White rural areas had fallen from one-quarter to one-twelfth. Thus the rural areas although nominally White (0.5 million in 1980) were, in terms of their occupants, predominantly Coloured (0.6 million) and Black (4.6 million).

However, despite official concern, the social and political aspects of White rural depopulation were largely ignored, and in 1970 the Report of the Commission of Enquiry into Agriculture was more interested in an efficient agricultural industry. Plans therefore devolved on the means of assisting farmers of uneconomic holdings to leave the land, even if the gap between the numbers of Whites and non-Whites in the rural areas widened yet further. Active attempts in this direction through the stock reduction scheme and incentives to leave the land, have contributed to the rapid drop in the number of holdings in the 1970s. However, the threat of border incursions and guerilla warfare in the Transvaal has forced some reconsideration of the movement. Politically and militarily it is considered that a White family upon the land, on a cattle station, would act as an important source of assistance to the army and police in the conduct of a campaign. Subsidies for border farmers have been offered under the Promotion of Density of Population in Designated Areas Act of 1979, but it is too early to see how effective this approach is likely to be, as generally it is the basic infrastructure and the marginal profitability of beef ranching which have caused farmers to abandon their land. However, a return to the attitudes of the previous century is discernible, where farmers acted as the first line of defence on uneasy frontiers.

6

Landscapes of commercial agriculture

Unlike pastoralism, commercial agriculture is, with a few notable exceptions, of fairly recent origin. As De Swardt (1970: 3) stated: 'Apart from the coastal strips South African agriculture has been market orientated for barely three generations. In most cases this period is of shorter duration.' This has been due to the pastoral impress upon the heritage of most farmers in the White areas of South Africa, and the physical environment which has limited agricultural potential. As has been seen in Chapter 5 most of the country was laid out for pastoral farming and only the upsurge in industrial and commercial activities late in the nineteenth century, caused agriculture to be seriously prosecuted outside the coastal belt.

The poor physical endowment of South Africa has resulted in only limited areas being suitable for arable farming. Once those areas which are too mountainous or where the soil is too shallow or stony, or where the rainfall is too low (under 500 mm per annum), have been excluded; there remain approximately 15.4 million ha suitable for arable cultivation. Of this approximately 12.3 million ha have already been devoted to crop land. Thus the opportunities for expansion are relatively limited and the reserve is relatively low in terms of area per person, compared with world estimates. Although only 11.5 per cent of the area available for farming is under cultivation, it yields two-thirds of total production by value and makes an important contribution to the country's export earnings.

Official investigations have suggested that probably less than 4 million ha of arable agricultural land are of fairly high fertility – approximity 5 per cent of total available farming land. This most fertile portion of South Africa produces about 40 per cent of the total value of agricultural production. Conversely, cultivation has been extended to areas such as the western Transvaal, where the physical conditions are largely unsuited to the extensive cultivation of the dominant crop of maize. However, South Africa has not experienced the massive extensions and contractions of cultivation into semi-arid lands witnessed in other continents.

97

Government policies

Although most of the White areas of South Africa were opened up for pastoral farming, the initial settlement in the western Cape was designed to produce crop provisions for the ships of the Dutch East India Company plying between the Netherlands and the East Indies. Later British settlements in the eastern Cape (1820), the Ciskei (1855) and Natal (1850) were similarly designed as crop growing colonies run on lines not too dissimilar from contemporary arable farming in north-western Europe. In each case the settlements faced enormous problems of which plant diseases, crop failures and unsuitability of inherited cultivation practices, resulted in the failure of the original intention of the colony. The struggle to achieve self-sufficiency and later an export surplus was a long one, necessitating changes in techniques and in the basic economy, as livestock became a basic support element. The poverty of the environment was a fact which could not be comprehended in Europe, so that the same mistakes were repeated with each new planned settlement.

The landscapes which successive administrations planned were for small farms, usually 10–50 ha apiece, either with dispersed settlement (Dutch) or group village settlement (British). Only in the western Cape were these initial expectations realised, and then on a far more extensive scale than planned. This success was largely due to the degree of isolation from Black competition and the control which the Dutch East India Company was able to exercise over the colonial economy. One of the major reasons for the failure of many schemes, both large and small, was the ease with which settlers could either purchase subsistence crops from Black cultivators, or employ Black labourers to do the work for them. In the western Cape this option was not open as Khoikhoi numbers were small, and they do not appear to have cultivated sufficient to provide a surplus for sale. Thus slaves and indentured Europeans were introduced to the Colony within five years of its establishment, in order to provide the manpower necessary to undertake crop farming. This effected a degree of control over production which was lacking elsewhere until the introduction of Indian indentured labour to Natal, two centuries later. In addition the Company's control of the settlement through its management of trade enabled the farmers to sell their produce to a guaranteed, if poor, market. Until the twentieth century the costs of transport effectively limited the extent of settlement in the western Cape to within approximately 100 km of Cape Town.

The Natal coastal belt with its subtropical climate appeared to many of the mid-nineteenth-century settlers to offer considerable scope for agriculture. Certain diseases largely removed the option of turning to livestock raising, but other diseases attacked most of the crops with which the settlers experimented. Cotton, coffee, indigo and arrowroot were all cultivated but abandoned. Sugar proved to be the crop which would establish the second significant area of commercial agriculture in South Africa. The majority of the farms made available to settlers were small (under 10 ha) but it was the larger units which were able to produce a surplus for export. The early plantation required extensive areas for crops to feed its workers and animals, as well as timber for firewood for the mills in an age when each plantation erected its own mill. The organisation of the industry proved to be very different from the yeoman pioneer envisaged by the Government. Once more administrations were faced with the need for White managers of labour rather than White labour. In this case the labour came from India!

After these schemes the governments resorted to programmes of closer settlement. It was only with the development of the railway system from the 1880s onwards that such schemes became popular, as crop production had to be balanced by an accessible market. The railways played a part in the opening up of South Africa to crop farming, but the mainlines were built for urban and industrial interests, not for the expansion of a crop producing area. Closer settlement took two forms, the small irrigation plot and the larger dry land arable farm.

The various governments embarked after 1870 upon a series of irrigation schemes. Small patches had been irrigated on most farms, but the produce was for local consumption. The major irrigation schemes were undertaken at government expense, although a number of smaller ones were initiated by private individuals and companies, with official encouragement. The first schemes were undertaken in the Karroo where they were viewed as complementary to the development of the pastoral industry. In the main they were of a limited nature and were hampered by aridity and a lack of markets. The larger schemes undertaken since the end of the nineteenth century have been more successful, as more detailed preliminary investigations of their potential have reduced the chances of failure.

In the Cape Province a series of schemes on the Orange River has transformed the area from the confluence of the Orange and Vaal to the Augrabies waterfall (Fig. 6.1). Further up the Vaal, the extensive Vaal–Hartz scheme of the 1930s has resulted in the emergence of one of the major small irrigation landscapes in South Africa. Other major schemes at Loskop, Hartebeestepoort, and Pongola resulted in extensive new tracts of irrigated land coming into being since the First World War (Fig. 6.2). The size of farms laid out varied substantially from 10–50 ha, but they were markedly different from those in the dry land farming or pastoral areas. Many of the schemes were viewed as social investments by successive governments which regarded White land settlement as a major objective of government policy. On the smaller scale the state schemes at Winterton and Weenen in Natal resulted in the emergence of small specialised areas of irrigation. In the Cape, government assistance in the form of capital works such as dams has been substantial, but the various irrigation schemes have been largely left to individual initiative. Thus the Sundays River Settlement was a company, not an official, scheme. Smaller irrigation works were encouraged through state assistance to farmers who wished to irrigate a part of their land (Els, 1975). On the Fish River, Irrigation Board farms had only 3.1 per cent of their land under irrigation,

Fig. 6.1 Irrigated lands, Orange River Valley near Kakamas. The contrasts between the irrigated lands below the water furrow and the dry lands above are most marked. Whereas lands without water are devoted to stock farming, those with water are devoted to intensive cropping. Note the line of settlements immediately above the furrow. (South African Railways)

and differed little in size from their neighbours which were essentially pastoral (Daniel, 1975).

The Government embarked in 1962 upon one of the most ambitious development projects undertaken in South Africa. The Orange River Project has provided for the construction of a series of major dams across the River, to control the flow and provide a supply of water for irrigation and industry, and a hydroelectric power scheme. The first major dam, the Hendrik Verwoerd, was completed in 1971 and the second the P.K. le Roux in 1977. The former effectively ended the flood problem on the lower Orange River and through the construction of the 82 km Orange–Fish Tunnel, completed in 1975, has provided for a flow of water southwards to the Sundays River (1978) and to the industrial centre of Port Elizabeth. The latter, when the irrigation canals are completed, will make an additional 22 400 ha of irrigated land available on the lower Orange River. This is much more modest than the original project envisaged, as escalating costs (R500 million had been spent

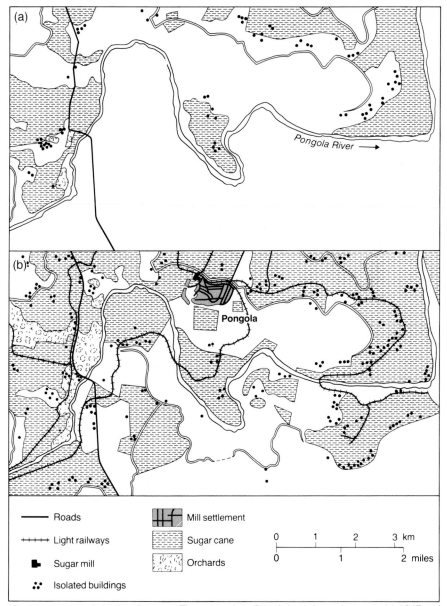

Fig. 6.2 Pongola Irrigation Scheme. The expansion of the irrigated area between (a) 1947 and (b) 1969 is most noticeable. However, large tracts even below the water furrow are not suitable for cropping and so remain as grazing land.

by 1978) caused the original objective of an additional 294 000 ha to be severely pruned; greater attention is now directed towards the industrial and household consumption of water.

In addition to the irrigation schemes, planned and unplanned dry land

101

farming schemes were undertaken. Since the 1870s the various governments in South Africa have sought, where possible, to subdivide large pastoral farms, either through the repurchase and division of properties, or through the encouragement of the Roman–Dutch law of divided inheritance. Official dry land closer settlement schemes were attempted in all provinces, but not all were successful as the potential of the land was often overestimated. However, units of under 500 ha were often made available after the original 2500 ha had been purchased for settlement. The programme was bound up with official concern for the maintenance of as many Whites as possible upon the land. In general the individual schemes were smaller and less ambitious than the irrigation schemes, and frequently paralleled rather than led economic trends.

Until 1970 when the Subdivision of Agricultural Land Act prevented further subdivision, the tradition of Roman–Dutch law had provided for all a man's heirs to divide his land between them. Thus once the open land frontier was closed at the end of the last century, pressure on the existing farms built up. By the first decade of the present century, subdivision, both physical and through undivided shares, had begun to transform the landscape of large areas of South Africa. Pressure for progressively smaller units built up so that over large areas of the Orange Free State and southern Transvaal in particular, many very small farms came into being. Often some amalgamation of holdings took place so that the whole process was in a state of flux, but the general tendency was for holdings under such a system to become smaller and often uneconomic. As a result, irrigation and arable potential were pushed to the limit with disastrous results in periods of drought. The subdivisional process was ended in 1970, but no complementary programme of farm consolidation or reform has taken place on the Australian or West European model with the result that major structural problems exist in the crop farming areas.

Landscapes of grain

In terms of area, nearly two-thirds of the land commercially cultivated in South Africa is under grain crops, covering 7.4 million ha in 1977. However, the area cultivated and the crops grown have undergone substantial changes in the present century (South Africa, Department of Agriculture, 1978). The first major grain production was in the south-western Cape where wheat was cultivated by farmers engaged in wine and fruit production, and also by those engaged in cattle and sheep rearing to the north and east of the main settled area. Production was highly extensive with large areas of farms in the production regions devoted to wheat and to a lesser extent, barley. It would appear that fallowing was practised and land was taken into use or abandoned to grazing as circumstances permitted. By 1806 some 14 000 tonnes were produced on an area of over 20 000 ha. By 1911 production in the Cape had increased tenfold and by the 1970s had increased a further fourfold. Although

Fig. 6.3 Extensive wheatlands, Worcester. Wheat cropping in dry lands is often irregular in pattern and variable from year to year. Here the light wheat fields contrast with the darker semi-arid Karroo bushes. (Anne Christopher)

yields have improved within these areas most of the increased production has come from a steadily extended cultivated area. The result has been the emergence of virtually continuous wheat lands to the north and west of the Cape Town–Stellenbosch area (Fig. 6.3).

Wheat was generally unsuccessful in the summer rainfall areas owing to the prevalence of rust and other diseases. As a result attempts by early settlers to grow wheat in the eastern Cape and in Natal failed. However, on the interior plateau extensive wheat cultivation has been possible, more particularly in the eastern Orange Free State and adjacent portions of the Transvaal. Here, a massive expansion has occurred since the 1930s, so that the Cape share of production has fallen from approximately three-quarters in the early 1930s to one-third in the latter 1970s, despite steady increase in Cape production. It is within the eastern Orange Free State that new varieties have been bred and also that mechanisation of wheat farming has had its most spectacular successes (Eloff, 1980).

The most important grain crop is maize, which proved to be particularly suitable for growing in the more humid parts of the interior plateau of southern Africa. Indeed the range within which attempts to grow the crop are made, are far wider than its suitability for cultivation (Gillooly and Dyer, 1979). Maize is not drought resistant and so makes a poor dry land crop. Furthermore it requires considerable heat in the growing period as well as plentiful water. However, at higher temperatures streak disease appears and this limits production to the north. Consequently only a part of the subcontinent is really suitable for its cultivation.

Although maize was introduced into the Cape Colony in the mid-seventeenth century, it was not until the nineteenth century that serious production commenced. It proved to be a highly successful food crop for both men and stock in the eastern Cape and later in the interior and Natal. At first the bulky product was grown on most interior farms, but purely for domestic use. The establishment of major urban markets at Kimberley and later the Witwatersrand, changed the whole economy. In the 1890s maize production expanded to fill the market and despite the disruption of the Anglo–Boer War, the first decade of the present century witnessed the start of maize exports. The improvement of the railway network in the 1900s and 1910s resulted in the spread of maize cultivation outside areas which were ideally suited to it, with the result that droughts led to substantial fluctuations in production. It is noticeable that the introduction of new hybrid seeds in the 1950s enabled production to be increased without a commensurate increase in area. In the early 1950s average production was 2.2. million tonnes and by the early 1970s it had reached 6.7 million tonnes. Between 1971 and 1978 South African production fluctuated between 3.3 and 9.9 million tonnes from a virtually static area of 4 500 000 ha. The low yields of 0.9 to 3.2 tonnes per hectare indicate the marginal and extensive nature of the cultivation.

The northern and eastern Orange Free State and the southern Transvaal have developed into the main maize production areas, with a high proportion

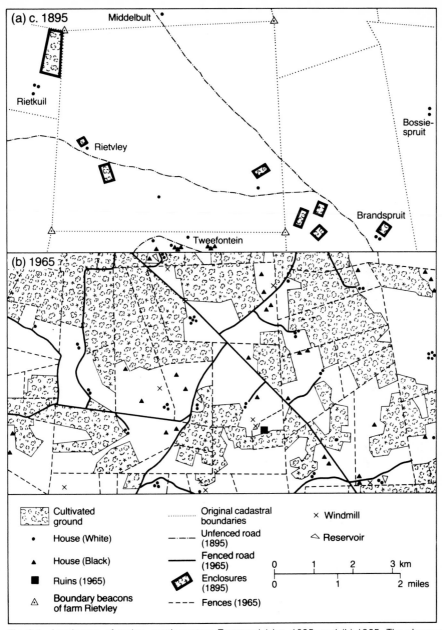

Cultivated ground

• House (White)

▲ House (Black)

■ Ruins (1965)

△ Boundary beacons of farm Rietvley

Original cadastral boundaries

Unfenced road (1895)

Fenced road (1965)

Enclosures (1895)

Fences (1965)

× Windmill

△ Reservoir

Fig. 6.4 Landscape of maize, south-eastern Transvaal (a) *c.* 1895, and (b) 1965. The change from a pastoral to a crop economy is apparent with the intensification of land use and multiplication of settlements. Even in a highly cultivated region large tracts remain as grassland, indicating a dual crop – livestock economy.

of the land under maize (Fig. 6.4). As such the landscape has undergone a substantial transformation, but the land is not continuously under maize and there has been little tendency towards the establishment of large company estates and resultant large-scale working of the maize lands. Farms have been subdivided, as outside the eastern Orange Free State the original units were standard (2500 ha), or often greater than standard grazing farms where the Government had not checked carefully. Thus a fairly dense rural population has resulted, more particularly Black, as the Maize Triangle (or Quadrilateral depending upon viewpoint) has few demarcated Black areas within it and squatting has become more prevalent. The increase in volume of production has resulted in the need for increases in storage capacity. So whereas the storage capacity in 1964 was only 0.9 million tonnes, by 1977 this had risen to 7.7 million tonnes. The grain storage facilities have contributed a new element to the landscape of the intensive maize region (Fig. 6.5).

Other significant crops of the grain areas include the oil seeds which have boomed since the end of the Second World War. During the war the oil extraction industry experienced serious shortages. Afterwards the Government launched a campaign to encourage the production of groundnuts. State control of prices and credit enabled some 200 000 ha to be planted by 1951, which was almost doubled within the following 20 years. Interest in other oil seeds, particularly the sunflower, developed as groundnuts, a tropical crop, are not really suited to the South African environment. New varieties of sunflowers were introduced in the 1960s and the area increased rapidly replacing large acreages of groundnuts in the Transvaal. These have generally been grown on grain farms to form part of the diversified landscape of grain growing.

Landscapes of sugar

The Sugar Belt is one of the most distinctive regions of South Africa, with a comparatively long and complex history of development. The initial success of experiments in the growing of sugar cane on the coastal lands of Natal in the 1850s and 1860s established a crop which has remained unchallenged in its position. At first the Natal north coast developed rapidly, then the more restricted south coast. In the present century the Zululand coastal belt was opened up in the long period between 1905 and the 1950s – overlapping into adjacent Transvaal and Swaziland. The most recent expansion has been inland into the Natal midlands where portions of timber land have been converted to sugar. As a result approximately 233 000 ha were under sugar cane in the late 1970s which was the second most valuable export crop for South Africa, after maize.

In the more intensively cultivated parts of the Sugar Belt as much as 80 per cent of the land lies under sugar cane, and all other crops have been dis-

Fig. 6.5   Maize silos have introduced some of the few features in an otherwise flat landscape. (Maize Board)

placed. This is a feature of recent origin. Early plantations placed comparatively small proportions of their land under sugar cane. Thus in 1911 only
12.0 per cent of the area of the Natal north coast was under cane. This proportion rose slowly until the Second World War, after which major strides
were made. The alternative land uses of food crops, fuel timber and squatter
cultivation were almost entirely displaced, as more extensive methods of cultivation were introduced. Thus the Lower Tugela district in 1971 had 62.4
per cent of its farmland under sugar cane – the nearest approach to a mono-
culture in South Africa.

Throughout the development of the sugar industry there have been three
major types of farm. The first, the planter–miller's estate, employed large
areas and embarked upon all the processes apart from the final refinement.
This was initially the general approach and the number of mills increased
rapidly as cultivation expanded. Thus in the late 1870s there were over 70
mills in operation but only 7000 ha under sugar cane cultivation. The number declined rapidly thereafter to only 18 in the late 1970s. The larger mills
were utilised by smaller planters and a series of light railways were constructed to link the mills with the cane fields of both the miller–planter and
planters. Nearly all the light railways have now been replaced by road transport. Centralisation into a few strategically placed mills was accompanied by
the large-scale purchase of land by the milling companies. Most of the milling groups emerged in the nineteenth century and became more significant
during the present century. Large holdings were acquired through the purchase of the earlier pastoral farms, which had been held by the land speculators,
rather than divided up into individual farms. In the main, the landscape impact was confined to the elimination of some of the smaller farming units,
but in general the big estates have been divided into semi-autonomous sections of approximately 600 ha apiece. Each is supervised by a manager, with
the assemblage of houses for staff, compounds for field workers and workshops for machinery. In addition decentralised field workers' quarters may be
located elsewhere on the estate to reduce distances to work. Approximately
40 per cent of the Natal coastal belt is held by companies.

The second type is the individual White holding which remains the most
important element within the coastal belt in terms of area held. The average
size in the coastal belt is a little over 100 ha and clearly farming is on a different scale from that practised by the milling companies. A close network of
farms and compounds characterises those portions still under individual tenure. In the main most hilltops are occupied by a farm house where sea
breezes can overcome the humid heat of the canelands (Fig. 6.6). Significantly the earliest experiments in plantation development in the 1840s and
1850s were aimed at this end-result, although the major immigration drive of
1848–51 had envisaged a far smaller 8 ha plot.

The third element is the Indian-owned farm. Indian identured labourers
were introduced to Natal from 1860 to 1911, mainly to work on the sugar
plantations. Although the terms of their indenture included returning to India,

Fig. 6.6 Landscape of sugar cane, Natal south coast. The farmhouse built on the crest of the hill, to take advantage of the sea breezes, is surrounded by the cane fields and outbuildings. (Anne Christopher)

many chose to stay and some obtained grants of land in lieu of their return passage. The majority, however, had to purchase small portions as best they could in the coastal belt where land prices were high. Thus by 1976 on the Natal coastal belt Indian farmers possessed a little under 40 000 ha or one-ninth of the total farm land. However, as a result of small–scale purchases and the division of holdings upon the death of the owner, they averaged under 20 ha in 1971. The pockets of Indian holdings represent a distinctive feature in the landscape as concentrated close settlements, almost approaching incipient villages in places, where subdivision has resulted in plots of under 5 ha. The problems of these small farms are substantial, but land usage is often intensive with virtually every portion of ground devoted to cane and with few of the fine ornamental gardens to be found on the White holdings (Greyling and Davies, 1970). Indian holdings are confined to the Natal coast-al belt as legislation in the present century largely excluded Indians from landownership in Zululand and the Transvaal.

Within the traditional areas of the Sugar Belt (the Natal north and south coasts) rural densities of population of approximately 100 per square kilometre are frequently met. The intensive cultivation of sugar, as well as intensive horticulture for the Durban market have enabled high densities of

109

population to live on the land, although the degree of subsistence obtained in some cases is low. The small Indian farms in particular have severe financial problems. Nevertheless, the large number of rural Indians have left an idelible imprint upon the landscape through the construction of temples, mosques and other buildings with Indian architectural elements. The landscape of the Natal coastal belt is one of the most complex entities in South Africa, having evolved through several stages and with diverse official planning policies. The initial mixture of standard-sized pastoral farms and small settlement plots has been carried through to the present, although both have been devoted to sugar cultivation.

The Natal interior has similarly experienced an adjustment of a pre-existing structure to the expansion of sugar cane cultivation. Sugar cane growing in the interior is essentially a product of the mid-1960s. The slump in wattle bark prices and the boom in sugar as a result of the decline in Cuban production, gave the impetus to develop the industry within the Natal midlands. New mills were constructed and a major reorganisation of farming enterprises was undertaken. The result has been the emergence of a mixed timber–sugar landscape in the heart of what was, between the 1920s and 1960s, the timber belt. Expansion has also taken place with the erection of a mill in the eastern Transvaal at Malelane. A new detached region has thus been added to the sugar areas. Significantly little of the expansion took place on the miller–planter estates, and none on new areas for Indian farming. Expansion has been concentrated upon the individual White farm.

Organisation of the landscape for sugar production from the start of settlement has been rare. However, the opening of Zululand to White settlement after 1904 was designed to provide sugar farms of approximately 200 ha apiece for individual planters. Both the large holdings of the milling companies and the small units of the Indians were expressly excluded. Further north in the Transvaal and northern Natal the Government organised the Pongola Irrigation Scheme for sugar production in the 1930s. Here, the previous pastoral farming landscape was erased and a new irrigation scheme was laid out. Both in Zululand and at Pongola the schemes were planned as a whole by the Government, complete with mills, rather than allowing the highly competitive system of the Natal coastal belt to develop.

Landscapes of vineyards

One of the earliest developments of White colonisation was the establishment of the vineyards of the western Cape. The first wine was produced in 1659 and through the endeavour of later governors, particularly Simon van der Stel at Groot Constantia, and the work of the French Huguenot refugees later in the seventeenth century, an export trade was built up. The main areas of vineyards were around Stellenbosch and on the eastern side of the Cape peninsula. Vinestocks were taken into the interior and most towns and farms in the country were able to produce their own wine and brandy. Apart from the Constantia varieties the wines were generally of poor quality until the present century, when superior wines and brandy have found a renewed place in the export market.

The original farms in the western Cape were small, ranging from 16 to 50 ha, and the cultivation of vines proved to be one of the most intensive and profitable enterprises possible in the eighteenth and early nineteenth centuries. However, probably no more than 3000 ha were planted with vines in 1806 and even by 1865 the area had only increased to 6500 ha, when the early period of prosperity declined and the value of exports dropped. The removal of most preferential tariffs in the British market by 1861 was a severe blow. Even more disastrous were the ravages of the phylloxera insect in the 1870s and 1880s, which led to the destruction of the existing vineyards and replanting with phylloxera-resistant strains from California. The desperate state of the industry in the latter years of the nineteenth and early years of the twentieth centuries resulted in the establishment in 1918 of the KWV (Koöperatiewe Wijnbouwers Vereniging), a cooperative to oversee sales. Through successive measures it now has control over production and sales so that a measure of stability has been achieved. It is through the promotional efforts of the KWV that wine consumption is being popularised in the important regions outside the western Cape. The export market accounts for only 10 per cent of production.

As a result the area under vineyards began to increase. In 1930 the area had reached 30 000 ha and by the late 1970s stood at approximately 110 000 ha. In part this reflected the wider spacing of vines from an average of 8000 per hectare a century ago to 3000 per hectare today. There has been a gradual filling in of the traditional vineyard region particularly in the Stellenbosch–Paarl area and the interior districts such as Worcester and Robertson. Vine plantings have also been extended up hillsides and on to areas previously shunned. New varieties have been bred to grow in the new environments and a steady expansion of cultivated area may be expected. However, urban pressures are such that some of the old established vineyards are being built upon. The Cape peninsula vineyards have fared badly with few now remaining. Pressure from the Cape Flats and indeed the internal growth of Stellenbosch, Paarl and Wellington are likely to increase, reducing established vineyards as new ones are brought into production.

The Cape vineyard region occupies a unique place in the history and landscape evolution of South Africa. The western Cape acted as the major cradle of White cultural development, particularly the evolution of the Afrikaner nation and the Afrikaans language, whose monument rises over Paarl Mountain. In landscape terms this has been paralleled through the evolution of a distinctive Cape–Dutch architectural style. The western Cape lacked good building stone and bricks were expensive to manufacture. Thus the walls of the first houses and sheds were of rough hewn rock, which were plastered and whitewashed. These were then thatched. This style was forbidden in Cape Town owing to the fire hazard and the flat-roofed buildings became

Fig. 6.7 Landscape of vineyards, Franschoek Valley, western Cape. The landscape of small farms and fields is inherited from the earliest land grants of the late seventeenth century, many of which were to French Huguenot refugees. High densities of settlement and cultivation result in a more intensively occupied landscape than in most of the commercial agriculture regions. (South African Railways)

general in the metropolis. In the country districts the white-washed thatched house and outbuildings became universal. The more prosperous farmers embellished their dwellings, and indeed some of their stores and distilleries, with gables and ornamentation of various designs. During periods of prosperity, as for example during the Napoleonic Wars, considerable rebuilding took place with the result that even comparatively humble farmsteads were built with gables (see Fig. 11.4). The evolution of this style was important as it became the norm for the more prosperous farmers in other parts of South Africa, when White settlement spread out from its Cape cultural hearth. Today the historic houses and farms of the western Cape form one of the major internal tourist attractions, and many farms make provision for entertaining visitors, just as the KWV has organised museums, restaurants and wine routes for tourists.

The landscape of the vineyard region is dominated scenically by the mountain chains (Fig. 6.7). Within the valleys is a fairly close pattern of farmsteads, with intensive cultivation of vines on the slopes and, in the western areas, the valley bottoms. The farm buildings vary from the major complexes with wine cellars and distilleries, to units with no more additional buildings than tractor sheds. In general, centralised wineries and distilleries have resulted in few functions of manufacture being retained on the farms, but rather transferred to major factory complexes scattered through the winelands. Little mechanisation has as yet taken place with the harvesting of the grapes, so that substantial labour forces are maintained in small hamlets and in suburbs of the towns and villages. The density of rural population is thus high and showed an increase between 1960 and 1970. Local rural densities of over 100 persons per square kilometre are to be met, which is rare outside the Black rural areas.

Landscapes of orchards

The range of climatic conditions in South Africa results in its suitability for a considerable range of tree and bush crops. The winter and summer rainfall areas and the temperate and subtropical regions complement one another. Areas are difficult to assess but approximately 80 000 ha are planted to deciduous trees and 60 000 ha to citrus trees and a further 10 000 ha to subtropical fruit trees.

The deciduous fruit industry is the largest horticultural industry in South Africa. It is mainly concentrated in the winter rainfall area, as the deciduous fruits grow best where the winters are cold and the summers dry and warm. The detailed topography of the Cape folded mountain belt has given rise to a number of specialised areas within the mountains, such as the Elgin and Ceres basins which are almost exclusively devoted to deciduous fruit, with smaller pockets of vineyards.

The Dutch East India Company started the fruit industry but it was not until the 1890s that major developments occurred, with the initiation of fruit exports to England in 1892. The export market provided the impetus for the development of the industry. In 1896 Cecil Rhodes started the Rhodes Fruit Farms in the Franschhoek Valley using expertise imported from California. Elsewhere cooperatives and a few big producers have organised the marketing under the Deciduous Fruit Board, established in 1939. The export market has dominated the industry with a peak export of 260 000 tonnes in 1976, but it is liable to substantial fluctuations according to climatic variations. Thus in the early part of the present century special railway lines were constructed to link areas such as the Langkloof with the ports. The packing facilities and communication system have been of vital importance to the expansion of the orchard areas. The most important are the apple and pear orchards which are

Fig. 6.8 Landscape of orchards, western Cape. The orchards, together with fruit bushes occupy only limited areas in the highly variable slope facets. The farm workers' housing is placed on land unsuitable for cultivation. (Anne Christopher)

a major feature of the Elgin and Ceres basins. On a much lesser scale are plums, peaches and apricots. Only small areas of deciduous fruit are to be found in the summer rainfall regions, mainly under irrigation in the northern Cape and eastern Transvaal, or at high altitudes in the Orange Free State where in addition the specialised cherry zone is located. In general, little of the summer rainfall area's production is exported, and the crops are used for the internal market and for dried fruit production.

Citrus fruit groves have been a major feature of the present century. Their geographical range is far greater than either the vineyards or deciduous fruit orchards, extending from the south-western Cape to the northern Transvaal. Throughout most of the subcontinent, however, irrigation is necessary either to supplement short periods of inadequate rainfall, or more generally as the basis of the trees' water supply. Thus as might be expected water supply is the major factor in limiting the area of the groves, and to a large extent it has been the regional availability of water which has determined the trebling of the citrus area since 1950. Most of the expansion has occurred in the northern and eastern Tansvaal.

Part of production is concentrated in the hands of a number of large estates such as the Zebedelia and Letaba estates of the northern Transvaal, where extensive sectors have been planned and planted as single enterprises. The result is one of the striking landscapes of southern Africa. The Zebedelia estate with over half a million trees on 2500 ha is claimed to be the largest citrus estate in the world. The organisation of such an estate and smaller enterprises has involved the construction of reservoirs, townships and factories. The estates thus became virtually self-contained units producing for an export market, for which Zebedelia was linked by a spur railway line.

Such larger estates are by no means universal in the northern and eastern Transvaal. Individual farms, often of under 100 ha, have the appearance of other irrigation areas in the southern Cape or Natal. A large number of farms are linked by means of a cooperative system to centralised storage, packing and transportation facilities. In terms of landscape the citrus groves are divided into smaller units with a dispersed farm pattern on the larger schemes, such as the Sundays River Valley. Elsewhere citrus trees may only appear in suitable pockets of land capable of irrigation, resulting in a less formal pattern of cultivation (Fig. 6.8).

Mechanisation in the fruit industry has only reduced the demand for labour to a limited extent. As a result farms and estates have had to provide large numbers of houses or barrack-style compounds to house their labourers. The latter is particularly common for seasonal workers contracted from the Black states. The former obtains in the western Cape where villages and hamlets are the dominant feature of the settlement pattern, and where rural population densities may exceed 100 persons per square kilometre. In the eastern Transvaal farms and estates make use of casual labour from the Black states, thereby obviating the need to establish workers' villages.

Forestry

Forests occupy approximately 1.2 million ha and consist mostly of imported species. The indigenous forests of the southern and eastern coastal belts have been substantially depleted and reduced to comparatively small areas. The indigenous species such as yellowwood, stinkwood and ironwood are extremely slow growing, with the result that the demands for constructional and other timbers in the eighteenth and nineteenth centuries, together with fires, largely destroyed the southern Cape forests. Those in the east of the country receded before the advance of agriculturalist and pastoralist, both Black and White. However, some areas of exploitable indigenous timber survive, particularly in the southern Cape, where the moist conditions make regeneration more rapid. Exploitation is largely limited to small quantities for furniture manufacture, in an attempt to conserve what remains. Probably only about 150 000 ha of indigenous forest now exist.

The indigenous forests are thus unable to meet the demand for timber, and recourse is made to the importation and planting of exotic species. Only limited areas are suitable for tree growth, more particularly the southern and eastern margins, where plantations have had to compete with other uses.

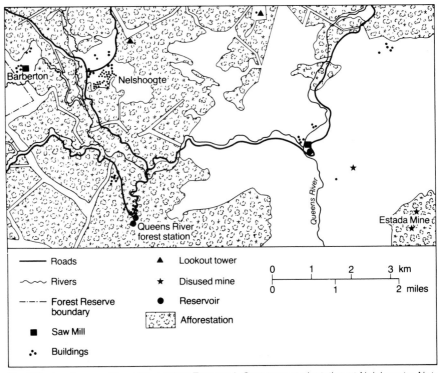

Fig. 6.9 Landscape of forestry, eastern Transvaal. Government plantation at Nelshoogte. Note the large areas not afforested, mainly the steep slopes, and the fire breaks. The district was the scene of mining activity late in the last century and early in the present, resulting in large numbers of small abandoned workings.

The initial impetus came in the 1890s from the interior urban markets and the demand for pit props from the mining industry. Subsequently private and mining company plantations were initiated close to the markets, particularly around the Witwatersrand. The trees preferred were the Australian eucalyptuses, which with a short growing period of 8–12 years, brought in the most ready return. The eucalyptuses had been widely used throughout South Africa as ornamental and shade trees, both on farms and in the towns and their rapid growth was readily appreciated. Soft woods presented less commercial incentive to plant as the imported price was relatively low, and their period of growth was longer, from 20 to 40 years. Thus coniferous tree plantation has been left entirely to state enterprise. The emergencies of two World Wars and the need to conserve foreign currency have encouraged both state and private plantations in the period from 1919 onwards.

Although the early plantations were close to the mining areas and the towns, improvements in the transportation system and the ravages of pests in a harsh climate encouraged private and state plantings in the more suitable growing areas. These were the eastern Transvaal, Zululand and the Natal midlands, with an outlier in the southern Cape within the indigenous timber areas. The eucalyptuses have proved to be particularly suitable for rapid growth and in consequence substantial plantings have taken place in the eastern Tansvaal and to a lesser extent in the Zululand region. However, plantations of eucalyptuses are present throughout the timber areas and they are often used as screens for conifer plantations. The rising demand for mining and constructional timber has been such that a steady increase in the area of plantations has taken place from 37 000 ha in 1918, to 152 000 ha in 1950 and 380 000 ha in 1978.

Softwoods, largely species of pine, have a wider geographical spread and come under marked state control. However, there has been a substantial increase in plantations for the manufacture of boxes, poles, boards and pulp. The response to wartime problems of supply was an increase in plantation area from 26 000 ha in 1918 to 560 000 ha in 1978. Demand for pulpwood for the southern African printing and paper industry has boomed since the Second World War and has resulted in further plantings. Thus several large plantations have come into being for the pulping industry in Zululand.

These large state concerns are usually extensive, covering thousands of hectares with as little as one-quarter of the ground actually planted with trees, owing to the rugged terrain and the need to preserve fire breaks (Fig. 6.9). The landscape of forest stations, processing plants and an elaborate road system for the continuous exploitation of the forests is highly distinctive. State 'forests' cover approximately 1.6 million ha, but 1.1 million ha comprise waste land unsuitable for planting, and only 240 000 ha are actually planted (220 000 ha to conifers), while the remainder awaits afforestation. The various industrial centres associated with the forests, sawmills, pulp mills, synthetic fibre plants and their ancillary board and creosote factories have resulted in a number of well marked settlements often in the form of company towns.

The wattle plantations in the midlands of Natal and the southern Transvaal represented one of the major forestry projects in southern Africa until recent times. Commercial planting began in the late 1880s when the wattle bark was successfully exploited for the extraction of tannin required by the leather industry. The wattle tree, introduced from Australia, has a fairly restricted tolerance of frost, drought and heat. Thus the midlands and the interior of the coastal belt of Natal, together with the adjacent parts of the Tansvaal, proved to be the most satisfactory areas for its cultivation.

The wattle tree is grown on an approximately 8–10 year rotation for optimum bark extract and mine prop production. The relatively short rotation thus provides a commercial basis for private enterprise and trees may be included as part of the general farming system, more especially with dairying. However, production is concentrated in a number of major plantations where wattle growing is the sole activity, and in more favoured areas wattle trees may cover thousands of hectares in plantation form.

Commercial planting took place rapidly in the 1890s, with 30 000 ha planted by 1904. The total area rose to a peak of 300 000 ha in the early

1960s. However, the industry which had expanded so rapidly in response to demands from Europe and later from North America and Asia was susceptible to competition, particularly from the South American quebracho tree. But latterly synthetic substitutes have also dealt a severe blow to the industry. As a result strict quotas have had to be applied to production and the small-scale growers were encouraged to withdraw altogether from the industry, under a rationalisation programme carried out in terms of the Wattle-Bark Industry Act of 1960. As a result of the decline in the wattle area to only 140 000 ha, there has been some re-afforestation with conifers and eucalyptuses, the expansion of dairying, and a major extension of sugar production into the Natal midlands. Thus considerable diversification has occurred within the timber belt with a marked effect upon the landscape, as the balance between the various uses is an uneasy one affected by the vagaries of markets beyond South Africa's control.

7

Landscapes of mining

The development of the mining industry has probably exerted the greatest influence upon the growth and form of modern South Africa. The considerable range of minerals present within the geological structures of the country has resulted in a high degree of independence of outside supplies and provided the means whereby the country would pay for imports (see Table 1.1). Further, most of the mining areas have developed in regions which were previously fairly sparsely populated. In some cases the result has been the restructuring of the South African space economy, as witnessed by the main gold and coal mines. In other respects, resources have been too poor to support any chain of events leading to major secondary growth, as is evidenced by the diamond fields and more recently in the case of the iron, copper and phosphate deposits. Mining activity of considerable antiquity is in evidence in the Transvaal with regard to iron, gold and copper. However, apart from the reports which early explorers brought back with them to Europe or to the coastal colonies, there is no continuity of gold workings between those of the 'Ancients' and more recent times. African iron mining activity appears to have ceased as imported ironwork undercut the locally produced item. The major mineral areas such as the Witwatersrand gold field were untouched by early Black miners, unlike the situation in Zimbabwe, where extensive mining had taken place. Despite the optimism of many explorers, early attempts to discover minerals, particularly gold, were unsuccessful. The Governor of the Cape Colony in 1685, Simon van der Stel, explored Namaqualand for copper deposits, but the inhospitable nature of the country precluded any exploitation for nearly 200 years. Other exploratory works, such as the silver mines near Port Elizabeth in the eastern Cape in the early nineteenth century, only scratched the surface and no major developments took place until the middle of the nineteenth century. One of the first large-scale 'mining' ventures in South Africa involved the exploitation of the guano islands off the west coast of South Africa and Namibia. In the 1830s and 1840s the value of the vast accumulation of guano was realised for agricultural fertiliser. The islands were then mined and swept virtually clean. However, accumulation is steady and control over mining was introduced when the islands, with such unlikely names as Plumpudding and Roastbeef Islands, were annexed to the Cape Colony. No permanent population is present on them.

Since 1850 mining has passed through a number of distinct phases. The exploitation of the Namaqualand copper deposits from 1852 onwards resulted in the first mining boom in South Africa. A large number of companies were floated but the mining population and production remained small, owing to the distance of the mines from the core of the country and the problems of transportation. The discovery of diamonds and later gold appreciably altered the situation, as although both were discovered in then peripheral parts of South Africa, the products were sufficiently valuable and the environment not so overwhelmingly poor, as to discourage an influx of miners.

The diamond fields

The initial discovery of an alluvial diamond on the bank of the Orange River in 1867 was highlighted two years later by the discovery of the stone, the 'Star of South Africa'. The result was the first mineral rush in South Africa which turned the prospecting and speculating of a few hundred men into a semi-organised series of mining camps on the Vaal River. The alluvial diggings attracted thousands from around South Africa and also from overseas. The area of the diggings was disputed and was largely without organisation until British administration was firmly introduced; so accurate figures of diamond production or even population are lacking. Workings at first were restricted to the gravel terraces and buried channels of the Vaal River, where the diamonds had been transported by the river from a then unknown source.

In 1871 wider prospecting discovered one of the intrusive 'kimberlite' pipes, which contained the diamonds. The main one, now the Big Hole, extended over an area of 15 ha and was soon divided up into a chequer board of mining claims. Three other pipes were subsequently discovered in the vicinity. As a result the main seat of mining moved to 'New Rush', which was later renamed Kimberley after the Secretary of State for the Colonies. The mining camp which was established was as irregular as the previous ones, but the longevity of the mining activity resulted in its permanence. The shanty town fixed the plan of the later city. The excavation of the pipe, originally a small hill, became progressively more problematical as claims were worked at unequal speed and increased mechanisation was required to remove the kimberlite, crush it and sift for diamonds.

Small-scale diggings gradually gave way to company workings, because individual diggers lacked the financial backing and technical knowledge to excavate deeply. Thus in the financial and legal battles which ensued, Cecil Rhodes's De Beers Company was able to establish a monopoly over production in 1889, and thereby exercise an effective control over the world market. The Big Hole was eventually excavated to a depth of approximately 300 m by the time it was closed in 1914 – clearly a task beyond the capabilities of the individual alluvial diggers of the early 1870s.

A part of the general reorganisation associated with the rise of the Company was the change in the composition of the labour force. The first White diggers on small sites had used their own labour, as in similar mining activities throughout the world. However, Black labour was soon introduced so that the hard manual digging and grinding was done by paid employees. A casual labour force was thus attracted to the mines with the promise of wages which would buy anything from trinkets to firearms. It also meant that a large group of Blacks was introduced to an essentially White mining settlement. White racial attitudes from the start prevented Blacks from taking part in the diggings for their own account, and strict control was exercised through fear of illicit diamond dealings. Compounds were devised as a means to exercise this control. Within fixed demarcated boundaries Black workers were supervised by their employers, who provided accommodation and food, and effectively restricted their movements. By 1877 there were 8000 Whites and 10 000 Blacks at Kimberley – mining had become Africanised.

Kimberlite pipes were discovered at Jagersfontein and Koffiefontein in the Orange Free State and at Cullinan near Pretoria. None gave rise to the size of settlement at Kimberley, although mining was on a similar scale (Fig. 7.1). The premier mine produced one of the world's largest diamonds, the Cullinan, in 1905. It weighed 3024 carats, and was presented by the Transvaal Government to King Edward VII to be subsequently incorporated into the Crown Jewels. Most of the other Kimberlite pipes in South Africa have been poorly endowed with diamonds and commercial mining has not been considered profitable except in a few localities.

Alluvial diamonds, the initial attraction to South Africa, continued to be worked by individual diggers after the rush to Kimberley, and small-scale operations are still in progress in the vicinity of the first works at Barkly West. Individual diggers also worked out the pockets of diamond-bearing gravels on the Lichtenburg Plain to the north of the Vaal. At the height of the workings in the late 1920s approximately 150 000 people (one-third White) were sifting the gravels. The resultant chaotic landscape of mounds and spoil heaps is all that remains in this mining venture.

The final stage in the exploitation of the diamond fields of South Africa followed the discovery of diamonds in the Namib Desert near Luderitz in German South West Africa in 1911. Further exploration to the south in the 1920s revealed diamonds of high gem quality in a series of marine terrace gravels at the mouth of the Orange River and at Port Nolloth. These were covered with 10 m of later deposits, mainly sands. The diamondiferous gravels are found up to 5 km inland over an extensive zone. Exploitation has been large scale, involving the removal of the overburden by open-cast mining techniques. This has involved considerable company investment and control. The mining operation on the southern side of the Orange River is based on Alexander Bay, which has been laid out in one of the most arid and inac-

Fig. 7.1   Koffiefontein diamond mine, Orange Free State. The open cast mine, similar to the Big Hole at Kimberley, is now being converted to a conventional shaft mine. (*To the Point*)

cessible parts of South Africa. Strict control is exercised through the compound system for the migrant Black workers, and a White township approximately 1 km to the north. Together they house 2600 people, half of whom are White. The whole complex is surrounded and divided up by security fences, while further fences restrict access to the diamond fields. In an effort to reduce costs, cultivation has been instituted adjacent to the river. However, the whole is dominated by the massive excavations and spoil heaps linked by a narrow gauge railway (Fig. 7.2).

Diamonds have been of considerable significance to the development of South Africa, as the first major mining venture which boosted the exports of the Cape Colony from approximately £2.5 million per annum in the late 1860s to £6.0 million per annum a decade later. The revenue derived from mining enabled the Cape Colony to raise capital to undertake major public works such as railways, roads and town improvement schemes which had been impossible while the country had been dependent upon wool and other agricultural and pastoral products for its exports. However, the Kimberley and later diamond mining centres did not prove to be industrial development

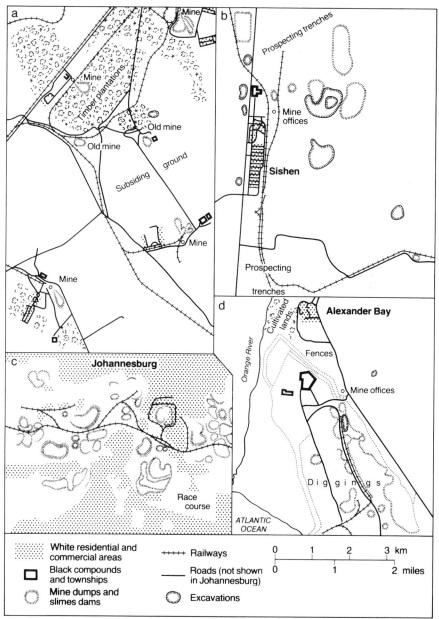

a

Mine

Mine

timber plantations

Old mine

Old mine

Subsiding ground

Mine

Mine

Mine

b

Prospecting trenches

Mine offices

Sishen

Prospecting

trenches

c

Johannesburg

Race course

ATLANTIC OCEAN

d

Alexander Bay

Orange River

Cultivated lands

Fences

Mine offices

Diggings

	White residential and commercial areas	++++ Railways	0 1 2 3 km
▢	Black compounds and townships	—— Roads (not shown in Johannesburg)	0 1 2 miles
	Mine dumps and slimes dams	Excavations	

Fig. 7.2 Mining landscapes: (a) coal mines, Witbank; dumps up to 50 m in height dominate the landscape. Note the self-contained Black and White mining settlements; (b) Sishen, northern Cape, open cast iron ore mines – a mixture of spoil heaps of overburden and large excavations; (c) central Johannesburg, relict landscape of gold mining dividing the city into two sections; (d) open cast diamond mines, Alexander Bay; extensive sifting of the sand dunes results in a highly disturbed landscape.

123

points (Van Der Merwe, 1975). Few other industries were attracted to Kimberley, which remained heavily dependent upon the mines. The other diamond mining areas have been or are likely to be ephemeral. Thus the prospect of the exhaustion of the Kimberley mines by the end of the century is cause for concern.

The gold fields

The discovery of gold, more than any other event, changed the economy of South Africa. Gold had been worked before the arrival of the Europeans, but it was only in the 1860s and 1870s that the metal was discovered in the eastern Transvaal. Mining at Pilgrim's Rest and later in the early 1880s at Barberton was on a relatively small scale. Mining camps sprang up around the alluvial workings and later shaft mines were developed, but although several thousand diggers were attracted to each one of the early fields and towns were established, the booms were short lived. The settlements remain either as ghost towns or tourist attractions. Production figures are sketchy, but it would appear from the colonial export figures that no more than 600 kg of gold were produced in any year, before the opening of the Witwatersrand gold field.

The discovery of gold on the Witwatersrand in the 1880s was followed rapidly by a sequence of events which established the area as the premier mining region in South Africa. In 1885 the gold-bearing conglomerate reefs were discovered, providing the rich deposits which had been searched for in vain elsewhere in southern Africa. In 1886 the town of Johannesburg was officially laid out, and in large measure the chaos of the Kimberley and previous mining camps was avoided. In 1887 the first major stamp mill was erected and in the same year coal was discovered at Boksburg and a year later at Brakpan and Springs. Unlike the leisurely approach to railway extension to the diamond fields, railways connecting Johannesburg to the ports of Cape Town, Port Elizabeth, Durban and Lourenço Marques (Maputo) were completed between 1892 and 1895. Initial mining activity was undertaken by numerous independent diggers, but as in the case of the diamond mines, technical problems associated with mining the steeply dipping gold reefs and crushing the ore, soon resulted in the displacement of individual diggers by a number of major financial enterprises. The first trenches rarely exceeded 20 m in depth, but in 1888 inclined shafts were sunk. In 1892 the initial deep level mining companies were formed relying upon substantial capital investment (Scott, 1951). The depth of workings increased rapidly, and in 1897 the Robinson Deep Mine had reached 730 m. By 1917 Village Deep had reached 1675 m, and recently depths of 3800 m have been attained at the Western Deep Levels Mine (Fig. 7.3).

Fig. 7.3 A modern gold mining complex. Western Deep Levels in the foreground is the deepest mine in the world at 3800 m. West Driefontein in the background is the richest gold mine. (Chamber of Mines)

The concentration of production into a few large concerns has continued as the older mines in the central Witwatersrand have been exhausted. Extensions to the Witwatersrand gold fields occurred as exploration of the Far East Rand and later Far West Rand proved the continuation of the gold-bearing reefs. The Far East Rand became the major production area in 1923. Other gold fields at Klerksdorp, Evander, and in the northern Orange Free State came into existence in the 1950s and contributed greatly to the substantial increase in production within the next two decades. Production, which by 1911 had reached 235 tonnes, only increased to 332 tonnes by 1950, although some substantial fluctuations had taken place in the intervening years, depending upon the state of the world economy and the official price of gold. Devaluations of the currency in 1932 and 1949 undoubtedly boosted production, just as the introduction of a floating price in the 1970s arrested the decline in production. Between 1950 and 1969 production increased to reach an all time peak of 1006 tonnes, since when it has fallen to around 700 tonnes in the late 1970s, despite the continued upward price of the metal in terms of world currencies.

The gold mining industry has relied heavily upon a high degree of organisation, and in 1889 the Chamber of Mines was established to guard the interests of the mine owners. One of the major problems has been the supply and housing of the labour force. White labour in the early mining areas lived on the mines and later in housing provided by the mining companies. Company settlements as time progressed have become larger with more sophisticated amenities. They have in some cases become fully fledged towns. The early miners of Johannesburg lived in the town, usually close to the mining area, but not in separate company towns. Now owing to the size of most gold mines the White employees are numerous, and the mining town is as large as many of the rurally based towns of South Africa unlike the company towns associated with agriculture or forestry.

The major feature of the mining settlement has been the expansion of the compound concept inherited from the diamond industry. The majority of workers in the gold mining industry have always been Black (Wilson, 1972). Thus in 1898, the last full year of production before the outbreak of the Anglo–Boer War, there were 88 000 Blacks working on the gold mines, in addition to 9000 Whites. As most Black workers came for only short periods of time under contract, and the demand for labour was high, the provision of a steady flow of mine labour was a problem. In 1893 the Chamber of Mines appointed a Native Labour Commissioner, and in 1896 the Witwatersrand Native Labour Association was established to recruit labour from Moçambique and territories to the north. Later the Native Recruiting Corporation was formed to obtain labourers from the adjacent High Commission territories (now Botswana, Lesotho and Swaziland). The Black labour force increased to nearly 300 000 by 1938 and stabilised at approximately 400 000 in the 1970s.

The Black miners have come, with few exceptions, on short-term contracts and without their families. Thus the mines have built large basic compounds in which their staff live as a virtually self-contained community. Contact between the mines and the outside world is minimised, but not to the same extent or for the same reasons as on the diamond fields. It has probably been the mines with their constant attention to economy which have presented the poorest image of migrant workers' conditions in the country, and over which there has been so much controversy.

The pattern of gold mining is therefore highly distinctive. The mine shaft and associated milling buildings provide the core to the settlements. Around this core are the various spoil heaps and slimes dams. The slimes dams are stepped, flat-topped waste heaps, where the waste is pumped in liquid form and solidifies with evaporation. For most of the gold fields the dump hills are yellow, providing a distinctive, often dominating new feature in the landscape. Although the transfer of waste sand dumps underground began in 1909, the mines produce more material than can be filled back underground. In addition the mines have railway sidings to bring in the vast amount of stores required, such as fuel, pit props and machinery. Internal tramways, conveyor belts and ropeways provide a redistributive system. Finally the distinctive White housing area with the amenities of sports facilities and schools, and the less attractive Black compounds complete the mining landscape.

Gold mining provided the boost to the economy of South Africa which finally transformed an agrarian into an urban based economy. The value of gold production in the Transvaal increased from £35 000 in 1886 to £38.7 million in 1912. The stimulus to industry and trade came through the demand for machinery and services to the gold mines. Although most machinery was imported at first, the incentive to produce locally was sustained. Similarly the demand for services such as transport, banking and insurance was such as to transfer the centre of commercial activity from Cape Town to Johannesburg within 10 years of that town's foundation. Although mining gave rise to Johannesburg and the Witwatersrand towns, the mines ceased to dominate them long before Kimberley ceased to be primarily a diamond mining town. The landscape of mining has left a belt of waste land through the Witwatersrand, much of it now abandoned, which separates the several towns into two halves.

It is a measure of the scale on which gold mining takes place, that the two most recent gold fields at Klerksdorp and the Orange Free State fields provided the opportunity to create an orderly series of towns, laid out according to the town planning principles of the 1950s. The phenomenal rise in the gold price since the ending of the fixed $35 per ounce in 1970 to reach $500–$800 per ounce in 1980, has resulted in a marked improvement of the position of most mines. The expected lifespans of a number have been extended as poorer grade ore can now be profitably worked. Further active prospecting for payable gold has been stepped up and new shafts to existing deposits have been sunk. The capital costs of new ventures are high, as a new mine

127

(1980) on the Orange Free State gold field costing R320 million illustrates, but the dividends are obviously worth while.

The coalfields

Coal was vital to the evolution of an industrial society in South Africa. The demand for coal came first from the railways, and then for mining at Kimberley and later on the Witwatersrand. Initially the coastal cities imported coal, but a search for the local product was undertaken, although specimens from Natal in the 1850s were deemed unsuitable. However, in 1859 coal was discovered in the eastern Cape at Cyphergat, and five years later production was commenced at Molteno. Further discoveries at Indwe and the linking of the coalfields to Kimberley by railway, sustained production of a field with essentially poor, highly volatile coal. Production reached a peak of 209 000 tonnes in 1899 and declined thereafter, leaving little beyond the settlements and a few abandoned mines.

Revived interest in Natal coal in 1880 resulted in the discovery of beds of steam and coking coals. Progress was slow and by 1889 there were only seven collieries in operation and only 29 000 tonnes of coal were raised. However, once the fields had been linked to the railways, expansion was rapid with 434 000 tonnes mined in 1898 and 2.8 million tonnes in 1913. The fields originally exploited around Dundee were extended northwards to Newcastle, Utrecht, Paulpietersburg and Vryheid. Many of the early mines were adits in the hillsides where the strata are virtually horizontal. However, the major mines have engaged in incline shaft mining. The field revealed considerable problems of firedamp and in its early years was highly dangerous. Growth is now limited as the reserves of better coal, particularly anthracite, are conserved.

The most important coalfields are those of the south-eastern Transvaal and adjacent portions of the Orange Free State. Although coal was known to exist in the Transvaal by the mid-nineteenth century, commercial mining had to await the discovery of gold on the Witwatersrand. The exploitation of the initial deposits approximately 100 km to the east, which necessitated a wagon journey, gave way to a shorter distance when the deposits at Benoni on the Witwatersrand were discovered in 1887. The transport of coal was improved by an internal railway system constructed in 1890 and known as the Rand Steam Tram, due to the opposition of some Republican parliamentarians to trains as such! The demand for coal resulted in some 1.9 million tonnes being raised by 1898. By 1913 this had risen to 6.0 million tonnes from the Transvaal and adjacent Orange Free State field. Since the First World War, production has become increasingly concentrated in the Witbank–Bethal area where exploitation of the coal is relatively cheap. Collieries have become steadily larger and hence more widely spaced to work more extensive areas. Self-contained mining settlements remain the dominant feature of the coal mining landscape.

The coal mining regions have partially been exploited to develop electricity and petroleum products. Thus owing to the bulky nature of the product, a series of major coal fired electricity generating stations and two oil from coal plants have been erected on the coalfields. The electricity power stations, with their adjacent coal mines dominate large parts of the eastern Transvaal, where a major programme of development has taken place since 1945. Once more self-contained settlements, sometimes of considerable size, have been created. Thus the Hendrina and Arnot power station settlements in the eastern Transvaal both enumerated over 4000 persons in the 1970 Census – a similar size to the neighbouring colliery towns. In layout they are also similar, but in this case the controlling company is the Electricity Supply Commission (ESCOM). The most recent power station, commissioned in 1979, with a generating capacity of 3000 MW, is one of the dominant features of the eastern Transvaal, with cooling towers rising over 130 m and chimneys over 200 m (Fig. 7.4). The adjacent coal heaps, ash dams, water ponds and distribution system complete the modern landscape of power.

The establishment of cheap generating facilities has enabled the country to be linked up through a national supply grid, thereby obviating the need to transport coal long distances to local generators. Thus coal transport has become relatively less important and local municipal generation of electricity has declined in significance. Most towns and cities are now linked to the national grid, and many of the smaller power stations have been retained only to generate emergency supplies, resulting in the erosion of an element of the industrial framework of the smaller towns.

Although coal is the main source for electricity supply, both for the national grid and for local generators, the long distance haulage of coal and the difficulties of long distance transmission, present a problem for the supply of the western Cape. This, the second most important agglomeration in South Africa, is over 1200 km from its nearest source of coal. The high costs of electricity generation, allied to the isolation of the region from the rest of the country persuaded the Government to establish the first nuclear power station at Koeberg on the coast, to the north of Cape Town. Thus an economic alternative to burning coal for electricity generation may result in changes in exploitation policies. However, with over three-quarters of current primary needs satisfied by coal, South Africa is in a unique position in the industrialised world.

Coal is a valuable raw material for the chemical industry, and more especially for the production of petroleum products. The South African Coal, Oil and Gas Corporation (SASOL) has developed an economic means of extracting oil from coal, which through constant experimentation and particularly as a result of the increase in the cost of imported petroleum products in the 1970s, has become a highly attractive proposition. The increasing threat of sanctions and trade boycotts, particularly the imposition of trade restrictions by Iran in 1979, gave a degree of urgency to the programme for establishing more oil from coal plants to make the country as self-sufficient as possible.

The first plant was established at Sasolburg on the Vaal River in 1950 and the second at Secunda in the eastern Transvaal in 1975, after feasibility studies had shown the viability of the project. Further projects are possible in the northern Transvaal. The two towns are once again essentially company towns devoted to a single product, but somewhat larger than is general. Sasolburg had attained a population of 29 000 by 1970 and a degree of industrial diversification was apparent, although most industries were dependent upon the plant's output of chemicals. The town plan integrated the elements of the White town, divided into a series of suburbs, a detached Black town (Zamdela) and between them the Sasol plant, the power station and the refinery to process crude oil pumped from the coast. The town plan as in the case of Welkom in the Orange Free State gold fields, is a marked break with the traditional grid pattern. Probably the extensive green zones within the residential areas are one of the most pleasing aspects.

The Sasol II and III plants at Secunda, in the eastern Transvaal, were established on land acquired by the State for the coal rights, as the demand for coal is expected to reach 12 million tonnes per annum when full production is reached. Planning of the town has again introduced a number of new elements. First the Sasol II plant is sited 2 km from the town itself and the collieries and power station are yet further afield. The internal arrangement of the town is also an innovation as the Black suburbs, which in South Africa have inevitably been planned as separate appendages to the main White town, have been designed as integral parts of the whole. Thus the town centre has been sited between the Black and White suburbs, rather than at the centre of the White area. The town planning scheme has also taken account of shopping developments and the centre is essentially designed for the segregation of motor transport, with extensive peripheral parking areas, and for pedestrians, with an internal mall which may be reached on foot from other parts of the town by means of green walkways. It is interesting to note that the majority of towns founded since 1940 have been established by one or other of the major state corporations.

Large-scale mining

In addition to the major schemes associated with the exploitation of gold and coal and, on a smaller scale physically, the diamond mines, South Africa possesses a vast number of minerals which have been mined in the present century. Although some are exploited on a small scale, it is the large project which has been most marked since 1945. The exploitation of the iron ore reserves at Thabazimbi in the western Transvaal for the iron and steel plant in Pretoria, was an early example of massive open-cast mining excavation. More recently it has been in the northern Cape that mining activity has been

Fig. 7.4   Kriel Power Station, eastern Transvaal. The cooling towers and chimneys are the only 'relief features' in an otherwise flat landscape. (ESCOM)

most impressive. The Sishen and neighbouring open-cast mines were originally opened to supply the growing local demand for iron ore in the 1950s. However, they have been greatly expanded as a result of the development of the export trade. Output from the mines increased from 4 to 22 million tonnes per annum between 1974 and 1979. Most of the increase (from 1 to 15 million tonnes per annum) was for export. The areas involved in the mining activities are extensive, as each mine may cover several kilometres. However, owing to the arid nature of the local environment this constitutes little interference with previous activities. The town of Sishen, established for the mines, expanded its workforce from 1200 to 4500 in the space of six years, and in 1980 comprised a community of over 8000 persons. On a similar scale is the exploitation of the Phalaborwa Complex in the eastern Transvaal, which processes phosphates. In 1951 the State Phosphate Corporation (FOSKOR) was established, and by 1970 the resultant mining settlement housed 7500 people.

One recent development has been the entry by South Africa into the large-scale mineral export trade. Certain strategic minerals such as chrome ore, manganese and platinum are mainly exported, with little of the production being retained in South Africa. The export of minerals has largely financed the industrial development of the country. However, exports have been dramatically increased as a result of two major schemes, the Sishen–Saldanha iron ore export scheme and the Richards Bay coal export scheme. Both involved the opening of new mines in existing mining areas and the construction of a railway to link the inland mines with the new export point. Added to this the export points are designed to develop into major industrial processing areas helping to eliminate the high levels of rural underemployment in the western Cape and KwaZulu.

Mining has played a vital role in the development of South Africa. The fortuitous combination of geological structures provided a base for the exploitation of a considerable range of minerals, although gold has dominated the production pattern since the 1890s. As a percentage of Gross National Product, mining accounted for 27.1 per cent in 1911, but with the rise of manufacturing in the Second World War the proportion fell to 14.0 per cent in 1960. The boost in mineral production in the 1970s arrested the decline so that mining contributed 14.8 per cent to the Gross National Product in 1978. The numbers employed in mining have been substantial: immediately before the First World War over 300 000 were engaged, three-quarters of whom were employed on the gold mines. By the late 1970s some 700 000 persons were engaged in mining.

Mining settlements constitute a most significant feature of the South African landscape. Few mining areas were sufficiently small, or ill-organised to result in dispersed settlement. Thus they have been urban in character both in time and in geographical extent. The initial mines in Namaqualand and in the vicinity of Kimberley differed little from mining camps in other parts of the world. However, individual White miners were quickly supplemented by a large Black labour force. At Kimberley the authorities felt this force required a substantial degree of supervision owing to the prevalence of illicit diamond sales. The introduction of the compound system whereby the Black labour was housed and fed by the mining companies, and thus segregated from the remainder of the population of the mining towns, proved to be highly popular in other mining spheres where the original need for security was lacking. Thus the gold and other mines worked on the same basis, recruiting labour on short-term contracts and allowing no permanence for the Black miner.

The mining settlement in South Africa therefore developed a distinct variant on the typical mine, with its two separate residential areas: the White town with its extensive facilities and the Black compound. This dualism is present in most of the company towns developed for special processing, and is in turn a reflection of the development of South African towns in general. The mining centres appear to have led the way in this type of segregation and possibly the mining industry has influenced the development of the other urban landscapes very extensively.

8

Landscapes of small towns

The South African space economy has been the subject of many interpretations, but probably the core–periphery concept first propounded by Fair (1965) and expanded by Board et al. (1970) provides one of the best starting points (Fig. 8.1). The core of the major metropolitan region, together with a number of lesser metropolises are surrounded by a periphery, which is underdeveloped and partially poverty stricken. The major core of the Witwatersrand has since the 1880s appropriated, to a high degree, the greater value of production in South Africa. Also as Fair (1976) stated 'South Africa's major metropolitan centres are, outstandingly, national centres of both production *and* consumption'. Thus the eight largest centres accounted for nearly three-quarters of the Gross Domestic Product of South Africa.

Overview of the urban system

In historic perspective the mercantile model of development expounded by Vance (1970) appears as valid for South Africa as for Australia (Heathcote, 1975) (Fig. 8.2). Mutual trade between the Imperial metropolis and the Colony resulted in major transformations of the economies of both. The state of dependency of the Colony upon the Imperial metropolis lasted in varying forms from the establishment of the Dutch Colony to the Second World War. The trade in staple products produced in South Africa as exports to the metropolis in Western Europe, was complementary to the goods and services imported for redistribution to the Colony. Early European contacts were not trading orientated as in West Africa, but directed towards settler production of crops, pastoral products and, later, minerals. The agricultural export staples were weakly developed in the colonial period, leaving much of South Africa outside the market economy; while the mineral export bases were exploited against a background of semi-subsistence agriculture, which whether Black or White, responded to the demand. Thus within only a few localised areas agricultural development followed the creation of an urban and industrial demand. This is not strictly analogous to the base-export theory

134

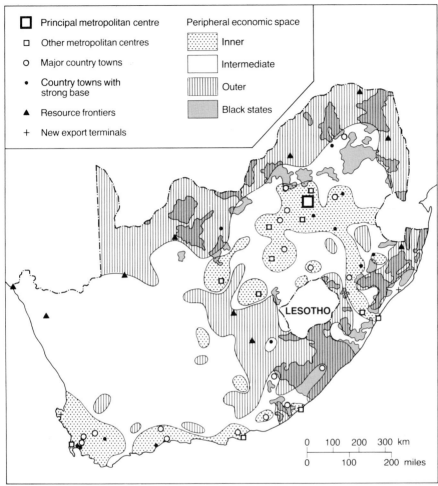

Fig. 8.1   The structure of the South African space economy. The core–periphery nature of the South African space economy is evident from the concentration of economic activity in the southern Transvaal. (Adapted after Board *et al.*, 1970)

(Browett, 1977), but undoubtedly the agricultural and mineral exports of the nineteenth and early twentieth centuries contributed to the economic growth of the metropolitan areas and some of the rural areas.

Thus the pre-1870 pattern of a series of ports linked to agricultural hinterlands with a low level or urban development had changed markedly by 1910. Whereas in 1870 there were probably only the three ports of Cape Town, Durban and Port Elizabeth with populations exceeding 10 000 inhabitants, by 1911 the number of such towns had increased to 21, ten of which were in the interior of the southern Transvaal. This transitional period was vital to the development of South Africa as the new pattern which emerged has proved to be remarkably resistant to later changes. The major metropolitan

135

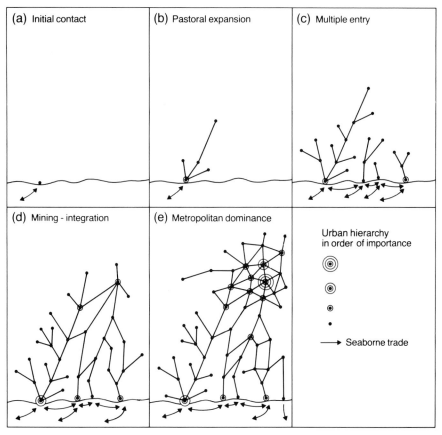

Fig. 8.2 The mercantile model of development applied to South Africa. The emergence of a Christaller style urban system in the interior is a later successor to the linear mercantile system.

core with a number of less important metropolises (including the three ports) are surrounded by a poorly developed periphery. Within this a marked national hierarchy has developed, in place of the separate systems of the nineteenth century (Van der Merwe and Nel, 1975).

Davies, R. J. (1972) identified 474 towns established in South Africa before 1960. Of these only 32 had been created by 1835. Between 1835 and 1870 some 199 were founded as the urban system was extended to most of the state territory; while between 1870 and 1933 a further 304 towns were established, at a rate of five per year. Between 1933 and 1960 only a further 20 were founded. The rate of foundation has risen again as the urban subsystems of the Black states have been elaborated. Recent town foundation in the White areas has usually resulted from state decisions to establish mining and manufacturing centres. The result is probably an oversupply of towns in parts of the country, where the agricultural resource base is insufficient to support an essentially nineteenth-century pattern of urban foundation.

Table 8.1   The South African urban hierarchy 1966

Order	No. in South Africa	Theoretical Christaller $K = 3$ lattice
1. Primate metropolitan area	1	1
2. Major metropolitan areas	3	2
3. Metropolitan areas	8	6
4. Major country towns	17	18
5. Country towns	61	54
6. Minor country towns	178	162
7. Local service centres	333	486
8. Low order service centres		1458
Total	601	2187

Source: Davies (1967); and Davies and Cook (1968).

As might be expected a new urban hierarchy has developed, based upon the primate metropolitan area of the southern Transvaal. The hierarchy has changed radically as the primate metropolitan area has expanded and assumed a dominance over the national system, as it was integrated in the late nineteenth and early twentieth centuries. Although the main structure of the hierarchy has been reasonably stable since the First World War, there has been considerable mobility in the middle and lower echelons. This reflects many different factors ranging from the effects of prolonged rural depopulation reducing the needs for services in the country towns, to the booms associated with mineral and industrial development.

The urban hierarchy has thus experienced nearly a century of integration and appears to have developed many of the classic features of Christaller's central place theory (Beavon, 1977). In common with many other areas, it is his marketing principle, whereby the maximum range of central services may be provided by the smallest and most economic number of central places, which appears to provide the best fit for the South African urban hierarchy (Table 8.1) (Davies and Cook, 1968). Thus the lattice which evolves is $K = 3$, where the number of central places in each successively lower order of the hierarchy increases threefold. The fit is reasonably satisfactory, except for the lower end of the scale where the local and low order service centres are concerned. Possibly problems of identification and calculation may be responsible here, as the hierarchy has been determined, in the main, by places with census statistics and separate telephone exchanges. Identification of separate physical entities would extend the tail substantially, but still not approach the theoretical number of places.

Within the hierarchy the metropolitan areas appear to be larger than might be expected (Davies, 1967). However, the other categories of towns and service centres fit the theory more closely. Nevertheless, it is questionable whether the order 1 urban centre of only one million is still valid, as the size of metropolises has increased markedly since the date of Christaller's work

50 years ago. Furthermore the widening of the gap between the size of the metropolitan areas and the smaller urban places has continued, despite attempts to control the metropolises in South Africa and other countries.

Thus in 1911 the 336 enumerated towns and metropolitan areas housed a population of 1.5 million. By 1980 the number of urban places had doubled and the number of urban dwellers had increased ninefold to 14 million. The upper ranks of the urban hierarchy were sorted out in the 25 years between the discovery of gold on the Witwatersrand and the first Union Census in 1911. The main feature since that date has been the widening of the gap between the metropolitan areas and the remainder of the hierarchy. In part this has been achieved through the incorporation of previously separate towns into the metropolitan agglomerations. However, the proportion of the urban population living in the four largest agglomerations (the Witwatersrand, Cape Town, Durban and Pretoria) has remained reasonably constant since 1911 at just over half the total urban population of South Africa. In 1980 two-thirds of the urban population lived in the 12 designated metropolitan areas, so that approximately 4 million people lived in the remaining 600 or so smaller urban places.

In terms of urban patterns the variety of the physical landscape and the political boundaries between Black and White has resulted in only limited appearances of the Christaller network. One of the recognisable areas of uniformity, the Orange Free State, has, after the emergence of the initial network pattern, been subjected to deformities of mineral discoveries and industrialisation. However, in areas such as Natal the mercantile model is still markedly in evidence. One interesting feature has been the emergence of a subsystem in Transkei, which as a result of political development has been able to promote its own 'metropolitan growth'. This is in marked contrast to the towns of the Ciskei which are firmly linked to the South African system (Cook, 1980).

Town foundation

The present urban network of South Africa is the result of White colonisation and economic and political activity in the period since the establishment of Cape Town in 1652. Within South Africa none of the major indigenous towns survived the destructive wars of the early nineteenth century. The large Tswana towns which escaped destruction in Botswana housed a high proportion of the total population, and in 1911 half the population of that country was grouped into six towns. However, the Tswana towns within the area which became South Africa in 1910 were destroyed and the succeeding villages were composed of much smaller groupings of houses. Elsewhere some of the temporary towns such as the Zulu royal kraals at Chakas Kraal and Ulundi housed several thousand people at their height, but they were essentially movable sites and lacked a modern urban base. Black participation in town foundation after the White conquest was negligible, and has only become of any significance in the present century. The programme of major reorganisation of the Black areas has resulted in the establishment of a large number of urban centres with layouts and functions reminiscent of the eighteenth and nineteenth century agro-towns established by the White colonists (Smit, 1979; Smit and Booysen, 1977). However, although planned for Blacks, most have been planned either according to White standards and forms, or by Whites. Black participation in the town planning process, even in the Black areas, has been minimal.

Hence town foundation, and the town planning process has been almost exclusively in the hands of the White population, either as administrators, traders, missionaries, miners, or soldiers. The town planning process has been subject to a wide variety of influences from Europe and elsewhere, and is a distinctive part of the more general colonial response to laying out towns in a new country where none existed before. The imprint until recently was largely Dutch and British, although current international approaches are presently recognisable. However, in each general style of planning, distinctively South African strands are evident which give a unique character to the townscapes (Fig. 8.3).

The European immigrants carried a highly developed urban and village settlement concept in the cultural baggage which they brought to South Africa. Thus the first settlement at Cape Town was an urban trading post. As the early settlers spread out so the first village was established at Stellenbosch in 1679. This acted as an administrative and ecclesiastical centre to serve the people who lived in the area across the sandy Cape Flats from Cape Town. Other centres were founded as church and administrative points in the ensuing century and a half. However, the small number of settlers and the often self-sufficient nature of many of the larger farms meant that the demand for goods and services was small, and this was usually satisfied by the traders and artisans of Cape Town. Thus few of the 'growth points' achieved any size even in the south-western Cape, until well into the nineteenth century, and contacts between the settlers and officers of the State and ministers of religion were infrequent.

A second strand in town foundation was the establishment of the mission stations. The first permanent station refounded at Genadendal in 1792, was followed by several others extending throughout South Africa in the first half of the nineteenth century. The earliest mission stations were founded as towns where communities of Coloured people could be Christianised without the influences and pressures of the frontier farmers or Cape Town. These towns were planned and organised centres with small industries and a supporting townland area, to produce as self-sufficient a community as possible. As the missions grew so new ones were founded, until the middle of the nineteenth century, when nearly one-tenth of the population of the Cape Colony lived in the missions. The form of the mission changed in the Black areas, where few attempts were made to establish large self-contained villages, as the Black population retained their traditional population patterns.

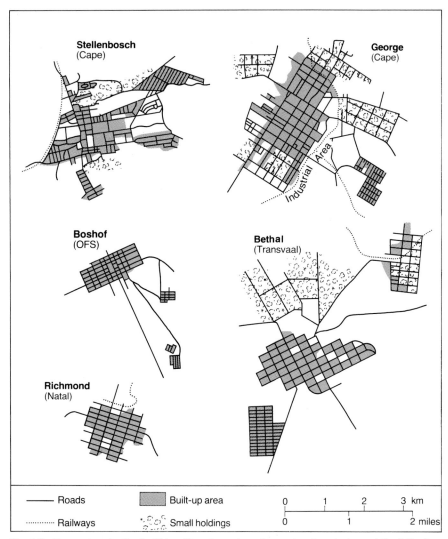

Fig. 8.3   Town plans in South Africa. The plans show the contrasting designs of the following: Stellenbosch – 300 years of piecemeal growth; George – grand design with the central axis focusing upon the residency and the second street on the church; Bethal – grid plan with addition of smallholdings and Black location; Boshof – town with detached Black and Coloured locations; and Richmond – not yet filling the original grid.

The exception was in the Tswana country and this may be ascribed to the greater urban background of the Tswana people.

The period of casual town foundation associated with the Dutch East India Company administration ended with the period of government by the Batavian Republic (1803–06) and the final British occupation of the Cape Colony in 1806. A more systematic approach was introduced with the establishment of a relatively large number of towns in a short period of time (Lewcock,

1963). The new towns were seen essentially as administrative centres with the seat of the representative of the Government, together with the churches, schools and stores. Indeed the towns were envisaged as centres of civilisation for the rural areas of South Africa. At the same time a series of forts was established on the eastern frontier, in an attempt to control the conflict between the Xhosa and the White settlers. Some of these had towns laid out around them, while others were abandoned.

The period of activity from 1815 to 1825 under the governorship or Lord Charles Somerset, son of the Duke of Beaufort, witnessed the introduction of a more grandiose plan than was evident in the earlier towns and missions. The first settlements had tended to grow in a haphazard manner, although usually later town plans minimised the irregularities. The grid-iron plan, the provision of wide streets, large blocks and plots, and extensive townlands for the use of the citizens, all indicated that urban centres were now envisaged rather than the relatively small villages of the Dutch period. Some of the features of the first settlements were retained: The system of water courses to allow for the irrigation of the town plots was one noticeable feature which was widely used in the Cape and indeed elsewhere. Lord Somerset was largely responsible for the development of the concept of the vista. Streets were lined with oak trees, as the main streets of Cape Town had been at an earlier stage, while buildings were usually of a fairly uniform style enhancing the vista concept. Further, major buildings often terminated the vista. Thus the residency at Worcester or the Church at George became focal points for views of a more urban nature. The towns also helped to emphasise the new official interest in the interior, as did the frequent naming of towns after the governor (Somerset East), his family (Beaufort West) and his king (George).

Later, the Great Trek resulted in the establishment of a large number of towns in the eastern half of South Africa. Most foundations followed plans and designs of Cape origin. The grid-iron plan was almost universally adopted and as in the case of Lord Somerset's towns, the number of plots laid out was often substantial. It was assumed that the farmers would possess a plot in town where they could reside when required to visit the magistrate, attend church, or engage in trade. The result was the emergence of a distinctly South African town, which was reproduced throughout the nineteenth century as new areas were opened up and towns were laid out by the State, the Church or private individuals (Croft, 1970; Haswell, 1979). In general the founders of towns were highly optimistic as to the future of their foundations with generous provision for anticipated, if often unrealistic, expansion.

In contrast to the ambitious plans of the immediate post-Napoleonic War period and the Trekker towns, most purely British planning was firmly fixed upon the village concept of a settlement in which farmers, together with agricultural craftsmen such as millers, blacksmiths, etc. would reside together with the parson and a couple of traders. This theme recurs frequently. In 1820 a series of villages was established by the British settlers in the eastern Cape. In the main the settlers chose to live on their rural plots, so that

141

the villages shrank to contain little more than the service buildings – a group of churches and trading stores. The settlement of Natal in 1850 resulted in another bout of village foundation. Although the majority followed the path of the 1820 villages to disintegration, a few survived and developed into towns, as government administrative functions were added soon afterwards.

In 1857 another series of villages was established for the German legionary settlers on the eastern Cape frontier. Again these villages met with mixed success, but probably they were more long lasting than any of their predecessors. Village settlement held a fascination for settlement scheme promoters, whether government or private. Most irrigation schemes were planned with adjacent villages until the Second World War, despite the marked tendency in each case for the farmers to move out and locate their dwellings on their agricultural plot.

Town foundation has remained largely the preserve of the Government and official bodies, although some private enterprise towns have been established. They, like their official counterpart, adopted the same approach to town planning and are virtually indistinguishable from them. In the more densely settled parts of rural 'White' South Africa, especially in the western Cape and Natal, a more spontaneous and unplanned village formation has occurred for farm workers. The general tendency for farmers to provide agricultural accommodation, virtually as tied cottages, has resulted in places in the emergence of small blocks of houses on farms and independent groups of houses elsewhere. Services in such settlements are usually poor, with little more than a general store and possibly a primary school. As such they are too small to enter the urban hierarchy, but they constitute an important element in the landscape where they may house several thousand people or only a few dozen.

Most towns and villages were established with a rural service base, but specialised fishing villages were founded to exploit the resources of the Atlantic Ocean. The cold Aghulas Current off the Atlantic coast has considerable marine life which supports a flourishing small-scale fishing industry. The early whaling industry was more generally located at a series of stations from Walvis (Whale) Bay to Durban. However, the whaling bases were mostly abandoned as high seas fleets replaced local whalers in the present century. Fishing, being limited to the Atlantic coast, is mainly small-scale resulting in the creation of a series of small villages on the Cape peninsula and vicinity. For example Hout Bay and Kalk Bay are predominantly fishing communities each with constructed harbour and village. On the Indian Ocean coast the warm waters and the lack of suitable harbour sites have largely precluded this form of settlement.

Town plans

The form of the small South African town varies substantially, reflecting its origins and later growth, yet there are certain traits common to most. Three basic plans may be distinguished: the grid-iron, the modern geometrical, and the haphazard. The plan of the core of most towns is usually a grid of straight streets intersecting at right angles. This was virtually the only form of plan in the nineteenth and early twentieth centuries, when the majority of South African towns were founded. The earliest villages were, however, relatively unstructured, despite the example offered by the metropolitan centre at Cape Town. Early eighteenth-century towns were relatively small and the later additions introduced the grid plan while surveyors attempted to tidy up the irregularities of earlier times. Significantly many nineteenth-century towns were planned on such a scale that no subsequent additions have had to be made, apart from those required by the Natives (Urban Areas) and Group Areas Acts. Towns established since the 1930s as well as additions to existing towns have adopted geometrical plans, akin to planning practice in other parts of the Western world. Whereas this is a significant element in the landscape of the metropolitan centres, it has had comparatively little impact on the majority of South African towns.

The first Dutch village foundations, such as Stellenbosch, Swellendam, Tulbagh and Paarl, were all small, with little more than a main street and either, or both, a church and a magistracy set in its own grounds. Some of these streets, such as Church Street, Tulbagh and Parsonage Street, Graaff Reinet constitute some of the finest examples of Cape–Dutch townscape surviving in South Africa. The irregular pattern of Stellenbosch has survived as each extension took place, and the result is one of the most interesting small towns in South Africa, reflecting 300 years of growth. The church, parsonage and magistracy, together with the square and powder magazine, provide the basic elements in the landscape. Around them the houses of traders, craftsmen, artisans and servants were built. The central area has since been partially rebuilt, but unlike the more important commercial and industrial centres, the rebuilding was incomplete, so that a fair proportion of eighteenth- and early nineteenth-century townscape survives (Smuts, 1979). The University of Stellenbosch has occupied a portion of the old town but not seriously infringed upon the historic core. Indeed as in other university towns such as Grahamstown and Potchefstroom the influence of the university has been such as to slow the forces of change.

The grid pattern for town layouts and extensions was almost universally adopted in the nineteenth and early twentieth centuries. It took many forms, depending upon the size of plots offered and the positions of major public buildings and open spaces. In size, plots ranged from 1 ha to less than 0.1 ha. The larger sized plots were designed to enable the owners to grow their own fruit and vegetables, and to keep their own horses and cattle in sheds at night. In addition to housing the occupier's family, a number of servants were also accommodated. Each plot, when occupied, thus became an agricultural smallholding, a residence and often a place of business. It was only with the advent of the residential plot for industrial towns or expansion of the metropolitan areas that sizes were markedly reduced.

Fig. 8.4 Queenstown, established 1853 on the eastern frontier of the Cape Colony. The un-usual hexagonal plan was designed for defence. The central area served as a market place. Prominent sites were allocated to the Church of England and the Dutch Reformed Church, while the more recent extensions beyond the railway include school sports fields. (South African Railways)

In arrangement a high degree of standardisation was achieved. In general, wide streets were surveyed, often with the idea of enabling an oxwagon to turn, and widths of 30 m were not uncommon. Streets were frequently lined with trees and water furrows. Plots of uniform size either extended from street to street or were half that extent. Usually subdivision of plots began at an early stage so that the street to street plot was rare after 1850. The plan produced uniformity, except where local topography necessitated curved, and therefore more expensive to survey, streets.

The plans were usually interrupted for open spaces and public buildings (Fig. 8.4). Open spaces were of three types: the market square, church square and gardens. The market square functioned as a place where merchants and farmers met and sold and exchanged goods, often on a regular basis. Such squares had to accommodate large numbers of wagons and oxen, as well as goods, and often occupied an entire block in the town plan, extending over several hectares. The market square declined as such in the present century as transport became mechanised and specialised markets were built. Thus new civic centres, gardens and parking lots have been established on the sites of many of the old market squares. Some towns were planned with more than one market square and a variety of uses have since been found for them. In King Williams Town, public buildings, market facilities, a bus station, and ornamental gardens are to be found on the sites of old market squares. Church squares, as the land was deeded to the Church, whether Dutch Reformed or Church of England, have had more stable histories. Initially the square was used for the assembly of the rural community for a quarterly communion service, 'Nagmaal'. Later a church was erected, and rebuilt, often several times. Church square was frequently one of the central points in a town so that the church provided a focus for street vistas. The idea of squares for parks and botanical gardens was more restricted, and such land was often on the edge of town; nevertheless several parks were established in the centres of nineteenth-century towns. It is significant that few squares were designed as parade grounds in a country which relied upon a mounted militia rather than a regular infantry. Worcester is one of the exceptions.

A further element in the town plan is the provision of townlands or commonages for many of the towns. The areas involved were often extensive, with 3000 ha or more provided. For example the commonage at Middelburg in the Transvaal measured 13 000 ha, and several others were almost as large. Commonages initially provided for the grazing of the citizens' animals, and those of visitors to market and church. In addition they supplied the firewood, thatching reeds, quarrystone or clay for bricks. Later commercial exploitation ran to timber plantations and temporary cropping. More recently a variety of uses such as landing strips, industrial sites and Black and Coloured housing estates have been evident in many towns. Many of the commonages were of such a size that they remain open, and large tracts are available for the future expansion of the majority of South African towns. By contrast the towns established in the 1850s with the Natal settlement schemes and some of the more recent foundations have been without commonages, and have therefore had considerable problems with regard to expansion.

Town planning until the twentieth century was little beyond land surveying. Apart from the elements of the town plan, with its squares, and the commonages there were few refinements. Internal differentiation between various uses and between different classes is largely a product of the present century. The sole differences might be between large irrigated plots and small unirrigated plots in several Transvaal towns, but a town planning scheme was lacking until recently. Generally in the smaller towns more has survived from the period immediately following foundation, as redevelopment has often been minimal. Thus many of the nineteenth-century townscapes of South Africa are to be found in the smaller and declining towns (Picton-Seymour, 1977).

Town functions

The non-metropolitan towns amounting to approximately 600 towns, form the lower part of an urban hierarchy which is markedly top heavy (Davies, 1967; Davies and Cook, 1968). However, in terms of size over half the urban places were in the two lowest orders of local and low order service centres. Significantly, few towns are declining in population but nearly all those urban places classified as towns, minor towns or service centres are losing White population which, because of its significant spending power, has marked results. First, spending power is reduced and the numbers of functions offered by the town is likely to decline, thereby continuing its downward path. The relative poverty of the urban places of the Karroo region illustrates this feature. Second, the introduction of the Group Areas Act to the small rural towns has resulted in the town core emptying its Coloured, Asian and Black population at the same time that the White population is in serious decline; leaving a virtual dead heart to many of the smaller settlements, while the 'location' grows and in most cases far exceeds the population of the parent settlement.

The present hierarchy reflects the relative success of the town foundations developing into viable units and attracting more functions. It is noticeable that the majority of towns were established for either administrative, ecclesiastical or market purposes, although the motives of most town founders seem to have been mixed, and often highly ambitious. It is also evident that little control was exercised over town foundations except in the Orange Free State where no town might be established within 32 km of another, except for special purposes – usually mining. Originally (1863) the distance was set as 12 hours by horse ride apart (Moll, 1977; Van Zyl, 1967).

Administrative functions were important in selecting sites and in planning layouts of towns. The Government in selecting a site for a magistracy usually desired to bring the Government closer to the frontier and the rural population, and often chose an existing site or farmstead for the purpose. There was no equivalent of the grand colonisation design apparent in the United States or parts of Australia. The establishment of a magistracy was vital to a town as the farmers had to pay their taxes including farm rentals at the designated offices and legal matters usually had to be settled there. In the present century the civil service has multiplied rapidly as state services and supervision have increased. Administration has become far more labour intensive, as decentralised ministries and departments have established offices in the urban centres. In the Cape Province an additional tier of administration, the Divisional Councils, responsible for roads and limited planning functions, also operate. The current reorganisation and reduction in the number of councils is thus being resisted by those centres which will be losing a function. However, education possibly is one of the most significant of the present administrative functions, as small rural schools have largely been closed and the education of all races is now urban based. Declining numbers attending

White schools in many parts of the country, reflecting the decline in rural population, adversely affects the schooling provided in the smaller towns. Thus higher forms at school are centralised in the larger towns and the small town school declines.

Ecclesiastical functions were of importance for those towns which were established from the start as church settlements. The quarterly communion service of the Dutch Reformed Church was a vital element of rural society. The site chosen over the years tended to attract other activities and a formal decision to build a church and lay out a town often followed. The central position of many churches still reflects this significant step. In similar vein the mission stations for the Coloured and Black population reflect the same tendency, although few major church towns emerged in the Zulu and Xhosa areas, where there was no background to community life on that scale; although the major mission hospitals might achieve the size of a large village, as at Holy Cross in Transkei.

Most towns, whatever the object of the founders, relied upon the financial and commercial base which they attracted. The market in the colonial economy was a vital element in the transfer of goods between the countryside and the metropolitan power. It was the market which provided the means of barter and sale, where farmers could dispose of their products and acquire the necessities and luxuries offered by an industrial society. Thus the market place and outspan for the wagons and their oxen were elements of most town plans prior to the First World War. In more recent times permanent covered markets have been built in some of the larger towns and in the smaller towns the market place has been utilised for parks and government offices. Individual traders and services were permanently established in the towns although purpose built shops and offices only began to be erected late in the nineteenth century (Fig. 8.5). However, it is worth noting that most South African farms were remarkably self-contained and that the range of urban trades was restricted through lack of a market until the nineteenth century. Financial concerns only appeared in the second half of the nineteenth century, when banks and building societies were established and the money economy introduced. Shops in the towns were also late comers. Wholesalers appeared as the rural economy was integrated with the world economy. The trade was a two-way affair, with imported goods being distributed to the towns and countryside, and a reverse flow of agricultural products from the rural areas to the towns. Some towns, such as King Williams Town or Mafeking relied heavily on the Black trade, which was more specialised and restricted in nature than elsewhere. Thus warehouses, often now converted for other purposes, constitute a significant element in the townscapes concerned. Retail shops emerged as the urban population increased. The general trading store was joined by bakeries, butcheries and dairies as the local population ceased to bake its own bread or keep its own livestock on the commonages. In other words the towns become less rural in aspect, although such a process has not progressed far in the smaller South African towns. Naturally towns without

Fig. 8.5 Indian-owned general store, Dundee, Natal. The Indian trader supplied a cheaper class of goods than the average White urban shop and thus created a special niche in trade and a distinctive shopping street in most towns in Natal and the Transvaal. (Anne Christopher)

a rural foundation acquired this degree of differentiation earlier than those with it. In the present century the rise of electrical and motor trades has resulted in a new range of commercial enterprises, as the farms have come to rely increasingly upon services from the towns.

With increased prosperity, professionals such as doctors, dentists, lawyers, auctioneers, surveyors, bankers and auditors have joined the earlier arrivals, the administrators and the clergyman. These persons, usually with higher than average incomes, have built larger and more distinctive houses, and established higher class suburbs, where social segregation has become a feature of even small towns and where there are more and less desirable areas, reflected in housing styles. Other services such as hotels, motels, cafés and garages for the travelling public reflect another change in urban function where the passing trade is catered for. Obviously only those towns on the main routes have shown such influences, which the construction of a bypass may adversely affect with regard to trade. So far few complexes in South African towns have approached the visual impact of the American motel-fast food–gas station landscape.

New trades and services are introduced to towns as they grow, or are displaced as they decline. Davies, R. J. (1972) found that there were marked threshold populations required to sustain various activities. At the upper end a department store required a population of at least 8000 although the average population per store was twice that value. Most professional services required 2000–5000 inhabitants, while shops were established at lower threshold populations. As a greater complexity is introduced so the demand for specialised accommodation arises. This may range from the conversion of houses into offices to the building of shopping and office complexes. In landscape terms the latter leads to a high degree of uniformity as most chain stores or institutions erect similar looking buildings whether it be in the northern Transvaal or the south-western Cape.

Manufacturing industry has played a significant part in the development and growth of most towns (Davies and Young, 1969). The local industries associated with food and drink have a long history. Milling, together with the processing of agricultural products provide the industrial base for most small towns, and remain a significant element even in larger towns. Davies and Young (1970a and b) found that only for towns over 80 000 inhabitants did the proportion employed in food and drink cease to be the most important manufacturing activity. In small towns of 2000–5000 inhabitants the proportion averaged 41.0 per cent. Although great efforts have been made by most towns to attract manufacturing industry, it remains a metropolitan and large city activity, with low levels of activity elsewhere except for basic services. Industrial areas have been laid out by many towns but oil storage, warehousing and repair facilities are as much as the majority of towns rise to. Consequently towns with a significant manufacturing component are limited in areal extent.

A more specialised form of town is that established for the railways. Rail-

Fig. 8.6 Railway settlement, central Cape. The railway station failed to attract other functions to itself, and the settlement thus remained limited to the station, station master's and workers' houses, storage shed and stock pens. (Anne Christopher)

way functions and workshops gave rise to spectacular growth often followed by gradual decay. Although the main workshops were established in the metropolitan areas, others were set up further into the system. Touws River, Noupoort, De Aar, Waterval Boven represent interior junctions and workshops with towns expressly established for the purpose. Other workshops such as Ladysmith have acted to diversify the local urban economy. The transfer from steam traction to diesel and electric power has often made the smaller settlements redundant. Thus Rosmead (Cape) in 1979 lost the majority of its White population when the main line was converted. At the other end of the scale many railway settlements remained small (Fig. 8.6).

Only in the most recently planned towns, or in extensions to existing towns, have town planning regulations introduced any marked segregation of land uses. Thus commercial, financial and professional services, and even industries, occupy sites originally designated for residential or agricultural use. The conversion is rarely completed for an extensive number of blocks except in the major towns. The smaller South African towns exhibit many of the features recognised in small English towns or villages (Best and Rogers, 1973), namely low population densities and high proportions of land under residence and gardens. The open, often garden-like nature of many smaller towns is particularly noticeable in the drier parts of the country where trees dominate the urban landscape, but are absent in the rural landscape.

Change in the towns – segregation and decline

Segregation in the small towns has been a well-marked feature since expansion began late in the nineteenth century. It does need to be stated however that the Coloured populations of the Cape towns were not under any legislative restriction on place of residence until 1950. Nevertheless, as in colonial times, with a few exceptions, social and economic position was in large measure a reflection of skin colour. The poorer quarters of town tended to be racially darker than the better off areas. There were though no clear-cut lines between such areas, and with the dominance of domestic workers living in at their place of work, the degree of segregation was slight. Blacks who came to the towns either squatted on the outskirts or were housed by their employers. The mission stations represent one of the earliest *de facto* attempts at small town segregation, in the belief that the indigenous population could only be saved from the corrupting influences of the White man by careful education and protection.

During the nineteenth century the numbers involved were small. In 1911, outside the metropolitan areas, the urban population was only 540 000, of whom nearly half were White. They were distributed across more than 300 urban centres. The rapid rise in population, more especially the Coloured and Black populations placed strains upon the existing framework. The small Asian population had already been resisted by the Whites in Transvaal and Orange Free State towns. In the former case with little success, but in the latter with complete success. The Indian bazaars of some Transvaal towns are a legacy of this period. The influx of Blacks led to the enforcement of segregation legislation designed for the metropolitan areas but applied to the smaller towns. as well. Squatter camps become locations, either on the same sites or more rarely on new ones with some order introduced, usually after the outbreak of disease.

The introduction of the Group Areas Act in 1950 and the general enforcement of previous segregation legislation related to the Black population profoundly affected the small towns of South Africa. Townships for the Coloured population were now created, as in general the existing built-up area was proclaimed the White group area and it was the other races which were forced to move. Occasionally existing predominantly Coloured areas became the Coloured Group Area and a buffer strip was established through the town. Thus even for the smallest size of settlements a dual element of 'twin' towns emerged. The new townships were reasonably simply constructed as the townlands were used for this purpose and no acquisition of farmland was generally involved.

It is worth noting that the majority of towns were losing White population between 1960 and 1970 and this trend has continued in the most recent inter-census period. Thus the decline in the central portion of the towns has been very substantial, resulting in low density settlements, but with a high density appendage. Appendage is probably an apt description, as the locations and townships are usually dependent upon the main town for all services. Even the towns now included in the Black states started in this form and it has largely been a wealthier class of Black administrators and entrepreneurs who have since occupied the original 'White' town. Similarly towns such as Verulam, which have become Indian, have substituted one class for another within the central core. The distinctive form of the South African town has thus survived political changes.

The growth of the Coloured and Black populations in the South African towns has resulted in the Whites becoming a minority in all but a handful of cases, although with few exceptions political control has remained with the White population. Furthermore, purchasing power has remained essentially in White hands due to the wage gap between the races, reinforced by class groupings. Thus few of the new Coloured and Black townships have more than rudimentary commercial and financial facilities, reflecting the essentially 'dormitory' planning attitudes of the administrators. Further, many of the towns lack the financial resources to build housing for the Black and Coloured population to the standard laid down by the central government. Hence many appear ramshackle. Recent government recognition of the scale of the rehousing programme is illustrated by the decision in 1978 to upgrade the Black township in Graaff Reinet rather than rebuild it 10 km away.

The number of small South African towns is in excess of the present needs of the rural population and hence many do not possess the services necessary to provide for a community. Thus a spiral of decline begins where services are withdrawn, making the towns less attractive to the community. Whereas concern has been expressed in several circles about the problems of the small towns, little practical aid has been forthcoming, as most development aid has been diverted towards the Black States and the metropolitan areas outside the Witwatersrand.

The problem of decay has affected only a minority of towns to the extent that physical contraction has taken place, and that buildings have been abandoned. Far more noticeable has been the loss of economic base in the form of shops and mills. Whereas the White population has left the towns, the opportunities for Coloureds and especially for Blacks have been far more limited. Unemployment and underemployment have thus become the major problems of the small towns. A few have been designated growth points, either for the Coloured population in the western and central Cape and elsewhere for Blacks. In general only the larger towns have been designated and little has been offered to the smaller towns. The downward spiral seems likely to continue with declining White and Coloured populations, leaving behind a large number of unemployed, dependent upon the remittances of those with jobs in the metropolitan regions – reminiscent of other peripheral areas.

The South African small town

Bearing the aforementioned in mind, it is possible to provide a sketch of a 'typical' South African town. There are many exceptions but the broad features may be discerned. First it consists of two portions, an old White town, with a new Black or Coloured appendage. The majority of the population lives in the latter, although it is the smaller half in terms of area. Occasionally there are two appendages, one Black and one Coloured, but the generalisation remains the same. The original town, mostly nineteenth century in origin, was usually laid out with generous sized plots (0.25–1 ha in extent). Except in the commercial centre of the town many of these have remained intact and provide a semi-rural aspect, where small-scale farming activity with

Table 8.2   Population of Laingsburg 1904–80

	Town		Rural district	
	White	*Coloured★*	*White*	*Coloured★*
1904	618	647	1700	5193
1911	662	605	2233	2401
1921	965	610	2060	2844
1936	1007	823	1765	2014
1951	1123	1218	847	2951
1960	1047	1791	727	3343
1970	896	2229	675	2604
1980	775	2383	522	2695

★ Including Blacks and Indians.

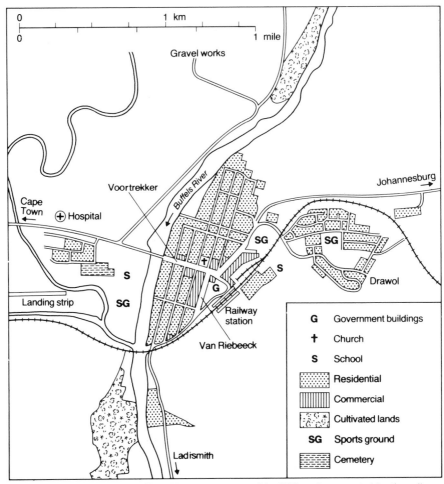

Fig. 8.7 Plan of Laingsburg. The old town, now zoned for Whites, is separated by the railway line from the new suburb of Drawol, built for the Coloured population. In January 1981, the normally dry Buffels River came down in spate, flooding two-thirds of the old town and destroying most of the buildings in the two blocks closest to the river. The disaster cost over 150 lives and caused damage worth R12.3 million within the town. It seems probable that the section of the town closest to the river will be abandoned and that rebuilding will take place elsewhere.

crops and orchards is undertaken. In the centre of the town the dominant building is invariably the church, usually with a spire, set either in a square of its own or close to the centre of the street grid. The commercial centre generally consists of two streets, the one containing the main bank edifices, the major shops, petrol stations, town hall and hotel. The other street, or sometimes the other end of the main street, is also occupied with shops, usually poorer looking edifices, often originally Indian, but now usually immigrant White owned, catering for the Black and Coloured trade. The commercial façades of both streets are seldom complete, with houses remaining close to the centre of the commercial area and in the side streets leading off

Fig. 8.8 Voortrekker Street, Laingsburg. The main communication axis is dominated by the Dutch Reformed Church, but is lined with hotels, school hostels, petrol stations and stores. (Anne Christopher)

the main street. The age and style of buildings range from those built at the foundation of the town to modern or modernised, with a preponderance of the former.

Most of the original grid of the small South African town is devoted to housing. Sizes and styles vary substantially, but generally a range exists within each town from comparatively wealthy to poor. The housing styles reflect the locality and history of the town, including a predominance of nineteenth century, single storey houses, with verandahs and corrugated iron roofs. Some are large and ornate reflecting the flamboyance of the late Victorian and Edwardian eras, while others are small and plain. Owing to the general stagnation of the smaller towns, new housing estates dating from the post-Second World War era are not extensive, although most towns possess such an area. Sometimes it was recognised that part of the town would consist of small houses, used only occasionally by local farmers on their visits to transact business or attend church, or by retired farmers, as opposed to permanent inhabitants. In several cases the water supply affected the appearance of the townscape, as many were irrigated with water channels along the sides of the roads, while others used boreholes and windmills for their supply. In general the older parts of the town were planted with trees and gardens, either ornamental or productive, were laid out. The initial appearance is thus often luxuriant with comparatively little evidence of housing when viewed from a distance. In other cases less water was used and the houses are more tightly packed. In virtually all instances the old town has been zoned White in terms of the Group Areas Act.

By contrast the Black or Coloured sector or location is smaller, with plots of 1/30 ha on average. Little cultivation has taken place in the gardens and trees are few and far between. The housing styles are generally uniform and of fairly recent vintage, dating from the establishment of the location and later, as it is here that growth is taking place, compared with the stagnation or decline in the White sector. There is a conspicuous lack of land use variation with few shops, but again the townscape is dominated by a number of churches. The two sectors are separated by open ground, usually unused except for grazing. Such a picture is repeated through South Africa with a number of minor variations.

Laingsburg in the Cape Province has been taken as an example, as it has no particular distinguishing features to set it apart either in historial background or in physical layout. It is a minor town under the Davies (1967) classification and remained so in 1980. The town was established in 1881 on the railway then being built from Cape Town to Kimberley. The population

Fig. 8.9 (*Above*) Old Town, Laingsburg. The landscape is dominated by the trees and windmills in the grounds of the houses, which vary substantially in size and style. Note the barren nature of the surrounding hills and the 'oasis' aspect of the town. (Anne Christopher)

Fig. 8.10 (*Below*) Van Riebeeck Street, Laingsburg. The main commercial street is lined with its cooperative and Indian-owned stores, most of which date from the turn of the century. (Anne Christopher)

Fig. 8.11 Drawol, Laingsburg. Standard-style housing for the Coloured population is interspersed with extensive playing fields and open spaces. (Anne Christopher)

grew to reach a little over 3000 inhabitants by 1970 (Table 8.2). However, the White population has been in decline since 1951 and thus the financial base of the town is in decline. This is even more serious when the depopulation, both White and Coloured, of the rural areas is also considered.

The town is physically divided into several parts (Fig. 8.7). The earliest section was laid out as a grid of streets (10–14 m wide) about a central axis, Voortrekker Street (47 m wide), extending from the railway station to the Buffels River. Most of the streets are therefore laid out parallel to the contours, although no town irrigation system was constructed as water was only available from boreholes. The windmills in most gardens are a distinctive feature of Laingsburg, as of many South African towns. Most of the plots were relatively small, 1/10 ha apiece, and provision was made for the church and government buildings on the main axis. The Dutch Reformed Church, built in late colonial style in 1904 is the dominating feature of the townscape with its spire rising above the trees (Fig. 8.8). Most of the houses built in this section of the town also date from the colonial period before 1910, although there is a sprinkling of later ones of various dates to the present (Fig. 8.9). In common with most South African towns no shopping area was planned, but one grew up on the main axes of communication, namely Voortrekker Street on the main Cape Town–Johannesburg road and Van Riebeeck Street, the road to the south towards Ladismith and Prince Albert. The former is lined with garages, a hotel, general store, the banks and a couple of general traders. The latter is the main retail hub with the cooperative, several Indian stores and general traders (Fig. 8.10). It is evident from the grander shop frontages that the early part of the present century was one of wealth for the town.

The second element is the extension to the core, which has been established as two separate entities on the two main roads. On the road to Ladismith, an extensive layout of plots has been used only for occasional residence and agriculture, while the more recent layout along the road to Cape Town has a number of new houses, together with the school and hospital. Owing to the decline in the White population the new residential suburbs include large tracts of vacant land.

The third element in the townscape is the Coloured township of Drawol, which is physically separated from the remainder of Laingsburg by the railway line and sidings, and sports grounds. This is a new township with highly uniform and standard types of building closely spaced. Within it extensive school and sports grounds break up the monotony, but unlike the older White areas, trees are absent or are still young, and the impression is bleak (Fig. 8.11). In area it is under half the size of the original town, although it now houses more than half the total population.

The remaining elements of the townscape are associated with the townlands which originally covered some 4000 ha. Much of this is now farmed, but the remaining area provides space for the two cemeteries, brick fields, landing strip, and for any future expansion.

159

9

Metropolitan landscapes

The metropolitan areas of South Africa fall into three categories. The first comprises the major port cities, Cape Town, Port Elizabeth, East London and Durban to which may be added other centres of similar origin. Owing to the colonial source of the South African space economy, these were the original points of contact between Europe and the interior and it was through these centres that a two-way trade developed. They are thus the oldest and in many ways the most complex metropolitan landscapes in the country. The second category comprises the major mining centres, of which Johannesburg and the Witwatersrand are the outcome of a process of metropolitan accumulation, converted from a mining area to the financial and commercial hub of southern Africa. It is significant that no other mining centre achieved the same degree of transformation. The third category includes the administrative centres. The various colonial and other capital cities can lay claim to metropolitan status through their accumulation of functions and political power.

The ports

The ports have played a vital role in the development of South Africa as the point of contact between Europe and the African continent. They represent in Vance's work (1970) the great entrepôt cities where the wholesaling of goods, both incoming manufacturers from Europe and outgoing raw materials and foodstuffs from the colonies, was organised. The distributive functions of the ports resulted in a distinctive set of landscapes and relationships with the interior. However, owing to paucity of suitable sites on the South African coast the number of ports was never very large and the hierarchy of ports has been fairly restricted in numerical terms.

The first major point of contact – Cape Town, has remained one of the most significant centres in South Africa. The site was utilised by Portuguese and other navigators in the sixteenth and early seventeenth centuries as a watering place on the long voyage from Europe to India and the East Indies.

However, the inhospitality of the indigenous population effectively prevented any permanent occupation. The Dutch in the mid-seventeenth century increasingly found their station on St Helena inadequate and sought a permanent base elsewhere. In 1652 improved reports from the vicinity of the Cape of Good Hope prompted the Dutch East India Company to formally occupy the site at the foot of Table Mountain where the fresh water streams flowed into Table Bay.

The first settlement was confined to the fort which was constructed to protect the watering place and the gardens which were planted adjacent to it. However, in 1657 certain of the Company's servants were given freedom to pursue their own businesses, and the first 'town' was laid out. It was limited to the area beyond a line 500 m from the fort, where a road and ditch were constructed, the Heerengracht – now Adderley Street. In the course of the seventeenth and eighteenth centuries, the town was expanded as blocks were laid out and the formal arrangement of the Company gardens, parade ground and warehouses along the beach front was designed. The city blocks were small, usually only 100 m × 100 m, with main roads 20 m wide and side roads 12 m wide. This cramped situation has presented the city planners of Cape Town with major problems in the present century.

Cape Town became the administrative, commercial and ecclesiastical capital of the Colony – only losing some of these functions in the present century. The bulk of the trade of the subcontinent passed through the port until the 1850s, and even then, in passenger terms, Cape Town retained its pre-eminence. Harbour works were minimal until the 1860s when a series of docks were constructed, culminating in the 1940s in the reclamation from the sea of the foreshore, an area of several hectares, which became an extension of the congested Central Business District. More recently the Schoeman Dock and the container berths have added appreciably to the port's competitive position (Fig. 9.1).

The search for other port sites along the coast was intense as European settlements spread into the interior and the exploitation of such resources as the forests of the southern Cape began. Sites at Mossel Bay, Plettenberg Bay and Knysna were used, together with such virtually private ports as Port Beaufort. However, few rivers were navigable for even a couple of kilometres from their mouths, so that it was the bay sites which were favoured. It was only in 1799 that Algoa Bay was selected as a suitable site and a fort erected. The town was laid out 16 years later and named Port Elizabeth 5 years after that.

The site of Port Elizabeth was restricted. At first only one street was laid out with plots on both sides, constrained either by the sea or an old marine terrace. The port, with access to the produce of the developing eastern Cape, grew rapidly and overtook Cape Town by 1860 in terms of value of trade, as wool became the staple export of the Colony. Harbour works were constructed comparatively late with the breakwater only being completed in the 1920s. Extensions in the 1930s and 1970s appreciably improved the facilities

offered by the port and ensured a share in the growing volume of southern African trade.

Further expansion associated with the eastward movement of the colonial frontier necessitated the search for further port sites (Clark, 1977). A quest for a port for Grahamstown in particular resulted in attempts to develop the site of Port Alfred, but the physical restrictions were too great. East London was established to serve the frontier, but its physical disadvantages, particularly silting and small size, have retarded its development. Alternatives to East London have proved to be hard to locate. The development of Hamburg by the Ciskei and one of the estuaries in Transkei may add to the number of ports, although the expense of developing them will probably be prohibitive.

The Colony of Natal included the large lagoon of Port Natal, where Durban was established. Although silting was a problem, with the growth of the bar across the entrance to the Bay, engineering works in the 1880s enabled ships to enter the Bay (Hart, 1967). Durban as the port for Natal and later the nearest South African port to the Witwatersrand, soon became the most important in terms of tonnage in South Africa. However, constant improvement of facilities had by the early 1970s virtually exhausted the Baysite, and relief for Durban became imperative.

The search for additional port sites has been a continuing endeavour. In the nineteenth century prospective sites such as Port St John's, Lake St Lucia and Walvis Bay were annexed by Great Britain before any interest in the interior was evident. Indeed the hinterland of Walvis Bay was later annexed by Germany! In Natal some, such as Scottborough and Port Shepstone, developed a limited coastal trade but the advent of the railway killed the port functions. It was the specialised mineral export ports for the Namaqualand copper mines, such as Port Nolloth, which were most long lived and which pointed to the future development of bulk mineral export terminals. In the 1970s Saldanha Bay and Richard's Bay were built for iron ore and coal exports respectively, and both were linked to the mines by new electrified railway lines. The advent of the two ports had an immediate impact upon the port hierarchy, as in 1979 they occupied first and third places in terms of tonnage handled, although most of this was direct export with comparatively little processing activity. Government control of the railway and harbour system has been such that the port hierarchy has otherwise been little changed in the last 100 years.

In the course of the 1970s significant changes have occurred in the main import–export ports with the advent of containerisation. This has resulted in major transformations as new terminals have had to be constructed on reclaimed land and new access routes designed as increasing quantities of freight have been allowed on to the roads. It is not insignificant that from a customs point of view, Johannesburg has become the most important con-

Fig. 9.1 Cape Town harbour. The new container-handling wharves are evident, as are the high-rise buildings of the reclaimed land of the foreshore, which constitute a major part of the townscape. The city is backed by the spectacular Table Mountain. (*The Argus*)

tainer 'port' in the country. The appearance of the dock areas has changed as warehouses have given way to extensive open spaces for the stacking of the containers. Owing to the high degree of mechanisation the turn around time at the container terminals is much less than at the traditional cargo quays, so that the ports appear less congested despite the increased volume of goods passing through them. The need for specialised zones for bulk ore and oil handling, containers, general cargo and pleasure craft has led to increased differentiation within the harbour areas, although significantly the passenger services have virtually ceased.

Townscapes of the port cities

The ports represent one of the few areas of long-term urban growth beyond the initial plan. The steady spread of the coastal cities is in marked contrast to the explosive growth of the interior metropolitan region, where expansion usually took the form of planned suburban and semi-rural areas, and where few areas of evolution of street and settlement patterns are present.

Cape Town, as the oldest, largest and most complex port city, illustrates the process well. The original grid was extended until the early nineteenth century, with a pattern which showed little change from that envisaged in the late seventeenth century. As a result of the boom in colonial trade from the 1840s onwards, the population grew and suburbs, beyond the control of the City Council, expanded. Industrial areas were sought outside the restricted site of the original plan. Owing to the fact that there was only one route to the interior most industrial sites lay close to this route, resulting in ribbon development. The construction of the railway in 1860 enabled workshops, workers and employers to move further out and the decentralisation of the City continued. The introduction of horse trams and later electric trams accentuated this tendency up to 1914. The infilling of road pattern and the growth of settlement around the railway stations followed the form recognisable elsewhere in the industrialising world. Thus the suburb of Woodstock close to central Cape Town exhibits a range of land uses, building styles and densities which is lacking in the more orderly and planned towns and extensions of the later period. A mixture of industry, commerce and residence, with gradations of the latter, provided a degree of community which is lacking in later cities. This pattern is repeated in the string of settlements originating in the period before 1914. Thus Cape Town City housed only 40 per cent of the population of Greater Cape Town in 1911, before the extension of the municipal boundaries to include the suburbs.

The complexity of urban landscapes built before the introduction of formal town planning schemes gives the port cities a unique character (Dewar and Uytenbogaardt, 1977). The lack of a town grid, or more often the fitting of grids between the main streets, distinguishes them from most interior cities. The complexity of land uses, particularly in those areas suitable for the erection of factories and workshops is highly noticeable. Residential class segregation emerged in the nineteenth century as merchants, administrators and other wealthier members of society were freed from dependence on walking to their place of work. Larger houses in substantial gardens were the main features of the landscapes of suburbs built in Cape Town immediately to the east of the Table Mountain block. The older suburbs with a mixture of modified Cape–Dutch style and English Gothic were succeeded in the twentieth century by more universal style houses ranging from English Queen Anne to Spanish Mission. Each of the port cities developed higher class suburbs as the tram system was extended. In general they were raised sites above the level of the original town, such as Oranjezicht in Cape Town, the Hill in Port Elizabeth and the Berea in Durban. The relationship between altitude and social class reflects occurrences in Victorian cities elsewhere.

Allied to the physical expansion of the port cities was the internal differentiation from the 1860s onwards. The central area of Cape Town containing as it did virtually the entire population in 1855, was residential in character. Businesses were carried on in private houses and the main differentiations were the warehousing facilities nearest the shore and landing places, and the blocks of government land. In the second half of the nineteenth century a sorting-out process took place. The Dutch style town centre with its small blocks, open drains, trees and raised verandahs in front of the one- to two-storey houses gave way to more utilitarian structures. The reserve of the gardens provided land for a host of government projects such as the Anglican Cathedral, the South African College, later the University, the Public Library and the Houses of Parliament. After 1860 the Central Business District emerged as special purpose buildings were erected, replacing houses. The trees and verandahs were removed and by the 1880s Adderley Street had taken on the form of a commercial thoroughfare. Firms vied with one another to erect higher and more impressive buildings. Stuttafords Stores reached five stories in the 1880s. By the turn of the century seven-storey buildings had been erected and after the introduction of lifts the skyline of the Central Business District steadily rose. Shops and offices occupied the new structures and a high degree of localisation took place. Competition between the banks to erect magnificent and imposing edifices is reflected in massive Victorian structures which survive in the townscape of today, although the Victorian Post Office and Railway Station have been demolished to make way for more intensive uses of the land in Adderley Street.

Davies's (1965) Central Business District delimitation of Cape Town found a remarkable correspondence between the CBD and the eighteenth-century town grid with the hard core delimitation based on Adderley Street. The restrictions upon the extension of the Central Business District were largely those of barriers imposed by blocks of municipal and central government offices in the south-east, the railway in the east, the sea to the north and the gardens to the south. Thus expansion had tended to be, as the original eighteenth-century town had been beforehand, towards the west. Within this transition zone, automobile, industrial and wholesale users survived but were under pressure. Relief was provided in the 1960s with the development of the foreshore on reclaimed land (Davies and Beavon, 1973). The CBD has expanded rather than decentralised within the Greater Cape Town region as new office and hotel blocks were erected in the 1960s and 1970s on the reclaimed land. This has resulted in a revival of the pre-existing CBD with the construction of an underground mall system of shops and restaurants under Adderley Street and adjacent streets. The mall is linked to the new Golden Acre centre, designed as a prestige regional shopping complex, complete with extensive parking facilities.

Cape Town, alone of the port cities has, retained a central government capital function. This function beginning with a fort, the second of which still stands with associated barracks and parade ground, formed a major part of the original settlement. The construction of the governor's residence, slave lodge (later Supreme Court and finally museum) and municipal building extended the block of government ground. More recently the multiplication of national and local government functions has resulted in extensive tracts of land and portions of buildings coming under government control, and acting as barriers to the expansion of the Central Business District. Even on the foreshore extension, substantial tracts have been devoted to the railways, other state and municipal offices and the Opera House.

Residential areas have survived in central Cape Town. The well-marked Malay Quarter and other residences lie beyond the main automobile and wholesale regions of the west. To the south the gardens and government land provide a barrier which results in a buffer between the Central Business District and the residential area. Interestingly no high rise flatland has evolved on the edge of the CBD, but has appeared at the secondary centre on the Atlantic coast where the holiday industry is based.

Particular attention has been directed towards Cape Town as the original port and the centre of the main coastal metropolitan area. Other port cities exhibit many of the same features of growth and internal differentiation (Fig. 9.2). Port Elizabeth owing to its highly restricted CBD site has developed a certain degree of decentralisation in North End on the main access routes from the port to the interior (Beavon, 1970). Durban alone has had few barriers to the expansion of the CBD beyond the railway lands (Davies, 1963). Most features of the port cities follow those of Cape Town in the evolutionary nature of their expansion before any degree of planning control took place. However, although forts were established at Port Elizabeth (Fort Frederick), East London (Fort Glamorgan) and Durban (Old Fort), they were less significant features in the landscape and the subsequent government reserves were relatively less important, as none became colonial capitals. Thus within the CBD the blocks of government land set aside for town halls, government offices, etc. are largely surrounded by other uses (Fig. 9.3). In this manner the usual metropolitan skyscrapers encircle the monumental buildings of an earlier age. The more recent development of the port cities has fol-

Fig. 9.2 Plans of selected parts of Port Elizabeth: (a) Central; (b) New Brighton (Black suburb); (c) Sunridge Park (White suburb); (d) Greenbushes (smallholdings).

lowed the model of the main metropolis on the Witwatersrand, reflecting a greater measure of control.

The Witwatersrand

The development of the Witwatersrand metropolitan region has been one of the most remarkable features of the historical geography of South Africa (Fig. 9.4). Following the discovery of what proved to be the richest gold

reefs in the world, a string of towns was proclaimed in 1886 extending from Krugersdorp to Springs. At first, mining was concentrated in the central Rand around Johannesburg, but as this declined so the East and West Rand assumed greater importance. To this rich mining area came men and women to seek their fortunes, not only in mining, but in the provision of services for those engaged in mining. Hence Johannesburg became one of the largest mining camps in the world. However, unlike Kimberley and many other mining areas, a degree of permanence was soon achieved. Regular towns were laid out and substantial stone and brick buildings were erected. Within six years of the discovery of gold the gold fields were linked to the coast by rail lines, and Johannesburg had become the economic hub of the subcontinent. Within 10 years the same population as the established port of Cape Town was enumerated.

Population figures prior to the Transvaal Colonial Census of 1904 are unreliable, but a 1896 municipal survey of the area within a 5 km radius of the centre of Johannesburg enumerated 102 000 persons, half of whom were White. Some 15 000 buildings had been erected, of which 45 per cent were of brick and stone. Such an instantaneous spurt of activity inevitably resulted in acute problems, and a landscape very different in appearance from those which had evolved over a long period of slow growth in the port cities. Although it would be unfair to say that there was no planning in the development of the Witwatersrand in its formative years, little coordination was evident between township developers, miners and others operating the urban land market. The various township grids laid out on the various plots were not effectively linked to their neighbours. Little attempt at industrial segregation was made, and even the first dynamite store was sited close to the Johannesburg centre. As a result, a jumble of houses, mines, factories and works developed, which have presented major problems for planners of the present era.

The initial plans had provided small town blocks and lots with comparatively few open spaces. Within the confines of the centre of Johannesburg, businesses, trade and finance facilities were established. The Stock Exchange, Chamber of Mines and other organisations were set up in the first few years of the town's existence. In 1896 nearly 3000 businesses were enumerated in Johannesburg. This business and financial dominance has been maintained and strengthened ever since. The Central Business District was established within the restricted site bounded by the gold mining ground to the south, the railway and hill to the north and industry in the west. On the east, room for expansion was available, while more recent expansion of government functions north of the railway has relieved pressure (Hart, 1969). Central Johannesburg, through the construction of the largest assemblage of high-rise buildings in South Africa, has been able to expand its office facilities and still

Fig. 9.3 Central Durban. Note the contrast between the government land (City Hall, Post Office, Cathedral, Railway Station and parks) in the foreground, and the commercial areas of the Central Business District. (Durban Publicity Association)

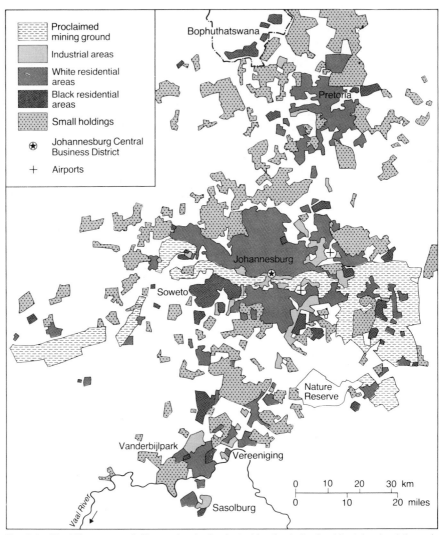

Fig. 9.4   The Witwatersrand. The region is dominated by the belt of gold mining land through the centre. The separate mining towns have now grown together, as the Witwatersrand, Pretoria and Vereeniging areas are now in the process of forming a single conurbation. Note the small area devoted to housing the Black majority in the region.

is capable of considerable vertical expansion, as well as encroachment into the zone of transition to east and west (Fig. 9.5).

Around the Central Business District extensive suburbs were developed, separated into two distinct halves by the belt of mining land. The northern more prestigious suburbs have grown rapidly, despite the marked fluctuations in the trade cycle (Hart, 1977). This northward spread of high class suburbs began in the 1890s when Park Town and other more spacious suburbs were laid out (Hart, 1976a). The trend has since continued, producing land-

Fig. 9.5 Central Johannesburg. The concentration of high-rise flats of Hillbrow around the J. G. Strijdom Post Office Tower (foreground), and the Central Business District (middleground) create an impressive landscape of high intensity usage. (Satour)

scapes of great diversity. To the east and west of the main axis of northward high class development, relatively poorer housing has been erected, ranging from the inner terraces to more recent detached houses. It is within these inner areas that recent arrivals, such as the Portuguese community, have been housed (Browett and Hart, 1977). In addition a second centre, the high density flatland of Hillbrow has emerged to the north-east of the CBD. To the south of the mining land little expensive property development has occurred, and the area is shared by White suburbs and the Black residential complex of Soweto.

Beyond the core of the Witwatersrand, the outer zone has experienced a later and more ordered growth (Fair, 1977). Each of the other towns is smaller than Johannesburg and has organized itself as a separate entity (Cook, 1975). The central jumble of land uses is therefore marked, but the later planned segregated uses are even more marked. In particular the extent of the gold mining land is relatively larger and therefore development has been more confined. Although secondary industrial development has to some ex-

171

tent been decentralised from the core, the tertiary sector has become more concentrated so that the outer area of the Witwatersrand accounted for two-thirds of the gross geographic product of the region, even though mining amounted to only one-quarter of the region's total.

Owing to its size and importance many of the features of metropolitan landscapes are best illustrated by examples from the Witwatersrand, which is therefore examined systematically in the latter portions of this chapter.

Capitals

One of the unusual features of South Africa is its plethora of capital cities – past, present and future. The country possesses three official capitals, Pretoria for the administrative purposes, Cape Town for the legislature and Bloemfontein for the judiciary. For the parliamentary session the Government, together with all the attendant officials, diplomats, etc. move from Pretoria to Cape Town. In view of this current triplication of the capital it is scarcely surprising that old and new capitals should be scattered about South Africa, and that there is a lack of one national centre, which is the norm for most countries.

Political fragmentation both past and present has brought with it the foundation of numerous capital cities in South Africa. Cape Town alone has fulfilled these functions for over 300 years. With the development of new states and colonies in the nineteenth century so new capitals were planned and constructed. Great Britain established King Williams Town for British Kaffraria, Eshowe for Zululand and Mafeking for the Bechuanaland Protectorate, even though the town lay outside the territory. All these were ephemeral. However, it was the republicans who founded most capitals. Pietermaritzburg was planned in 1838 as the grandest of all these cities with over 450 plots, wide streets, open spaces and over 10 000 ha of townlands. Public buildings were constructed including the Church of the Vow, erected after the Voortrekkers' victory at the Blood River had secured Natal for them. Later as the capital of the British Colony of Natal a host of official buildings such as Government House, the Legislative Assembly, the Colonial Office, General Post Office and Church of England Cathedral were erected in the manner of other nineteenth-century British colonies. Many of these survived, lending a unique character to the city which since 1910 has been relegated to the status of a provincial capital only.

Other republican capitals such as Winburg, Potchefstroom and Lydenburg were relegated in status when new capitals were established at Bloemfontein and Pretoria, and little remains to show their previous status. Some such as Schoemansdal in the northern Transvaal were destroyed and not rebuilt, while Ohrigstad in the eastern Transvaal had to be abandoned as being too unhealthy. In the later nineteenth century a new series of capitals was established as republics proliferated on the borders of the Transvaal. Thus Vry-

Fig. 9.6 Union Buildings, Pretoria. Designed by Sir Herbert Baker for the Union Government offices in 1910 in Edwardian imperial style. (Information Services of South Africa)

burg (Free City) for the Stellaland Republic and Vryheid (Freedom) for the New Republic of Zululand, joined less spectacular developments such as Rietfontein (Kalahari Desert State) and Rooigrond (Goschen).

Republican town planning for a capital city differed little from ordinary town planning as government buildings were generally small and at first only occupied plots within the town, with few outward signs of opulence, Churches were the main focus of attention, such as that at the intersection of the two main streets in Pretoria. Only in the late 1880s and 1890s did Pretoria and Bloemfontein begin to construct the range of government buildings to be found in the British colonial capitals. In style though, their architects looked towards the Netherlands and Germany for inspiration, not towards England. Many of the major public buildings of this period have survived, and Church Square in Pretoria, even without its church, retains some of the characteristics of the prosperous late republican period.

At Union in 1910 the South African Government decided upon the somewhat cumbrous system of three capitals (Pretoria, Cape Town and Bloemfontein), rather than selecting one or building a new capital as the Australian and Canadian dominions had elected to do. The imperial imprint, however, was placed upon Pretoria, which was provided with Sir Herbert Baker's grand Union Buildings, one of the finest complexes of government offices in the then British Empire (Fig. 9.6). Since then government functions have expanded to such an extent that Pretoria has grown rapidly with the construction of new office blocks for the various government departments, although most are indistinguishable from the commercial offices alongside. Only a few spectacular official blocks have been erected, and those have mainly been for the municipal and provincial administrations. Other functions have been developed, so that the contemporary University of South Africa building dominates the southern approach to the city, and the University of Pretoria is the largest residential university in southern Africa. Most recently a city block has been devoted to the State Opera House, built on a scale as befits the premier national capital. Owing to the proximity of Johannesburg (50 km) there has been little tendency for private business to relocate in Pretoria, even for prestige purposes, as Johannesburg is sufficiently close to the seat of power for day-to-day contact to be maintained. However, in an attempt to broaden the employment base of Pretoria, the South African Iron and Steel Corporation's first steel works was established in the capital and several other state concerns have followed. This concentration of functions in Pretoria is symbolised by the transfer of the naval headquarters from Simonstown to the administrative capital in 1977.

Bloemfontein was selected at Union as the seat of the Supreme Court. Pressures for redevelopment have been less intense here than in many other cities with the result that the centre is still comparatively open, with government buildings dating from the independent republican, colonial and Union periods. The most prominent are the republican Council Chamber (Raadsaal), with its dome and Ionic pillars reminiscent of American state capitols; and the Law Courts, constructed in Edwardian imperial style. These are set in a distinctive government quarter adjacent to the main commercial area.

The latest phase in capital development has been associated with the movement of the various Black South African states towards self-government and independence. In all cases a new capital has been deemed as necessary as a flag or a national anthem, but seldom was there an obvious choice, as most of the towns remained within the White areas. Even those towns which had become administrative centres for the Black areas were usually outside the Black states themselves. Thus Mafeking, Eshowe and King Williams Town were not designated the capitals of Bophuthatswana, KwaZulu and Ciskei respectively. As a result the South African Government drew up guidelines for the selection of sites for new capitals. These included an open site, away from White influence, yet capable of economic development. Rather surprisingly the guidelines suggested that the site should have no strong historic ties (Best and Young, 1972a).

There were few obvious localities for the Black state capitals, indeed Umtata alone was an undisputed choice. The Transkeian territories had possessed a measure of self-government since the 1890s, and the territorial council had met in Umtata, where the Bunga or Parliament Building had been erected. Although nominally a 'White' town, the capital was transferred to Transkei on independence. This was the only inherited capital from the colonial period. Elsewhere the selection of the site was more complex, with contenders and various vested interests. Most of the sites were small towns or service centres with few amenities. Thus Ulundi (KwaZulu), Thohoyandou (Venda), Phuthaditjhaba (QwaQwa) and Giyani (Gazankulu) were chosen. Both Ulundi and Thohoyandou had strong historic ties with their former Zulu and Venda rulers. Greater diversity of choice was apparent in the selection of capitals for Bophuthatswana (Mmabatho) and Lebowa (Lebowakagoma), where open sites were selected from a number of possibilities, and new towns designed as capitals from the outset. In both cases the Black states' claims to the neighbouring White towns, Mafeking and Pietersburg respectively, were rejected.

The initial rejection of the Bophuthatswana claim to Mafeking resulted in the construction of the new capital, Mmabatho, some 5 km from the centre of Mafeking. Its subsequent incorporation of the latter in 1980 caused plans to be drawn up for the consolidation of the disparate parts of Mmabatho, Mafeking (renamed Mafikeng), Montshiwa township and Montshiwa Stadt, the traditional settlement area. The delay in political agreement is reflected in the bifocal city with separate government and commercial centres, dating from the brief, three-year period of the division of the urban area by an international boundary. Similar problems of adding new government sections to older residential and commercial areas are apparent at Thohoyandou, which incorporates the present administrative centre of Sibasa, and the two new towns of Makwarela and Shayandima, established in the 1960s (Venda Government, 1979).

Possibly nothing exhibits the problems of site selection more vividly than the choice of a capital for the Ciskei. The original proposal of the South African Government was Debe Nek, a small service centre in the middle of the territory. However, although conforming to the criteria laid down by the South African Government, it failed to satisfy the Ciskei Government, which chose Alice in preference. Alice was the seat of the University of Fort Hare, the oldest Black university in southern Africa, and of several other major educational institutions. However, Alice only became available as a result of the incorporation of the Victoria East district into the Ciskei in the late 1970s, and so no development work has been possible until recently. Several of the capitals have progressed little beyond the planning stage so that many of the administrative functions are carried out from provisional capitals, usually the Black townships outside a White town. Thus the Ciskeian Government operates from Zwelitsha, the Black dormitory town of King Williams Town, and the Lebowa Government from Seshego, outside Pietersburg. The whole question of inherited capitals is likely to be raised again following the incorporation of Mafeking, the old Bechuanaland Protectorate capital, into Bophuthatswana (1980) and the stagnation of the ambitious Lebowakagoma project. The question of incorporating other centres such as King Williams

Town and Pietersburg into the adjacent Black states will have a profound effect upon their designated capitals.

Apart from the inherited capital at Umtata, the new capitals have necessitated planning virtually from their origins. Even Umtata has experienced a major boom associated with independence, and the demand for government offices, houses and other official buildings. In addition the institution of a national air line and airport and a defence force has led to major public works around the capital. The newly planned capitals similarly require a range of public buildings for their executive, legislative and judicial functions. Each of the Black states has sought to improve its educational facilities with new colleges, and in Umtata and Mmabatho, national universities. All these activities together with the erection of monuments, renaming of streets and buildings, etc., are a part of the nation-building process set in motion by the governments concerned.

In the sphere of housing, impressive new structures have been built for the Presidents, Prime and Chief Ministers and their Cabinets. Bryntirion, the government enclave in Pretoria, has been taken as a model in many cases. Indeed unlike the situation in most Black townships in South Africa, a wide spectrum of society is present in the Black capitals, and gradually a full range of housing is being erected, from presidential palace to squatter's shack. It is the latter which is likely to be increasingly marked in the 1980s. Here the experience of Gaberone in Botswana may act as a guide. When built in the 1960s, it was planned for 5000, with provision for expansion up to 20 000 inhabitants. However, in 1976 it had reached 37 000 and it was estimated that by 1981 the population would be enumerated at 75 000, or nearly one-tenth of the national population (Botswana, 1977). Much of the population of Gaberone lives in controlled squatter settlements and basic facility housing, below the standards set by the Colonial Government, but more related to the resources of the Botswana population. Mmabatho and Umtata are exhibiting the first signs of the squatter influx, and previous standards are viewed as inappropriate to the new governments. The upgrading of the Ngangelizwe suburb in Umtata is axiomatic of a changed post-independence official attitude to 'informal sector' housing. In the case of Mmabatho the pull is not so strong, as the main economic opportunities are to be found in eastern Bophuthatswana, linked to the Pretoria and Witwatersrand metropolitan areas. Even so the major expansion of population is likely to take place within the traditional tribal areas, which are planned to be upgraded rather than replaced.

Industrial development

Industrial development within the metropolitan regions has passed through a number of stages. The early service and processing industries were widely diffused across the country and within cities, although some degree of internal differentiation was evident in the case of bulky or obnoxious trades. Thus in the older towns and metropolitan areas industrial plants are present within the Central Business District and immediately beyond its boundaries. Industrial plants established in houses, warehouses, even office blocks are an integral part of the central area of the metropolis.

However, the expansion of the towns in the second half of the nineteenth century was essentially associated with railway development. New and heavier industries were established. Railway workshops, engineering plants, glassworks as well as centralised flour mills and breweries were erected in the main centres, utilising the benefits of reduced transport costs. Most of these industries lay adjacent to the railways, and with them associated residence and commerce resulted in a complex pattern. Many of the early industrial areas suffered from cramped sites and expansion was only possible by moving to new areas laid out for the purpose. The older industrial areas then declined and were invaded by commercial and other uses, or factory sites were abandoned as unsuitable for any use. The result is a highly blighted zone.

From the 1920s onwards planned industrial areas with, or more recently without, railway sidings have been established. The size of the industrial estates has grown with larger plots, allowing for expansion, being established further from the centre of town. The industrial estates, with their segregation of land uses provide a complete contrast to the earlier mixed form of area. The older planned estates have generally been fully utilised with all space occupied by factories and their extensions. More recent estates are unconfined, with an attempt to create the impression of a spacious, evenpark-like, environment. Much of the open space represents room for expansion, so vital to the twentieth-century horizontal industrial layout. In contrast to the early mixed industrial areas, the industrial estate has shown a high degree of permanence without fluctuation and invasion by other uses, other than a limited commercial function. However, in line with the spread of the residential areas, industrial estates have been laid out in newer districts. These are usually 'clean' factories which require only road transport facilities (Young, 1973).

The leapfrog effect of industrial zones is but a reflection of the mobility of many firms which proceed through a series of stages of expansion, seeking new premises. Mobility and instability of firms are inevitably reflected in the large number of concerns which occupy unsuitable factories and therefore plan to move elsewhere.

The metropolitan areas have a further complication, in that the industrial areas are viewed as an essential part of the racial planning process. Buffer strips separating the residential areas of the various race groups are made even more effective through the planning of new industrial sites. Black areas, in particular, are sited adjacent to industrial zones and vice versa. Thus in theory the buffers are increased and social contact reduced.

The industrial areas of the metropolitan regions are growing at an irregular rate. The Cape Town region's share of national output fell from 22.1 per cent in 1916–17 to 11.6 per cent in 1970. At the same time the southern

Transvaal's share rose from 37.4 to 50.0 per cent, while the Durban region remained virtually constant at 11.7–13.2 per cent. The predominance of the southern Transvaal is such that moves to decentralise industrial development have been largely unsuccessful (Bell, 1973). Once more the overall strategy of separate development came into play as decentralisation meant moving first to the border industrial zones situated adjacent to the Black states, and later, location of industries within the Black states at designated growth points. Such moves have had only minimal effects upon the southern Transvaal and the attractive power of the region remains very strong. This may be illustrated by the development of the motor industry, which originally amounted to pure assembly work, and was located in 1922 in Port Elizabeth. The Ford Motor Company, General Motors and Volkswagen established major plants for the assembly, and later manufacture of cars and heavy vehicles in Port Elizabeth and Uitenhage. However, as the Government's local content programme assumed greater importance, so the attraction of the steel plants in the southern Transvaal, to say nothing of the major markets, exerted an increasing pull. Location within that region was sought by the majority of firms established from the 1960s onwards, with the result that approximately half the vehicles manufactured now originate from the southern Transvaal.

The concentration of industrial development and hence employment ran counter to the Government's policy of separate development, which aimed at reducing the flow of Blacks into the White metropolitan areas. Thus industrial decentralisation has been a stated policy since 1956 (Rogerson, 1975). This aimed, initially, at restricting development in the metropolitan areas by establishing fixed maximum Black to White employment ratios for new 'footloose' industries, and the offering of incentives to industrialists willing to relocate on the borders of the Black states, and later within the Black states themselves. A series of growth points were designated for the purpose, such as Butterworth in Transkei (Fig. 9.7).

Border industries have been most successful particularly where they are situated adjacent to the major metropolitan areas, and thus become an integral part of the whole. The Bophuthatswana enclaves extend to within 15 km of the centre of Pretoria, and the border industrial zones of Rosslyn and Babalegi have attracted a wide variety of industries as a result of the financial incentives offered by the South African Government (Best, 1971). Industrial parks with ample room for expansion have been laid out. The Durban region has also benefited from the proximity of KwaZulu, as has East London from the Ciskei.

Government control of state-owned metropolitan industry is more direct. The various state corporations such as the South African Iron and Steel Corporation (ISCOR), and the South African Coal, Oil and Gas Corporation (SASOL) have been powerful influences in the location of industry. ISCOR, established in 1928, provided for a state iron and steel plant to be established at Pretoria. In 1942 a second plant was established at Vanderbijlpark, on the

Fig. 9.7 Butterworth, Transkei; Growth is reflected in the new factories and houses erected in the 1970s as a part of the Government's decentralisation programme. (Anne Christopher)

Vaal River, south of Johannesburg. More recently a third plant was established at Newcastle in northern Natal. The iron and steel plants directly influenced later metal industries to move to the southern Transvaal, where a supply of steel was available. The development of an oil from coal plant was undertaken by SASOL at Sasolburg in 1950, and was sited on the Vaal River, close to Vanderbijlpark. Increasing world prices of crude petroleum led to the decision to establish two further plants at Secunda in the eastern Transvaal outside the southern Transvaal metropolitan area, while an additional private scheme in the northern Transvaal is under consideration at present.

The rural–urban fringe

One of the most noticeable features of towns and cities in the twentieth century has been their rapid areal expansion. The area of many South African towns has grown far more rapidly than their population. Yet at the outset a qualification needs to be made, as there are forms of urban sprawl in South Africa representing quite diverse origins and appearances: the first is the Western capitalist form of irregular expansion related to the free land market; the second is the controlled socialist form of planned housing development in orderly sequence; the third is the uncontrolled growth of squatter settlements on the periphery of the towns, which have been a feature of many developing countries. All three forms may be present around a single large town depending upon the degree of control exercised by the local and national authorities.

The free market fringe is restricted almost entirely to the White sectors of South African towns. Until the 1950s there was little or no planning control over its development and it therefore took on many of the forms of the United States or British sprawl. These might be summarised as the progressive conversion of the land from rural to urban uses. The initial stage being the withdrawal of farming land from active use. Hence farm buildings become run down, fences unrepaired, windmills neglected. In general such areas are placed under pasture and possibly rented to adjacent farmers as seasonal grazing. More likely organisations such as riding schools may temporarily use the farm facilities, or sports clubs rent them for a number of years for sports not requiring substantial infrastructures. Withdrawal and decay are symptoms of an anticipation that land is likely to rise in value when placed to other uses.

The first stage of more profitable use is usually associated with subdivision into smallholdings. These may be anything up to 25 ha in extent but represent the division of a farm into several smaller units. Although the intention of the subdivision may be agricultural, the majority are too small to support a family from the produce of the land alone and so some other income is necessary. The balance between agricultural and town income varies from holding to holding, but in general smallholdings may be regarded as an extension of the town rather than an intensified form of agriculture. Smallholding development was particularly prevalent in the period from 1920 to 1950,

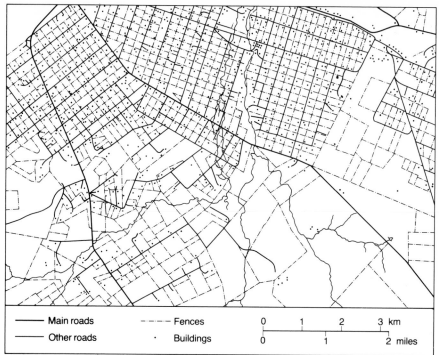

| — Main roads | - - - - Fences | 0 | 1 | 2 | 3 km |
| — Other roads | · Buildings | 0 | | 1 | 2 miles |

Fig. 9.8 Rural–urban fringe, Bloemfontein. South African towns have developed extensive semi-rural peripheries where the large plots and low taxes made rural living attractive to the urban worker.

more especially in the Transvaal where special facilities were offered under the Agricultural Holdings (Transvaal) Registration Act of 1919, which allowed subdivisions above 1 ha without the restrictions of the township laws. By 1955 there were probably 90 000 smallholdings in South Africa, of which nearly two-thirds were in the Transvaal. The area covered by them was approximately 400 000 ha. Owing to stricter control the number and area have probably not altered markedly since that date, as the provinces passed ordinances curbing excessive subdivision, while the 1970 Subdivision of Agricultural Land Act halted the movement.

The smallholding offered the urban dweller many of the advantages of rural living, such as more space, fewer restrictions and lower rates, while with the motor car and bus services he was within reasonable proximity to his work and urban amenities. The smallholding offered land for small-scale farming, often vegetables or fruit, or for keeping livestock, more especially pigs and horses. Thus in many of the poorer parts of the country smallholding development increased the volume of produce from a unit of land, although often only as a sideline for the owner. The smallholding with its secluded house, arable patch and paddocks linked by a series of usually gridiron roads has remained a feature around many larger South African towns (Fig. 9.8).

181

However, further intensification of usage has occurred as those smallhold-ings closest to the towns have been further subdivided for urban residential use. As the time of conversion rests upon the calculations of each individual landowner the process is a most untidy one, and indeed decades may separate the conversion of one smallholding from that of its neighbours. Further-more, the road plans of neighbouring holdings may not link up, as a series of separate housing schemes progress independently.

Thus at a given time the rural–urban fringe exhibits a complex landscape of abandoned and run-down farms, smallholdings, residential developments and open space, either with roads and plots demarcated or lying completely waste. The whole is determined by the state of the land market, and the per-sonal preferences, prejudices and calculations of the individuals involved in its operation (Christopher, 1973b).

The other two forms of rural–urban fringe are almost exclusively related to Black and Coloured urbanisation. Strict control in South Africa has en-sured since the 1960s, that urban expansion is generally highly ordered for Coloureds, Indians and Blacks. The essential difference when compared with the White fringe is the control which the Government, both national and loc-al, exercises over the land market. Land has been provided by government departments for the extension of townships and all planning and most con-struction is undertaken by the Government. The element of state housing has been less important in more affluent White portions of society and few areas of rural–urban fringe in the White sectors have developed along these lines. There is thus an abrupt edge between waste land and built-up area, with fre-quently a transition from farmland to dwellings separated only by a buffer strip.

The third form of rural–urban fringe is the unorganised or semi-organised squatter settlement. Here, it is worth noting that squatters are defined under the Squatters Act of 1951, as all persons living in wood and iron structures. Such settlements have emerged frequently in South Africa, particularly during and after the Second World War when housing provision was inadequate for the substantial flow of Coloureds and Blacks to the towns. A massive clearance and rehousing of the squatter population in the 1950s and 1960s, together with tight regulation through the pass laws on the influx into the towns, largely eliminatd such settlements. However, the 1970s have seen its recurrence as the increase in population is such that neither the existing rural nor urban facilities can cope. Although many of these settlements have come into being in the Black states, the western and eastern Cape have been the scene of rapid squatter camp construction. Unlike other rural–urban forms construction is often of high density, with corrugated iron as the main building element (Fig. 9.9). The government response has generally been to

Fig. 9.9 Crossroads Squatter Settlement, Cape Flats. The strong rural–urban migration has placed severe strains upon the resources of urban administrations. Many now face unmanage-able demands for housing. This is filled by the 'temporary' wood and corrugated iron housing assemblages which have reappeared in the 1970s. (*The Argus*)

bulldoze down the squatter shacks and send the Black population to their state area and the Coloureds back from whence they came. However, sheer numbers in the later 1970s have resulted in this programme breaking down, and delays in demolition being introduced. Thus the Crossroads squatter camp in the western Cape has eked out a precarious but increasingly permanent existence over a couple of years. Others which received less publicity have similarly taken on an air of permanence as the housing construction backlog has built up. In 1977 it was estimated that there were 23 000 structures housing 120 000 people in the western Cape. Decisions to improve rather than demolish may have a profound effect upon the future appearance of South African metropolitan areas.

Segregation in the metropolitan regions

One of the notable features of the larger towns in South Africa is the almost complete residential segregation of the races. Separate townships for Blacks have been enforceable since 1923, and indeed most of the larger towns had put aside areas for their African population not housed by their employers before that date. It was however the systematic implementation of the 1923 legislation together with the 1950 Group Areas Act which profoundly affected the appearance of most South African towns in the 1950s and 1960s.

The Group Areas Act provided for residential segregation and the zoning of towns for each of the racial groups present, together with industrial and other uses. Each Group Area was to be separated by a buffer strip, at least 100 m in width. Furthermore, as little contact as possible was to be permitted between Group Areas, so that direct road access between Black and White suburbs was to be kept to a minimum. Such an aim not only applied to future housing areas, but also to a 'sorting out' of existing residential areas where there was racial mixing. The sorting out process mainly applied to the cities of the Cape Province where Whites and Coloureds had mixed freely in the urban areas, and to a lesser extent to Natal and the Witwatersrand where Indians, Whites and Coloureds had mixed. Although large numbers of Blacks lived in the urban areas they were already more highly segregated from the remainder of the population, and the post-1950 era consisted mainly of moves to relocate them further from city centres.

The Group Areas Act and its associated legislation relating to Blacks, dating from earlier in the century, resulted in the emergence of two distinct features. The first, associated with the central city, was the removal of Coloureds, Indians and Blacks from the older parts of the city. The initial stages had been little more than the removal of squatter camps as a result of the health hazard. In this manner cities such as Johannesburg and Port Elizabeth rehoused Blacks from the centre of their cities before the First World War. Later in the post-1950 era removal involved mixed suburbs, where often all race groups were moved out or only the Whites were allowed to remain, and the removal of racially heterogeneous suburbs, which were zoned for White occupation. Wholesale demolition of properties then ensued leaving waste lands on the edge of the Central Business Districts of Cape Town (District Six) and Port Elizabeth (South End), or further out, Durban (Cato Manor), where the Indian portion of the Central Business District remained. In Johannesburg the demand for land was such that Sophiatown, for example, was soon rebuilt but this time as the White suburb of Triomf. Even 30 years after the passing of the Group Areas Act, the process is by no means complete and the waste lands remain. By the end of 1979 some 112 000 families had been moved and 23 000 remained to be moved under the Group Areas Act. Only 2.0 per cent of the families displaced were White.

The second and most striking geographical aspect of the segregation legislation has been the erection of the townships for the different racial groups, on the edges of the existing cities. The first moves in this direction were taken early in the twentieth century when irregular squatter camps were demolished and new sites established for the Black population in towns such as Port Elizabeth at New Brighton, and Johannesburg at Pimville (now part of Soweto). In both cases the sites were several kilometres distant from the White suburbs, and the housing was supplied by the authorities. Thus Black housing has been, and is largely seen as, the responsibility of the State rather than the individual. After 1928 new townships were built adjacent to the first, and distinct Black areas began to emerge, Johannesburg's Soweto (SOuth WEstern TOwnships) being the largest and most significant in the country.

During the Second World War house building ceased, and this allied to the massive industrialisation associated with the War, resulted in the need afterwards for a major programme of construction. Added to this was the segregationist desire of the vast majority of the White population, and the result was the initiation of a major building programme in the mid-1950s which lasted until the early 1970s. First priority was given to Black housing. Squatter camps were demolished and their inhabitants rehoused in the new townships. At the same time Blacks living in racially mixed areas and areas intended for other racial groups were rehoused. Thus half (50 000) the existing (1980) houses in Soweto were built in the period 1957–68. By contrast only 5000 date from the period 1970–79.

The major Black townships adjacent to the White-occupied towns are a remarkable feature of the South African landscape. The 'twin' nature of the urban areas is highly pronounced, as is their complementary nature. Thus, for example, Soweto for Johannesburg, Umlazi and KwaMashu for Durban, and New Brighton for Port Elizabeth, were planned as residential areas with little provision for industrial or commercial development. Indeed in Soweto 96 per cent of employed persons leave the township to go to work. Tracts of land were set aside for housing, both for family units and for single men and women's hostels (Fig. 9.10). Provision for trading stores and schools completed the planning process. As most housing was low cost, few civic

185

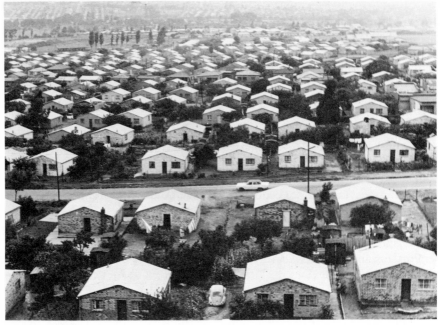

Fig. 9.10 Soweto housing scheme. The uniform style of both economic and subsidised housing schemes is the dominant feature of the townships. (*To the Point*)

services were provided. The civic centres were lacking because administrative functions were exercised by the main city government, which required only an office in, or at the entrance/exit from, the Black township. Only recently under the Community Councils Act of 1978 has an attempt been made to establish separate Black municipal governments.

It is the uniformity of the Black townships which is probably most noticeable. Low-cost housing of limited styles according to the age of the area is only alleviated by small areas of individually built housing. In Soweto only 2 per cent of houses have been privately built. This reflects the official attitude that the residents of the townships are temporary, and that anyone with money to invest in housing ought to move to one of the Black states. Housing has been provided to certain basic standards of space and construction, largely to the design of the National Institute of Building Research. As part of the reappraisal of the townships these standards have been brought into question, as building costs have risen faster than the poorer section of the community's ability to pay for them. Thus in 1979 the Minister of Cooperation and Development stated that these standards:

> were not so high given the environments of a developed Western economy, but when it is taken into consideration that South Africa is for a large part still experiencing Third World conditions, it becomes obvious that it is folly to impose unaltered standards of the developed world on our situation. (*Rand Daily Mail*, 16.10.1979)

Such a statement seems to suggest that the controlled squatter shack may have a place in the future South African city, on a permanent basis. At the other end of the scale, the recognition that Blacks are not temporary dwellers in the major metropolitan areas has led to greater attention being given to the needs of the more affluent members of the Black community.

The temporary nature of Black residence had been particularly emphasised after 1968, when Black leasehold rights were withdrawn, and an increasingly large proportion of government money was directed towards the development of the Black states. The 1976 Soweto riots, however, resulted in a major reappraisal of the position of Black urban dwellers and some relaxation of the restrictions placed upon them has been evident. The introduction of 99-year leasehold tenure, under the Black (Urban Areas) Amendment Act of 1978, and the consequent availability of finance for private housing and improvement, are expected to result in the amelioration of the appearance of many of the Black areas. In addition various schemes of betterment, such as electrification have begun, and organisations such as the Urban Foundation have been established to promote the quality of the township environment.

Furthermore, through a complex set of regulations, trading has been inhibited so that the major chain and supermarket stores have been excluded from the Black townships. Limits were placed, among others, on the range of goods (convenience only), shop area (150 m^2, later increased to 350 m^2), number of businesses (one), and employment (Black only). Tight restrictions were also placed on partnerships, and White capital was not allowed into the townships. Shopping facilities are therefore basic and restricted, in the main to small general stores (Davies, W.J. 1972). A recent study of Soweto (Morris, 1980) found that the hierarchy of shopping places was markedly ill-developed, with few large groupings and a highly restricted range. Liquor stores, general dealers, butchers and greengrocers predominate. The central civic and business site (77 ha) has remained undeveloped. Changes may be expected in this regard as many of the restrictions on Black trading were lifted in 1978. Thus in 1980 the first supermarket was opened in Soweto, but probably 70 per cent of the disposable income of Soweto residents is spent outside the township, mainly in the Johannesburg Central Business District. A similar state of affairs obtains in the other metropolitan areas.

The restricted physical extent of the Black townships is also noticeable. Soweto with a population in excess of one million is the largest single settlement in South Africa, yet its total area is under 10 000 ha. Thus the relatively high density housing, and the conditions of overcrowding which prevail within the houses, contrast markedly with the lower density White suburbs. On the Witwatersrand, White residential densities of 23 persons per developed hectare contrast with 100 persons per developed hectare in the Black areas. In Soweto where the *de facto* population is estimated to be up to twice the *de jure* population, the density may in reality approach 200 persons per developed hectare.

Whereas the Black townships have until recently been regarded, officially at least, as only a temporary or restricted element within the overall urban system of White South Africa those for Indians and Coloureds have been regarded as permanent and fewer areal and administrative restrictions were placed upon them. This is not to suggest that sprawl has been allowed to occur, but once construction began on a major scale, restrictions have not occurred in the release of further land zoned for Indian and Coloured housing. Once more the provision of housing has been regarded as a function of the Government and private house building has been limited in scale.

The major areas affected have been the Cape and Natal towns and cities, more especially Cape Town, Port Elizabeth and Durban, which between them possessed the largest populations requiring rehousing under the Group Areas Act determinations (Western, 1978). The zoning of cities for Group Areas was protracted, frequently resulting in the emergence of irregularly shaped areas which were a consequence of compromises. Completely new areas were settled such as the Indian township at Chatsworth in Durban, while others were continuations of existing townships such as Gelvandale–Bethelsdorp in Port Elizabeth. In Cape Town, the Cape Flats were utilised for a series of townships to house Coloureds and Blacks in the western Cape (Granelli and Levitan, 1978).

A recent development in Cape Town has been the construction of Mitchell's Plain, begun in 1974 and planned for completion in 1984, with a population of 250 000. As a measure of the scale of the project, it is equal in scope to the entire housing schemes of the City Council (35 000–40 000 houses) between 1945 and 1975. The venture has moved a long way from the uniformity of earlier locations and townships, by introducing a variety of housing styles to suit the requirements and financial resources of the Coloured community. Differentiation has been the keynote with the introduction of terrace housing, semi-detached and detached styles, at higher densities than have been usual in South African towns (Fig. 9.11). Plots of as little as 1/80 ha have been provided, although net densities have an average 45 houses per hectare on the 3100 ha site. The awareness of the need to conserve the limited land resources of the Cape Flats, and a change in attitude to high density housing, have contributed to the planning of such new styles, reminiscent of the English new towns of the 1950s and 1960s (Brand, 1979). The townscape reflects the objectives of the City Council to provide a new ideal for Coloured housing, shedding the 'low-cost' image and promoting better living conditions for a community achieving a measure of prosperity. Thus shopping and community centres, schools and tended open spaces constitute major elements in the scheme. However, at a distance of 30 km from the centre of Cape Town, the commuter problem will be substantial.

Another result of the need to build more houses has been the planning of the new city of Atlantis, 45 km to the north of Cape Town. Atlantis is designed to be self-contained in terms of employment, through the provision of new industrial areas to relieve pressure for land in Cape Town. For this

Fig. 9.11 Mitchell's Plain, terrace housing. A major change in density to conserve land has resulted in the construction of houses reminiscent of the English new towns. (City Engineer, Cape Town)

purpose the town has been given 'Border Area' status in the range of incentives offered to prospective industrialists. It is designed to link up with the mission town of Mamre, one of the more prosperous of the mission settlements. The final number of inhabitants will exceed Mitchell's Plain, reaching 500 000 early in the twenty-first century, when its areal extent will exceed 10 000 ha. The contrast with Soweto, with currently over twice the population on a somewhat smaller area is noteworthy.

Redevelopment and the planning process

The metropolitan cities are not static. The alteration of metropolises is such that even in times of depression, such as the late-1970s, people still moved to the Johannesburg, Durban and Cape Town regions in substantial numbers. The attractive powers of the metropolises have received attention from the Government which has embarked upon a policy of decentralisation. In part this is the result of the segregation policy in attempting first to attract industry to the borders of Black states and later to growth points within the Black states. However, the problems of urban congestion, more especially traffic congestion and water supplies, have also prompted an attempt to decentralise and slacken the flow of people and jobs into the metropolitan areas.

189

Fig. 9.12 Hypermarket, Port Elizabeth. Large hypermarkets or super-stores, with a dependence on motor transport, have been a feature of shopping trends in the 1970s. (P. Niman)

The southern Transvaal, however, remains the hub of the southern African economy and growth appears likely to continue. This has resulted in major developments within the industrial complex and a certain degree of decentralisation within it. Thus in the White residential sector new shopping businesses and light industrial areas have emerged. Prestige centres such as Sandton City, the Rosebank Centre and the various hypermarkets have to a large extent reduced White retail and financial dependence upon the city centre. The hypermarkets planned from the mid-1970s onwards have aimed at catering for the car-owning population. In planning such a project approximately 200 000 White people within a 40 km radius are estimated to be necessary for a viable hypermarket. A weighting to other groups according to level or car ownership is also included. Thus maybe 10 such markets would be sufficient for the entire country at its present state of development. With trading areas of 20 000 m² and the need for parking up to 2000 cars at a time, the land demands of the hypermarkets are of a different order from previous shopping centres (Fig. 9.12). Thus a minimum area of 10 ha is required, resulting in the likelihood of such markets being sited in the rural–urban fringe close to major freeway intersections. It is already apparent that some of the new hypermarkets have volume turnovers among the highest in the Western World.

Decentralisation has largely been on a racial basis as the city centres, although zoned for White occupation, have came to rely more heavily upon the growing Black trade. The Black townships lack major shopping facilities, with the result that most of the Black generated trade is focused upon the

Fig. 9.13 Transitional zone, Johannesburg. The expansion of the Central Business District of the premier financial and commercial city has been possible through the displacement of old housing and trading districts. (Anne Christopher)

city centre and its immediate vicinity. At first, this resulted in the emergence of two Central Business Districts, one for the Black and one for the White trade, based essentially on the quality and price of goods. As a result of Group Area removals and rising Black spending power the distinctions are being eroded. Indian trading sectors, with the noticeable exception of Durban, have been or are due to be removed to the Indian Group Areas. It was the Indian trader who most successfully catered for the Black market over the last 100 years. The removal of the poorer Central Business District has resulted in the emergence of new Indian trading areas, including the Oriental Bazaar in Johannesburg, and in space for the White CBD to expand. Under the Group Areas Act some 2120 business premises, mainly Indian, were moved between 1950 and 1979. The most symbolic example of this is the erection of the new Johannesburg Stock Exchange building in the old Indian trading area of the City (Fig. 9.13).

191

This has not meant that vertical expansion of the CBD has been unimportant. Considerable internal redevelopment has occurred throughout South Africa. Apart from government buildings the majority of structures on city blocks within the CBDs of the metropolises are post-1960 in date. Distinctive regional styles have been replaced by a certain degree of uniformity as the same banks, building societies, insurance companies and chain stores are represented throughout South Africa. Thus the distinctive republican styles of the Pretoria CBD have given way in the main to the styles of other parts of the subcontinent. Amalgamation of sites, even of city blocks, has been necessary to achieve the plan area for some of the more ambitious buildings. The Carlton Centre in Johannesburg occupied four city blocks comprising an office block 50 storeys high, a shopping complex and an hotel. Elsewhere in Cape Town and Durban similar projects have changed the face of the cities. The exception has been the preservation of public buildings, such as city halls, post offices and churches, which although originally the dominant buildings in their streets are now dwarfed by the multi-storeyed edifices around them.

Around the perimeters of the CBDs further changes are taking place. In general the first residential suburbs were immediately adjacent to the central areas. As urban development in the interior of South Africa was late, most suburbs exhibited a certain degree of social segregation. Thus the prestige suburb of Parktown contrasted with the more modest Vrededorp in the Johannesburg of the 1890s, and the railway tracks became as socially divisive in South African cities as elsewhere. However, as the cities expanded so pressure on the inner suburbs increased with regard to both residence and trade and industry. The residential pressures were such that several of the spacious suburbs of the late nineteenth and early twentieth centuries have been subject to infilling and rebuilding. Subdivision of properties to enable more houses to be built was followed by the construction of blocks of flats from the 1920s onwards. Flatland suburbs such as the Berea in Durban, Sunnyside in Pretoria and, most spectacularly, Hillbrow in Johannesburg have mushroomed, as plots have been converted from houses to blocks of flats. The process is a piecemeal one with a combination of houses and open waste spaces, within which flats of various vintages are intermixed. Such suburbs, with the advantages of proximity to the central city, have high densities of population which have resulted in the emergence of yet more decentralised shopping and entertainment centres including restaurants, cinemas and discos.

Other central suburbs have deteriorated, with houses being subdivided into flats on rooms, or indeed the residential function may have been partially replaced as a result of the conversion of main street frontages into shops and minor industrial premises. The emergence of 'motor towns' on the edge of the Central Business District has been a significant feature of all major Southern African cities. The main streets in such an area have been occupied by salesrooms and petrol filling stations, while the back streets have partially been converted into warehouses, repair works, spray painters, panel beaters, exhaust fitters and a host of other trades. The overall appearance is one of decay and decline – the true zone of transition. Among the industrial buildings, houses and shops remain, resulting in a highly mixed cityscape.

Possibly one of the more impressive features of metropolitan redevelopment in the period since 1960 has been the prominence given to motor transport, for both commuting and industrial haulage. Extensive freeway systems have been built in and around the main centres, with elaborate urban interchanges and flyovers. In an attempt to penetrate the cores of the metropolitan areas substantial demolition has taken place, although reclaimed land, such as the Cape Town foreshore and the Witwatersrand mining ground, has been used where possible. The result is frequently a new constriction to the Central Business District, as effective as the railway lines of the nineteenth century, but even more demanding in its requirements for land.

10

Landscapes of tourism

The landscapes of tourism and recreation may be divided into two basic categories: the wildscapes and those which are highly developed. In a sense both are the result of man's action, as no 'natural' area can survive without an elaborate legislative framework to preserve it and conserve the plant and animal life found within it. The wildscapes are, in a way therefore, a misnomer as the control of such areas is the concern of a body of rangers and ecologists concerned with the maintenance of a particular environment. Within this category may be placed the national and provincial parks and the private game reserves. In addition a few other state and privately owned areas, being unused for any productive purposes, either due to aridity or disease, may be included. At the other end of the scale are those areas developed for recreation and tourism, ranging from the extreme management of a 'natural' environment such as the coastline, to the channelling of people's interest in the tangible features of the past.

The question as to what tourists want or are led to want, is a matter of perception which was omitted from Chapter 3. The South African Government in its promotion of tourism, both internal and external, has to 'sell' the country by various means. Some of the descriptions are somewhat vague and flamboyant, as in a recent glossy brochure:

> South Africa: Where the welcome is warmer, the hospitality more generous and the value for money unrivalled
> Where the sunshine is taken for granted
> Where a greater profusion of wild animal and plant life flourishes than anywhere else in Africa
> Where the scenery and landscapes are as extravagantly varied as the peoples that inhabit them.

This statement indicates the continuity of current tourist propaganda with that designed to persuade settlers to come to the country in an earlier age. The natural environment is again depicted in glowing colours, without qualification; and in personal terms a highly selective image of South African society is presented.

194

In seeking to identify landscapes of tourism, a recent study had indicated that for international tourists, the main urban centres and the game and nature reserves attract most attention, while internal tourism is more beach oriented. Ferrario (1976) identified 15 tourist regions. The most important was the western Cape including Cape Town, the historical core region of South Africa, and the mountains to the east. The second most important region was the Natal coast based on Durban. The Pretoria–Johannesburg region, Port Elizabeth and Bloemfontein, although individually significant, were limited largely to a few attractions and did not constitute major tourist regions as the first two had done. The most extensive region was the eastern Transvaal including the Kruger National Park and Drakensberg. Here alone were 'natural' features dominant. Less significant regions such as the Natal Drakensberg and the Cape Garden Route, provided a greater mix of tourist attractions. Tourism is more limited in extent than might appear, as features such as the Augrabies Falls, Kalahari Gemsbok Park and the Karroo towns are sufficiently remote to deter most potential visitors. The concentration of coastal resorts together with the southern and eastern Transvaal reflect dominant tourist interests but the more remote areas, with often more fragile ecosystems and less commercialised facilities, have their followers.

Thus the 'natural' and the 'man-made' attractions of South Africa have been subjected to an ever increasing pressure. Internal and international tourism has increased rapidly, despite the setback of the early 1970s, and the adequate use of South Africa's tourist potential is a matter of some concern. It is noticeable that as yet most tourism is restricted to the White population and visitors from Europe, particularly the British Isles, and North America, who might be expected to have similar viewpoints. The attractions for visitors according to Ferrario were scenery and landscape, wild life, and natural vegetation in the first three zones of interest. These would rate highly for local tourists, so the wildscapes of South Africa are particularly important. The sun and the sea provide a second focus of tourist activity, while the inland resorts, whether man–made lakes, historic sites or special purpose holiday resorts, diversify the landscape of tourism.

The wildscapes

Most of South Africa was apportioned to some use in the course of the nineteenth century, before any real conservation feeling was evident in official circles. Thus the areas of untouched wildscape are few, and mainly confined to the problem areas of the country. In the arid lands of Namaqualand or the Kalahari, extensive tracts of land were too dry for pastoral farming. Whereas in the rugged mountainous regions of the south-western Cape and the Drakensberg farming and grazing could not be extended over the whole area; although it may be doubted if such areas were completely immune to the depredations of men and their grazing animals. The other major unused areas were those where diseases such as malaria and nagana precluded settle-

195

ment until the major mosquito and tsetse fly eradication programmes of the present century. Here large areas were nominally settled but often abandoned either permanently or on a seasonal basis.

The need to preserve areas of the country as National Parks was, in the main, the result of the depletion of animals by the pioneers as they entered the country. Vast herds of elephants and buck roamed South Africa at the time of initial European settlement, when African use of the wild animals had been limited and not disastrous. However, hunting parties armed with guns proved to be devastating. Hunts were organised, such as that for Prince Alfred at Bloemfontein in 1860, which resulted in the slaughter of between 20 000 and 30 000 large animals. Other large-scale hunts and the systematic killings for sustenance in the nineteenth century effectively depleted the number of wild animals. The vast herds of springboks in the Karroo were virtually wiped out, and some species such as the quagga were completely eliminated. Lions and hippopotamuses were exterminated in the Cape, and by the late nineteenth century only a remnant remained, in areas which were unhealthy for men and their stock. From this emerged the first steps in a conservation programme.

Attempts to create reserves or parks in other areas which were capable of agricultural or pastoral use were unsuccessful until recently. The Bushmanland Reserve and later Kalahari Reserve are two examples of the conservation principle being overtaken by events. Thus in the settled region, parks constitute no more than a few thousand hectares apiece, where land has been purchased or donated for the purpose. The extensive areas are invariably in the unusable regions. The National Parks amount to approximately 2.9 million ha. A further 1 million ha are in the care of provincial and other local authorities. In addition some 1.5 million ha are under the control of the Forestry Department, but unsuitable for afforestation. To this must be added the private game reserves, resulting in a total of approximately 5 million ha of preserved wildscape.

The most important areas are the Kruger National Park (1.95 million ha) and the Kalahari Gemsbok National Park (0.96 million ha). The origins of both rest with government decisions made in the 1890s although proclamation is more recent. The Kruger National Park was opened in 1898 as the Sabi Game Reserve. The land was designated through fear that people might one day not be able to see the indigenous animals such as the lion, rhinoceros, giraffe and elephant of South Africa, unless protected land was set aside for them (Fig. 10.1). Some of this land had already been granted to individuals and mostly acquired by land companies. It was only in 1926 that it was formally proclaimed and the National Park principle applied so that the other uses, such as grazing were discontinued. The Kalahari Gemsbok Park was established as a last refuge for the animals of the northern Cape, on some farmland which attracted no settlers at the final stage of White colonisation. These, together with a number of Natal parks for rhinocerous preservation, and the Cape parks for elephants at Addo, mountain zebra at Cradock, bon-

Fig. 10.1   White rhinoceroses in the Umfolosi Game Reserve, Natal. The White, square lipped rhinoceros at one time faced extinction, but with careful conservation the Natal Parks Board secured its future. (Satour)

tebok (antelope) at Swellemdam and antelope at Beaufort West and Graaff Reinet, were primarily envisaged as game reserves. A more recent category has been that devoted to the more spectacular scenic areas of the country such as the Drakensberg, the Augrabies Falls on the Orange River, or the Golden Gate Highlands on the Lesotho border. In similar vein the Tsitsikamma Forest National Park has attempted to preserve some of the remaining natural forests for posterity. The most recent form has been associated with dam construction and the utilisation of the land around the resultant lake as a recreation area.

In all cases, although conservation has been seen as a major element in the parks, the secondary element of tourism and recreation has developed as people have wished to see the fauna, flora and scenic features. In order to allow controlled access the National Parks Board and the other authorities responsible have constructed settlements where tourists may be housed and from where control may be exercised. These settlements in the Kruger National Park and other game reserves are fenced to keep animals out and walking is forbidden. The settlement consisting of the wardens' residence and tourist accommodation is often constructed in the style of African architecture with stone walled buildings and thatched roofs. These settlements are small and offer only limited accommodation to restrict the numbers in a given area of the reserve. Thus, the 13 resorts in the Kruger National Park provide accommodation for only 3000 people. Further, only a portion of the park is open at any given time and certain sections are completely inaccessible to the general public so that the ecology is not disturbed.

197

Added to the state intervention, private landowners have established private game parks. In the eastern Transvaal, adjacent to the southern portion of the Kruger National Park, nine private game parks with a combined area of over 250 000 ha act as an addition to the wildscape. The resorts within the private reserves vary from the game lodges designed to house small safari and hunting parties of maybe a dozen, to the extensive Shlaralumi Resort with accommodation for 1200 persons.

Not all areas of wildscape are in National Parks or are devoted to animal conservation. In the mountains of the southern and western Cape Province and in the Natal and Transvaal Drakensberg, tracts of state or private forestry and waste land have been opened for ramblers with a series of trails. Many of these involve walks of several days, with huts placed at intervals of a day's walk. The popularity of the first trails opened in the early 1970s has led to a steady programme of extension.

Specific scenic attractions such as the Cango Caves at Oudtshoorn and other limestone caves in the Transvaal have generated tourist traffic to particular sites, but often for no more than a stop en route.

The coastal belts

The coastal belts are highly specialised landscape areas, which in the present century have been closely linked with tourism and recreation. This has not always been so, and the development of the coastline, as opposed to a series of favoured points along it, dates from the end of the nineteenth century. The rise of the seaside holiday resort and more recently the drive to possess a beach 'cottage' among the White population have been powerful influences for change. The result could hardly be called a wildscape, and much human activity has been devoted to the transformation of the coastal zone (Steyn, 1974).

The initial modification occurred as a result of the rise in popularity of 'a holiday at the seaside'. Although bathing or just taking the sea air had been in vogue for several decades by 1900, little settlement had specifically been laid out for this purpose. However, increasing wealth and cheap rail transport enabled the earliest seaside resorts to develop in the period before the First World War. The initial centres were appendages to the existing port cities. Usually suitable beaches were developed and a new recreational centre to the town was established. Thus at Durban the beachfront expanded where it had previously been peripheral to the town (Fig. 10.2). At East London, Orient Beach, at Port Elizabeth, Humewood, and in the Cape peninsula, Muizenburg and other resorts on the Atlantic and False Bay coasts such as Sea Point, were all developed in this period, separate from, but close to, the original city. The initial provision of sea front facilities such as hotels, bandstands and promenades, but few piers, introduced a distinctive flavour to these resorts. The dualism between the seaside resort and the remainder of the town remains a feature today (Taylor, 1975).

Fig. 10.2 Beachfront, Durban. Note the chain of hotels on the beachfront and the low intensity uses behind them; as well as the recreational facilities along the shoreline. (Durban Publicity Association)

199

The rise in private car ownership, and therefore the freedom to venture further afield led to a further phase in coastal development (Steyn, 1975). The evolution of the coastal township began soon after the First World War. Plots were laid out adjacent to the coast for people to build holiday or retirement cottages. New towns came into being, especially on the Natal coast, where the holiday industry boomed. Land speculators, particularly after 1944, laid out large numbers of townships, many of which were situated too far from the sea to have any success. Approximately 22 500 township plots were laid out on the Natal south coast in the brief period from the end of the Second World War to the early 1950s, when planning control was more rigidly introduced. In general they were 0.1 to 0.2 ha in extent and covered a total area of approximately 3000 ha. In 1971 only 30 per cent had any form of construction upon them and the remainder stood idle. This is particularly true of the townships to the south of Port Shepstone which are more inaccessible to Durban than those to the north (Natal Town and Regional Planning Commission, 1974).

The south Coast of Natal became the classic example of ribbon development with a thin ribbon along the 110 km of coastline from the Umkomaas River to Port Edward on the Transkei border. Added to which, some 30 local authorities came into being, most with populations of under 1000. Each local authority attempted to establish its own services so that coordinated town planning was lacking until the Natal Town and Regional Planning Commission began to provide such facilities. In the 1960s and early 1970s the Cape passed through a similar phase until the provincial administration placed a partial ban on all new coastal townships. Along virtually the entire coastline of South Africa, except for Namaqualand, coastal townships were laid out. A gross oversupply of plots resulted, so that in most cases the townships are remarkably open with only a scattering of houses (Fig. 10.3). On the Natal south coast and parts of the Cape coast the oversupply became serious and steps were taken to restrict the number of new plots and townships, but as is so often the case the damage had been done by the time the planning machinery was put into operation.

However, a number of townships were highly successful. Those on the Cape peninsula from Muizenburg to Simonstown and on the Atlantic seaboard grew as holiday and also suburban areas, with a substantial retired population who were still close to town. Other centres such as Plettenberg Bay and Jeffrey's Bay developed into towns in their own rights, while the extension of the Natal coast and the western Cape Coast reflected an enlargement of the initial popularity of Durban and Cape Town. Both have attracted substantial numbers of permanent residents, including retired persons and those engaged in providing services for the holiday trade. The landscape of villas, hotels, blocks of holiday flats and caravan parks is common to all the resorts, although land use is more intensive in some than in others (Steyn, 1972).

The most recent development in the 1960s and 1970s has been the

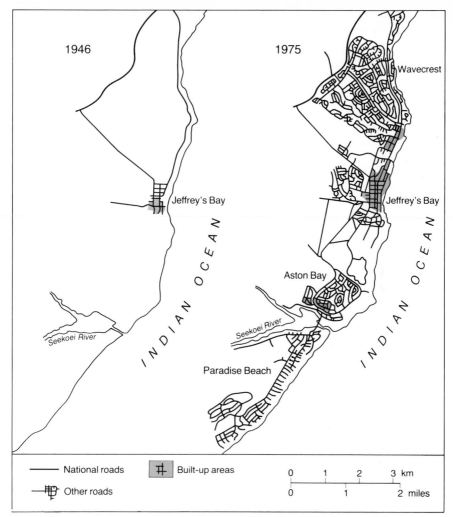

Fig. 10.3   Jeffrey's Bay, 1946 and 1975. The extensive development of coastal townships in the post-1945 era is a feature of much of the South African coastline.

evolution of the marina concept. So far few have been successfully operated. The idea of establishing a suburb as a holiday centre based on boating is not new; however, in a marina the idea is to provide a water frontage for each plot in the township, with facilities for boats and yachts. The Marina de Gama near Cape Town closely observes the principles, with what is an entirely man-made environment carved out of the sand dunes of the Cape Flats. Others such as Sanlameer on the Natal south coast have preserved more of the natural vegetation and a more touristic atmosphere, compared with the residential areas close to Cape Town.

Thus a vast range of coastal recreational landscapes may be determined according to the style of planning and the degree of success of the project.

The least successful remain as ghost towns, with a road pattern and maybe a few houses of various qualities. The majority have a partially suburban appearance with several streets of houses close to the beach, and a few other facilities such as shops, hotels and changing rooms. At the other end of the scale are establishments such as Umhlanga Rocks, which has developed into a town of several thousand permanent inhabitants with an impressive array of beach-front hotels. The beach cottage, however, has long since ceased to be sited on the beach.

The beach townships have been almost exclusively a feature of the Cape and Natal coastlines. The coastlines of Transkei and KwaZulu have remained virtually untouched, until recently. Owing to the unhealthy nature of the coastal strip few people lived there in pre-colonial times, and the sea has presented little attraction for the Black population. Thus the few resorts on the Transkei 'Wild Coast' were designed for the White population, but owing to their inaccessibility they have remained small. The largest at Port St John's possessed a population of under 2000 in 1970 prior to its incorporation into Transkei. It has since been transformed through the establishment of a commercial radio station in the town, and further attempts have recently been made to popularise the Transkei coastal belt.

Inland resorts

Inland resorts have a long history in South Africa. Mineral springs are found in several places and have been developed for curative and recreational purposes. The most prominent are those in Aliwal North in the Cape and Warmbaths and Machadodorp in the Transvaal. Numerous smaller warm springs occur throughout the country. The Aliwal North springs were developed as a spa with baths constructed and a number of hotels erected to house the visitors. On a rather different note at Warmbaths, the farm 'Het Bad' was sold by its owner to the Transvaal Government in the 1870s on the condition that those who asked for the healing power of the waters should receive them without payment. Later in the nineteenth century the Government constructed some cubicles and later still a camping ground was established, which remains in the centre of the modern town. The annual number of visitors exceeds 250 000, and the services necessary to cater for this influx necessitated the laying out of a township in 1920, which in 1979 had a population of over 8000. Numerous other mineral springs have been developed into holiday resorts, if on a less impressive scale than Warmbaths.

The construction of dams throughout the country has provided lakes which have attracted the holiday maker. Many settlements are small, with no permanent dwellings, but others have been developed as either resorts or holiday townships. Many of the major dams were constructed by the State and consequently it has been State, usually provincial, enterprise which has developed the resorts. Thus the Loskop Dam resort in the Transvaal is similar to the rest camps in the National Parks. On the lake behind the

Verwoerd Dam on the Orange River the workers town of Oranjekrag has been converted partially into a resort, while facilities have been established to enable trippers to launch boats and use the lake. The earliest such example was the Vaal Dam which was completed in 1923 and resulted in an artificial lake close to the metropolitan core of the Transvaal. Extensive use is made of its facilities.

Smaller resorts in the countryside, such as guest farms, change the landscape very little. Townships in scenically attractive areas such as the Hogsback in the eastern Cape are comparatively minor, yet distinctive, as they lack the basic functions usually associated with the agriculturally based village such as stores, offices and anything tending to disturb the residential image. These villages merge with the retirement or second home settlements which have evolved as the small towns have declined and investment in property has become attractive.

A significant development has been the planned recreational resort where the attractions are the social and sporting facilities offered, rather than the scenic or other physical characteristics of the area concerned. This type of resort is virtually self-contained, and although it was pioneered with the vacation centres, both private and provincial, it received a major impetus after the independence of Swaziland, Lesotho and Botswana. These countries took advantage of the strict gaming and censorship laws in force in South Africa, to establish resorts catering for the unsatisfied demand for gambling, and uncensored entertainment.

The success of the three countries' resorts prompted the Black states of South Africa to follow suit, on independence. Thus the Bophuthatswana and Venda Governments encouraged the construction of casinos in the main hotels of their capitals. Facilities were also made available for other entertainments, such as multiracial boxing tournaments. In Transkei a resort is under construction on the coastal border with Natal, in an attempt to extend the coastal holiday trade by providing casino, sporting and entertainment facilities. The Ciskei and KwaZulu authorities have also mooted plans to establish resorts at Hamburg and Ulundi when the legal situation permits them to change the laws. Others may be expected at a later date.

The largest and most prestigious holiday complex has been established in Bophuthatswana at Sun City in the Pilansberg, on the site of an old volcanic crater. The resort is some 150 km from Johannesburg and can be reached within 2½ hours by road. The potential is thus vastly increased as day custom can be catered for as well as the more usual residential use. Daily bus and air services from central Johannesburg have been instituted. As a result it was planned on a grand scale – R30 million was spent on its construction and R50 million extensions are in progress. The six-storey main building complex includes a 340 bed hotel, a conference centre, disco, theatre, cinema and casino (Fig. 10.4). In addition special sports facilities include an 18 hole golf course, artificial lake for sailing, etc. and swimming pools. The

landscape development involved considerable excavations and the importation of new soil and vegetation, including Saharan date palms. The whole has been designed to give an air of opulent fantasy. In addition a 60 000 ha game reserve has been established adjacent to the resort, and this has been stocked with elephant, rhinoceros, giraffe and various antelope, brought in from state and private game parks. The result is a virtually self-contained village employing 2000 people and housing at any given time substantially more.

Relict landscapes

Within the last 20 years there has been an increased interest in the tangible relics of the past. At first this was related to places with a significant historical association, either to an event, such as a battle or meeting, or to a person, such as his birthplace or house. Thus until recently much of the fascination with the past revolved around the monuments erected to commemorate significant events or individual buildings associated with them. South Africa possesses a number of major monuments, of which the most spectacular is the Voortrekker Monument outside Pretoria, built to commemorate the Great Trek. Vast facilities cater for the gatherings which take place here annually. More recently 'language' monuments have been erected in Grahamstown for English, and Paarl for Afrikaans. As features in the landscape, monuments are meant to be visible, and the larger form an aspect of the landscape for many kilometres around.

Individual buildings, because of their historical associations, have in certain instances been preserved. The result has often been incongruous, as through preservation orders one building survives and all its neighbours are demolished to make way for new ones. In general it has been the public buildings which have survived, although occasionally domestic structures have remained in the main centres, hemmed in by flats or office blocks. Thus in Pretoria, President Kruger's Residence in Church Street and Melrose House, the Victorian mansion where the Treaty of Vereeniging was signed, are preserved but their contemporary neighbours have gone. No more striking survival could be found than the single storey Old House Museum in Durban, surrounded today by blocks of multistorey flats. Such anomalies in the landscape are common in all the main centres, where redevelopment has taken place extensively in the period since 1960.

Recent interest has been directed increasingly towards historical landscapes, whether sections of towns or countryside. The idea of historic precinct preservation within cities is a new concept in South Africa, although in the major metropolitan regions comparatively few such areas exist within the core of the cities. Frequent redevelopment has obliterated the first

Fig. 10.4 Sun City. The largest inland resort in southern Africa is a creation of Bophuthatswana's post-independence economic development. (Southern Suns Hotels)

buildings and has often created landscapes of mixed architectural age and quality. Thus in Cape Town, apart from the public buildings and churches, only a handful of buildings date from before the British occupation in 1806. Those which do, tend to be larger than the average, judging from old paintings and sketches, and thus a false impression of the eighteenth-century town may be gained from the relics of the past. However, some historic areas have remained relatively untouched. The Cape Town Gardens and Government House, with the accretion of nineteenth- and early twentieth-century government buildings provide one example. In Pretoria, Church Square has changed comparatively little in aspect since the first decade of the present century, as the imposition of building height restrictions was designed to maintain the scale of the late nineteenth-century structures. However, the Transvaal Provincial Administration building, on an adjacent block, has through sheer size and proximity tended to dwarf the Square. Possibly, the two smaller nineteenth-century capitals of Bloemfontein and Pietermartizburg have more in the way of colonial and Victorian townscapes to offer. In the mining towns little beyond the street plans of the original centres survive. It is in the smaller country towns where the landscape has changed slowly that extensive townscapes of the past remain.

Townscapes such as Stellenbosch, Graaff-Reinet and Tulbagh retain some of the buildings of the period of Dutch administration. As growth has been slow and the commercial and industrial opportunities have been limited, the degree of redevelopment has been comparatively small and infrequent. Most houses were rebuilt or renovated in the nineteenth century and the shops again in the twentieth century. However, with few structures rising above three storeys the general townscape has remained that of a small town. Careful preservation measures and administrative interest have enabled such towns to conserve their heritage in the 1970s. Most of the smaller towns have a range of nineteenth-century public and private buildings, which are an asset in attracting tourists, although probably none can approach Stellenbosch and Graaff-Reinet in this respect. Both towns have the added advantage of fine hotels, converted from a Cape–Dutch farmstead, and an old residency (drostdy). Stellenbosch, which recently celebrated its 300th anniversary in 1979, has received extensive attention from many quarters, including past students of the University (Smuts, 1979). In contrast Graaff-Reinet has been carefully tended with the assistance of one of South Africa's top industrialists, who was born in the town (Henning, 1975). Tulbagh with its fine assemblage of Cape–Dutch houses and public buildings in Church Street, was restored as an entity after the earthquake in 1974 (Fagan and Fagan, 1975).

The small Karroo towns provide virtually complete Victorian townscapes, modified only by some new shop fronts and garages. Towns such as Aberdeen and Carnarvon retain many elements of the past, including the Karroo-style flat-roofed dwellings. The villages of the western Cape similarly exhibit few features of extensive modernisation. They range in scale from the smaller mission villages of post-emancipation times, such as Elim

Fig. 10.5   Matjiesfontein village, Karroo. A Victorian–Edwardian railway village has been successfully restored and converted to a hotel complex. (Anne Christopher)

or Mamre, to the larger almost town-sized settlements such as McGregor. The dominant Cape–Dutch architectural style provides the characteristic unifying element to the landscape. The mission stations in particular have exhibited few changes in the present century, although galvanised iron has replaced thatch on some buildings. Certain western Cape villages and towns have largely remained untouched as they are either in decline or have experienced little real growth in the last half century. As such they have become the attraction of an increasing number of tourists and artists searching for the past. A unique enterprise which is a tourist attraction in itself is to be found at Matjiesfontein in the Karroo. Here an entire railway village has been restored by the owner as a remarkable Edwardian-style hotel (Fig. 10.5). Pilgrim's Rest in the eastern Transvaal has similarly attracted considerable attention as an abandoned gold mining centre. Such complete townscapes give a real image of the past. Nevertheless none has been restored along the lines of Williamsburg in the United States, although tourist propaganda might suggest so!

In the rural areas relict features and landscapes are more difficult to define, and as a result have received less attention. Model Ndebele and Zulu settlements near Pretoria and Durban preserve or recreate the rural settlements of pre-colonial times, but the total landscapes around them are of recent origin. Farmsteads of early White pioneers survive, such as the corbelled houses of the Karroo, or the reed houses of Namaqualand, but few are lived in, and they mainly survive as storage huts. Pioneer farmsteads remain throughout the country, but the landscape around them has changed extensively in the intervening century or two (Walton, 1955). Most noticeably trees surround farmsteads where they were originally sited on open land, while fencing crosses the country where previously it was unconstrained. Thus in few rural areas may we look at a relict landscape, as opposed to some historic buildings. It is the western Cape, with its vineyards and Cape–Dutch farmsteads, which is the most popular specifically rural tourist magnet. The Wine Route, linking some of the finest buildings and vineyards, is a significant development in recent times.

In terms of industrial development, the early mining landscape survives in patches. On the Vaal River the uneven mounds of the diamond diggings remain. At Kimberley the area near the Big Hole has been converted into a mine museum by the De Beers Company, with historic buildings from Kimberley re-erected upon the site, in a highly successful reconstruction of aspects of the early diamond fields. On the Witwatersrand the old mine dumps and mining headgear survive close to Johannesburg as a reminder of the early period of mining activity, and an area has recently been converted into an outdoor museum. There are numerous small worked-out mines scattered across the countryside, sometimes with a fair number of buildings, rail lines and workings remaining. Few attract many visitors to become part of the landscape of recreation – usually they are in too insecure and dangerous a state for mass investigation.

Industrial archaeology is still in its infancy in South Africa. The early industrial landscapes have mostly been demolished to make way for new developments. Nevertheless the windmills and watermills of the pre-mechanical age have attracted attention, and restoration work has occurred since the 1930s (Walton, 1974). A range of these mills exists throughout the country, although once again the western Cape possesses a major share of them. Early factories have also survived, although invariably converted to other uses. However, lack of interest and pressure from other uses annually takes its toll of the small stock present. The various transportation systems have similarly left a share of relict features. Bridges, toll houses and abandoned tracks mark the earlier stage of road transport. Within the railway network extensive modernisation has removed many of the old railway stations in the main centres, and old lines are soon overgrown or taken back into agricultural use. However, parts of the country still operate a steam train system, as well as special scenic lines which run holiday specials. Thus the major steam junctions at Klipplaat, Touws River and Noupoort appear as the last of the major steam train centres and attract large numbers of locomotive enthusiasts, particularly from countries which have replaced steam engines with electric or diesel models. In special cases such as the *Apple Express* from Port Elizabeth to Loerie or the *Lilliputian* from Estcourt to Weenen, narrow gauge steam trains attract numbers of tourists on a regular basis.

The relict landscapes of varied type are receiving increasing attention, and efforts are now being made to convert them into tourist attractions. This applies not only to the more spectacular inheritances, but also to the less spectacular. Hence Port Elizabeth, with a mixed heritage of nineteenth- and early twentieth-century public and domestic architecture, has established a heritage walk for visitors to the city (O'Brien, 1979). Other towns have similar schemes providing a cross-section of the sites of historic and other interest to the tourist. Significantly the Historic Monuments Commission has been declaring an ever increasing number of domestic as well as public buildings as National Monuments, which are therefore retained in the urban fabric of rapidly changing towns. This policy has its opponents as current redevelopment may become impossible if too much is retained from the past. A balance is thus needed between the preservation of a meaningful visible heritage and the redevelopment of the cities according to the changing demands of the age.

Tourism has become significant in the present century as White South Africans have increasingly had the time and money to divert to it. It has taken many forms. The coastal holiday, either to bathe, walk, take the air, or do as little as possible, had an immediate impact in establishing the coastal re-sorts, first as offshoots of the main coastal cities and later as independent en-tities. The striving to establish an individual beach cottage as a second home gave rise to the spread of the coastal township, a movement which is still by no means complete despite the extensive changes to the appearance of the coastline, which they have wrought. The environmental impact has been se-rious and little conservation work has been undertaken as the coastal vegeta-tion is removed for building, thus pressure on the fragile environment is often damaging.

The most important impact upon the landscape has been the preservation of large areas as National and Provincial Parks. South Africa, in possession of the Kruger National Park, probably has the finest game reserve surviving in contemporary Africa, with a controlled population of the major fauna of southern and central Africa. The more speclialised parks elsewhere in the country also act as preserves of the natural flora, where agriculture and grazing have destroyed the ecosystem outside the boundaries. The newly established Karroo Parks at Graaff-Reinet and Beaufort West are attempting to re-create the natural Karroo environment, complete with the animals whose habitat it was two centuries ago. It is regrettable that a number of species which should be present in these parks, such as the quagga, no longer exist. Through the preservation of a portion of the country's wildscape, tourism has played a significant role in landscape evolution, much of which has come through state intervention.

The resorts, whether for mineral waters, gambling or enjoyment of the natural or historic landscapes are well represented throughout South Africa. Facilities at these and more generally at hotels, camping grounds and caravan parks reflect a high degree of mobility in the country. New resorts are opened periodically as the old ones become more crowded, and the advance booking becomes more pressing. Except in Transkei, Bophuthatswana and Venda, state-controlled resorts are segregated, so that either people other than Whites may not stay in them, or separate resort facilities are provided. Indeed a separate private, Blacks only, game reserve has been established close to the Kruger National Park. With the rising demand for recreational facilities the planned resort, rather than the extensive game or nature reserve would appear to be the most likely development, along the lines of the highly successful Pilansberg scheme in Bophuthatswana.

11

The changing landscape

The landscape is not static, but one of constant change. Its tangible history in South Africa is short, compared with countries of old civilisations where structures, or at least the major ruins and outlines of structures, are evident from a long period of human endeavour. The visible record in the landscape of South Africa is relatively brief, and as a result has comparatively little tradition to go by. Hence changes are acceptable on a scale which would be rejected in the more stable countries of the world. Several factors have led to rapid change, in the recent past, and are likely to result in accelerated change in the future. The most important, because of its ripple effects, is the high rate of population growth. South Africa exhibits many of the demographic features of Third World countries, with an annual population growth rate of approximately 3 per cent. This has resulted in a rapid rise in rural densities and a massive migration to the cities.

The population shifts have caused the build-up of great pressures within the metropolitan areas, where problems of housing and employment have been severe. Established patterns have become untenable and major re-appraisals are currently in progress, which may result in extensive changes in job opportunities and housing provision. It is possibly in the political arena that changes have been most remarkable. Acts of Parliament control who may do what and where, to a high degree. Thus many landscapes can only be explained in terms of the relevant legislation. Change, of some currently unknown nature, is projected for the 1980s and it may be expected that to some extent areas will be transformed through the direct intervention of the State. As a reaction to change, increasing concern has been felt among the dominant White community for the need to maintain a link with the past. Thus the preservation of the symbolic landscapes of South Africa is as much an element of change as the change itself.

Population growth

The impact of the growth in population has been remarkable. The population of South Africa has increased in the present century from 6 million in 1911 to 28 million in 1980. In the 20 years 1960–80 the population virtually doubled and is likely to do so again by the end of the century.

These figures alone give some idea of the immensity of the problems facing South Africa. In the remaining 20 years of the century almost as many houses will have to be built as were built in the previous 200 years. Growth has not been uniform in geographical extent, nor is it expected to be so for the remainder of the century. The urban areas and the Black states have experienced the highest rates of population growth, with the attraction of the opportunities in the towns and the restrictions on the movement of population from the Black states. Thus the urban population which stood at 1½ million in 1911, exhibited a ninefold increase to 14 million in 1980. Separate figures for the Black states are not so readily available, but they would appear to have increased in total from 2 million to 11 million in the same period.

The growth of the towns has been a phenomenon of the first order. Towns, apart from the major mining and port cities, remained small until the 1930s. In 1936 only two cities exceeded 250 000 persons. In 1980 there were eight such cities, four of which exceeded 1 000 000 persons. The basic reason for this explosion was the development of manufacturing and service industries. The Second World War was a period of economic impetus for South Africa and out of it came the self-generating growth of industry, which has demanded more and more workers in the towns. Opportunities however attracted more than the number of jobs available with the resultant emergence of the slums and shanties of the 1940s and 1950s. There followed a major restructuring of the South African town and the virtual elimination of the shanties by the late 1960s. However, in the 1970s, under pressure of recession, slums became a significant element of South African towns once more. Extensive housing schemes are again projected and the removal of all shanties remains an official objective. However, in 1976 a shortage of over 300 000 houses was estimated. As between 1961 and 1976 under half that number had been built, the elimination of slum conditions in the foreseeable future appears unlikely, despite a rapidly expanding formal urban area. As living standards rise so better houses are required, hence it is Mitchell's Plain rather than the standard township/location house which may be in evidence in the future (Fig. 11.1). Thus after a period of uniformity in Black and Coloured housing provision, divergencies between shack and house are likely to increase in the 1980s.

The Black states have exhibited high rates of natural increase, together with a significant inflow of 'repatriated' people. The result has been increased pressure upon the land resources and an incipient urbanisation, whereby tracts of the Black states are functionally little more than dormitory suburbs for workers in the White areas. The classic use of the rural areas as an insurance policy where families can live, children can be brought up, and to which the old worker can retire, results in the unbalanced social structure of the Black states. The result is the core–periphery relationship within South

Fig. 11.1   Modern housing at Mitchell's Plain. (City Engineer, Cape Town)

Africa, with an apparent widening of the economic gap between the two. The attempts to create job opportunities in the Black states to stem the flow of labour to the White areas is only one part of a decentralisation programme to reduce the gap between core and periphery. The rehabilitation of the land has been one of the most significant aspects of plans to improve the conditions in the Black states and to cope with a rapidly increasing population. Several replanning strategies have been undertaken, but the results suggest that the dormitory aspect is increasing in significance and the agricultural output is decreasing in relative importance (Daniel, 1980).

The political imprint

The political imprint upon the landscape is profound, with a high degree of government regulation of economic activity and population movement. The basic division of the country into Black and White areas, which as yet have no fixed boundaries, has had a major impact upon the landscape. Hence the redetermination of boundaries which has taken place and is projected for the future, has resulted in extensive areas having their previous landscapes virtually erased and new ones imposed. The probable scale of redetermination in the 1980s would appear to be greater than in the 1970s, as the 'meaningful' consolidation of the Black states takes place. Consolidation has increasingly involved the resettlement of Blacks in areas previously

213

farmed by Whites. Often the process has created a considerable increase in the density of population and change in land usage.

Within the White areas, where a mixed population is regulated by a multitude of laws concerning who does what and where, legislation and subsequent regulations have determined rural production through substantial state intervention in agriculture within the commercial sector. The State has determined who farms which areas and has more recently restricted who shall live in the rural areas. Thus changes in the rural landscape reflect not only changes in technology, but also increased government intervention.

The urban areas are subject to the greatest degree of legislative control. Town planning schemes have been the usual appendage to most municipal government projects in recent times, regulating which areas should be zoned for various uses. In South Africa, the added regulations of racial zoning of residential and business areas have resulted in the distinctive South African city, with its separate suburbs for the various population groups. The disentangling of the groups has in turn usually resulted in the original town with its Central Business District and industrial area being zoned White, and the other groups being rehoused in locations or townships at some distance from the town centre. Thus by and large, the poor live on the periphery of the town as in the pre-industrial city. For many towns the generous provision of townlands by previous governments has enabled the new suburbs to be accommodated without much loss of farmland, and in an ordered manner.

The continuation of the programme of racial sorting appears uncertain. The fates of two Black townships situated in predominantly White sectors of their respective towns show divergent trends. In 1979 Walmer township in Port Elizabeth was finally declared non-conforming and its inhabitants will have to move to proclaimed Black areas. In the same year Alexandra township in Johannesburg was allowed to remain. Possibly the major re-zonings and population movements associated with the Group Areas Act of 1950 are nearing their end.

Although population growth has been substantial, the flow into the cities from the Black states has been partially stemmed through the legislation of influx control. The system attempted to regulate the number of Black people living in the towns according to the job opportunities available. Outside the Cape Province the policy has been largely effective, once the initial immigration of the 1940s and 1950s had been accommodated. Only in the Cape Province, where the Coloured population has not been subjected to influx control, have the squatter townships re-emerged, outside the Black states. The squatter settlements within the Black states have grown substantially, as little control has been exercised over the shifts in population within them – only between them and the White areas. The urbanisation of the Black states along the boundaries of the White areas noted in the Transvaal and Natal is likely to be increasingly felt, as state boundaries mark ever more noticeably different landscapes. The political programme to stem the potential and actual flow of Black workers from the Black states into the White areas has taken several forms, each with its own landscape impacts. Rural development programmes to provide a greater livelihood from the land were tackled in the 1960s, and are likely to remain a significant element in landscape transformation as the South African and Black states' Governments attempt to improve rural living standards. The South African Government also embarked upon a decentralisation programme, with the creation of first the border industrial areas and then the growth points within the Black states. New towns and industrial centres were planned and developed as a result of decisions on a national level.

The imprint of central authority upon the landscape also applies to the new capital cities which have arisen, as well as to the prestige projects which have been undertaken in both the Black states and the White areas. For example the holiday complex at Sun City (see Fig. 10.4) and the University of the North (see Fig. 2.1) are the direct consequence of government intervention creating new activities in the Black states for political reasons in the White areas, whether they be the ban on casinos or the segregation of University education.

Within the White areas decentralisation, which as yet has had com-paratively little impact, is likely to have new urgency as the problems of the Witwatersrand become more serious – particularly the water problem. Major projects similar to the Saldanha Bay and Richards Bay terminals, or the Secunda plant may continue as the South African Government invests its income from the gold mining industry in projects of a capital nature. The National Physical Development Plan envisaged growth points throughout much of the country and the redistribution of wealth and population under government control is a probable feature for the remainder of the century. This is possible recognising that few places will have to be planned for decline, and that planning involves the distribution of growth.

Control of expansion through the Physical Planning and Utilisation of Resources Act (1967) and the National Physical Development Plan (1975) aimed at the creation of new metropolitan areas to relieve pressure on the existing major metropolitan areas. New development axes, including a highly speculative one through the northern Cape, are designed to substantially change the economic pattern of the country. However, control will have to be considerably tighter than during the initial decade of planning, when the majority of applications to contravene the Act were allowed. It is probably through the distribution of government spending that some measure of redistribution is likely to occur.

Symbolic landscapes

Most landscapes are in part symbolic (Meinig, 1979). All countries have a vision of their own landscape and elements within it. It may thus be questioned: Is there a symbolic and distinctive South African landscape? First

215

Fig. 11.2   Cenotaph and City Hall, Durban. (South African Railways)

a qualification must be introduced. The country lacks the massive constructions of the indigenous peoples such as those present in Zimbabwe, which are symbolic and inspiring for that country. In the built environment few indigenous constructions are unique to the country, and it is often from the remainder of Black Africa that inspiration is sought. Next, if the immigrant groups are considered, the British introduced colonial styles, recognisable in Canada or Australia, and little that was especially South African. Landscapes deliberately created as symbolic, such as the Durban City Hall and Cenotaph (Fig. 11.2) or Kroonstad Church Square (Fig. 11.3), are not unique as they are the products of their age rather than country. Similarly the Indian immigrants introduced their own landscapes akin to those implanted by emigrants to the West Indies or Mauritius. The major innovative group to date has been the Cape–Dutch or Afrikaner nation.

Early Dutch settlement attempted to re-create the Netherlands at the Cape. The towns and villages reflected strong Dutch influence, but owing to the plenteousness of the land, they were not as crowded or as restricted as in the metropolis. Modifications became apparent and a unique Cape–Dutch architectural style emerged, with thatched roofs, whitewashed walls and the distinctive gable (Fig. 11.4). The style in its association with the Dutch–South African heartland, became a truly national style, and was transported

Fig. 11.3   Kroonstad War Memorial and Dutch Reformed Church. (South African Railways)

as part of the cultural baggage of the White population across the subcontinent. Further, it was perceived as a South African style by the British who copied it. Thus not only is the gable to be found throughout the republican Orange Free State and Transvaal, but it was adopted for such contrasting entities as Hilton College, the private school for boys in Natal and the Duke of Westminster's estate designed by Sir Herbert Baker, in the Orange Free State (Fig. 11.5). The construction of areas such as Bryntirion, the government enclave in Pretoria, similarly looked to the Cape heartland for inspiration.

Domestic architectural styles have continued to be influenced by the Cape–Dutch heritage, despite a slackening of interest in the late colonial period when the prevailing British styles became popular. Nevertheless, the gable continued to be attached to many British colonial buildings. In the present era Cape–Dutch has become one of a proliferation of styles represented in the new private housing estates, particularly in the White areas, although this is invariably mixed with 'Spanish Mission', 'Contemporary', and numerous others. Thus 'Cape–Dutch' houses are to be found throughout the country. Significantly, the smaller houses originally built in the mission stations and the Malay and Coloured quarters and British Settler regions have not inspired modern domestic architecture.

If a building style has become symbolic, are there other elements which can be viewed as a distinctively South African landscape? The vineyards and mountains of the western Cape are commonly advertised and presented as the cradle area of the country and representative of the historic base from which White settlement originated. The 'English settler' country of the eastern Cape is more nebulous. The Karroo landscape of the extensive plains and isolated flat-topped hills is a common image of the centre of the country, yet largely shunned as too bleak; although it is possibly one of the other significant White South African images of the rural landscape. In the Black areas images of complete landscapes are recognisable, but are often idealised (Hugo, 1975).

It is the towns which provide further images of South Africa. Little could be more symbolic than the mine dumps and skyscrapers of Johannesburg as representing the transformation of South Africa through its mineral wealth. But just as the slave quarters and the poorer villages are forgotten in the image of the western Cape, so the shanties and locations are lost in the projected image of Johannesburg. Symbolic landscapes are highly selective in their form, and liable to changes of fashion with changing times as witnessed by South Africa's northern neighbour within the course of 1980.

Fig. 11.4 (*Above*) Cape–Dutch homestead (Boschendal, Groot Drakenstein), western Cape. (South African Railways)

Fig. 11.5 (*Below*) Duke of Westminster's estate homestead, 1904. The estate buildings were designed by Sir Herbert Baker in the Art and Craft style prevalent in England, but with some South African touches, such as the gable. (Anne Christopher)

Landscapes are emotional entities which have deep political connotations. Thus the landscape of South Africa reflects the political as well as the economic history of the country, in a way which makes even its appearance contentious. The recognition of this fact may prompt a more careful study of the landscape, and its reinterpretation and evaluation in the light of present circumstances.

Bibliography

Acocks, H. P. H. (1975) *Veld Types of South Africa*, Botanical Research Institute, Pretoria.

Adam, H. and Giliomee, H. (1979) *Ethnic Power Mobilized: can South Africa change?* Yale University Press, New Haven and London.

Beavon, K. S. O. (1970) *Land Use Patterns in Port Elizabeth*, Balkema, Cape Town.

Beavon, K. S. O. (1977) *Central Place Theory: a reinterpretation*, Longman, London.

Bell, T. (1973) *Industrial Decentralisation in South Africa*, Oxford University Press, Cape Town.

Best, A. C. G. (1971) South Africa's border industries: the Tswana example, *Annals of the Association of American Geographers*, **61**, 329–44.

Best, A. C. G. and Young, B. S. (1972a) Capitals for Homelands, *Journal for Geography*, **3**, 1043–55.

Best, A. C. G. and Young, B. S. (1972b) Homeland consolidation: the case of Kwa Zulu, *South African Geographer*, **4**, 63–74.

Best, R. H. and Rogers, A. W. (1973) *The Urban Countryside*, Faber, London.

Blenk, J. and Von der Ropp, K. (1977) Republic of South Africa: is partition a solution?, *South African Journal of African Affairs*, **7**, 21–32.

Blignaut, C. S. (1975) Thoughts on rural reform and factors which influence the location decisions of farmers, *Agrekon*, **14**(3), 8–15.

Board, C. (1962) *The Border Region*, Oxford University Press, Cape Town.

Board, C., Davies, R. J. and Fair, T. J. D. (1970) The structure of the South African space economy: an integrated approach, *Regional Studies*, **4**, 367–92.

Bophuthatswana (1977) *The Republic of Bophuthatswana*, Chris van Rensburg, Johannesburg.

Botswana (1977) *National Development Plan, 1976–81*, Government Printer, Gaberone.

Bradlow, F. R. and Cairns, M. (1978) *The Early Cape Muslims*, Balkema, Cape Town.

Brand, J. G. (1979) *Building a new town: city of Cape Town's Mitchell's Plain*, City Engineer's Department, Cape Town.

Browett, J. G. (1976) The application of a spatial model to South Africa's development regions, *South African Geographical Journal*, **58**, 118–29.

Browett, J. G. (1977) Export base theory and the evolution of the South African space economy, *South African Geographical Journal*, **59**, 18–29.

Browett, J. G. and Fair, T. J. D. (1974) South Africa 1870–1970: a view of the spatial system, *South African Geographical Journal*, **56**, 111–20.

Browett, J. G. and Hart, T. (1977) The distribution of White minority groups in Johannesburg, *South African Geographer*, **5**, 404–12.

Bundy, C. (1979) *The Rise and Fall of the South African Peasantry*, Heinemann, London.

Byrne, J. C. (1848) *Emigrants' Guide to Port Natal*, Effingham Wilson, London.

Chase, J. C. (1843) *The Cape of Good Hope and Algoa Bay*, Pelham Richardson, London.

Christopher, A. J. (1971) Colonial land policy in Natal, *Annals of the Association of American Geographers*, **61**, 560–75.

Christopher, A. J. (1973a) Environmental perception in southern Africa, *South African Geographical Journal*, **55**, 14–22.

Christopher, A. J. (1973b) *Land Ownership on the Port Elizabeth Rural–Urban Fringe*, Institute for Planning Research, University of Port Elizabeth, Port Elizabeth.

Christopher, A. J. (1974) Government land policies in southern Africa, pp. 208–25 in Ironside R. G. *et al.* (eds) *Frontier Settlement*, Department of Geography, University of Alberta, Edmonton.

Christopher, A. J. (1976a) The emergence of livestock regions in the Cape Colony 1855–1911, *South African Geographer*, **5**, 310–20.

Christopher, A. J. (1976b) The variability of the southern African standard farm, *South African Geographical Journal*, **58**, 107–17.

Christopher, A. J. (1976c) *Southern Africa*, Dawson, Folkestone.

Ciskei, Department of Agriculture and Forestry (1976) *An Outline of the Keiskamma Irrigation Scheme*, Ciskei Government, Zwelitsha.

Ciskei (1980) *Report of the Ciskei Commission*, Conference Associates, Johannesburg.

Clark, E. A. (1977) Port sites and perception: the development of the southern and eastern Cape coast in the nineteenth century, *South African Geographical Journal*, **59**, 150–67.

Cole, M. M. (1961) *South Africa*, Methuen, London.

Cook, G. P. (1975) *Spatial Dynamics of Business Growth in the Witwatersrand*, Department of Geography, University of Chicago, Chicago.

Cook, G. P. (1980) Scattered towns or an urban system?, pp. 30–47 in Charton, N. (ed.) *Ciskei: Economics and Politics of Dependence in a South African Homeland*, Croom Helm, London.

Croft, L. T. (1970) A comparative study of the South African urban scene, pp. 65–88 in Watts, H. L. (ed.) *Focus on Cities*, Institute for Social Research, University of Natal, Durban.

Daniel, J. B. McI. (1973) A geographical study of pre-Shakan Zululand, *South African Geographical Journal*, **55**, 23–31.

Daniel, J. B. McI. (1975) *Survey of the Cape Midlands and Karroo Regions, Vol. 5-A Geographical Analysis of Farming*, Institute of Social Economic Research, Rhodes University, Grahamstown.

Daniel, J. B. McI. (1980) The development of Ciskeian agriculture, *South African Geographical Journal*, **62**.

Davenport, T. R. H. (1971) *The Beginnings of Urban Segregation in South Africa: The Natives (Urban Areas) Act of 1923 and its Background*, Institute of Social and Economic Research, Rhodes University, Grahamstown.

Davies, D. H. (1965) *Land Use in Central Cape Town: a study in urban geography*, Longman, Cape Town.

Davies, D. H. and Beavon, K. S. O. (1973) *Changes in Land-Use patterns in Central Cape Town, 1957–1964*, Department of Geography, University of the Witwatersrand, Johannesburg.

Davies, R. J. (1963) The growth of the Durban metropolitan area, *South African Geographical Journal*, **45**, 15–44.

Davies, R. J. (1967) The South African urban hierarchy, *South African Geographical Journal*, **49**, 9–19.

Davies, R. J. (1972) *The Urban Geography of South Africa*, Institute for Social Research, University of Natal, Durban.

Davies, R. J. and Cook, G. P. (1968) Reappraisal of the South African urban hierarchy, *South African Geographical Journal*, **50**, 116–32.

Davies, R. J. and Rajah, D. S. (1965) The Durban C.B.D.: boundary delimitation and racial dualism, *South African Geographical Journal*, **47**, 45–58.

Davies, R. J. and Young, B. S. (1969) The economic structure of South African cities, *South African Geographical Journal*, **51**, 19–37.

Davies, R. J. and Young, B. S. (1970a) Manufacturing in South African cities, *Journal for Geography*, **3**, 595–605.

Davies, R. J. and Young, B. S. (1970b) Manufacturing and size of place in the South African urban system, *Journal for Geography*, **3**, 699–713.

Davies, W. J. (1971) *Patterns of Non-White Population Distribution in Port Elizabeth with Special Reference to the Application of the Group Areas Act*, Institute for Planning Research, University of Port Elizabeth, Port Elizabeth.

Davies, W. J. (1972) *Urban Bantu Retail Activities, Consumer Behaviour, and Shopping Patterns: a study of Port Elizabeth*, Institute for Planning Research, University of Port Elizabeth, Port Elizabeth.

De Jager, E. J. (1964) Settlement types of the Nguni and Sotho tribes, *Fort Hare Papers*, **3**, 19–30.

De Swardt, S. J. J. (1970) Subsistence and commercial agriculture, *Agrekon*, **9**(2), 3–9.

DeVilliers, A. (1978) A new approach for the planning and development of smallholder irrigation schemes in the Black states of South Africa, *Agrekon*, **17**(4), 8–13.

Dewar, D. and Uytenbogaardt, R. (1977) *Housing: a comparative evaluation of urbanism in Cape Town*, Urban Problems Research Unit, University of Cape Town, Cape Town.

Du Preez, P. H. (1975) Agricultural development in a dualistic framework, *Agrekon*, **14**(1), 7–12.

Eloff, C. C. (1980) *Oos-Vrystaatse Grensgordel*, Human Sciences Research Council, Pretoria.

Elphick, R. and Giliomee, H. (eds) (1979) *The Shaping of South African Society 1652–1820*, Longman, London.

Els, W. C. (1975) Die Groot-Visrivierbesproeiingstelsel as 'n geografiese probleem, *Acta Geographica*, **2**, 66–84.

Fagan, G. and Fagan, G. (1975) *Church Street in the Land of Waveren*, Tulbagh Restoration Committee, Tulbagh.

Fair T. J. D. (1965) The core–periphery concept and population growth in South Africa 1911–1960, *South African Geographical Journal*, **47**, 59–71.

Fair, T. J. D. (1976) Polarisation, dispersion and decentralisation in the South African space economy, *South African Geographical Journal*, **58**, 40–56.

Fair, T. J. D. (1977) The Witwatersrand – structure, stage, strategy, *South African Geographer*, **5**, 380–9.

Feely, J. M. (1980) Did Iron Age Man have a role in the history of Zululand's wilderness landscapes? *South African Journal of Science*, **76**, 150–2.

Ferrario, F. (1976) *The Tourist Landscape: a method of evaluating tourist potential and its application to South Africa*, University Microfilms International, Ann Arbor.

Gillooly, J. F. and Dyer, T. G. J. (1979) On the spatial and temporal variations of maize yields over South Africa, *South African Geographical Journal*, **61**, 111–8.

Granelli, R. and Levitan, R. (1978) *Urban Black Housing: a review of existing conditions in the Cape peninsula, with some guidelines for change*, Urban Problems Research Unit, University of Cape Town, Cape Town.

Great Britain (1901) *Report of the Land Settlement Commission, South Africa*, Cd. 627, HMSO, London.

Great Britain, Emigrants Information Office (1888) *Handbook No. 9 – Cape of Good Hope*, HMSO, London.

Greyling, J. J. C. and Davies, R. J. (1970) *Indian Agricultural Holdings on the Natal North Coast – land subdivision, land ownership and land occupation*, Natal Town and Regional Planning Commission, Pietermaritzburg.

Guelke, L. (1976) Frontier settlement in early Dutch South Africa, *Annals of the Association of American Geographers*, **66**, 25–42.

Harris, R. C. and Guelke, L. (1977) Land and society in early Canada and South Africa, *Journal of Historical Geography*, **3**, 135–53.

Hart, G. H. T. (1967) The bar problem of Durban Harbour, *South African Geographical Journal*, **49**, 95–103.

Hart, G. H. T. (1969) The structure of Braamfontein: its nodes and surfaces, *South African Geographical Journal*, **51**, 73–87.

Hart, G. H. T. (1977) Business cycles and the housing market in the core of the primate centre, *South African Geographical Journal*, **59**, 117–29.

Hart, T. (1976a) The evolving pattern of élite white residential areas in Johannesburg 1911–1970, *South African Geographical Journal*, **58**, 68–75.

Hart, T. (1976b) Patterns of Black residence in the White residential areas of Johannesburg, *South African Geographical Journal*, **58**, 141–50.

Haswell, R. F. (1979) South African towns on European plans, *Geographical Magazine*, **51**, 686–94.

Hattingh, P. S. (1973) Population counts and estimates in a Bantu rural area, *South African Geographical Journal*, **55**, 40–7.

Heathcote R. L. (1975) *Australia*, Longman, London.

Henderson, H. J. R. (1967) Towards the statistical definition of agricultural regions in South Africa, pp. 491–508 in Davies, R. J., Preston-Whyte, R. A. and Young, B. S. (eds) *Jubilee Conference Proceedings*, South African Geographical Society, Durban.

Henning, C. (1975) *Cultural History of Graff-Reinet*, Bulpin, Cape Town.

Holzner, L. (1978) Processes and patterns of urbanisation in the Republic of South Africa, *Geographia Polonica*, **39**, 123–42.

Hoskins, W. G. (1955) *The Making of the English Landscape*, Hodder and Stoughton, London.

Hoskins, W. G. (1978) *One Man's England*, BBC, London.

Hugo, M. L. (1975) Die Waardebepaling van Natuurskoon as Buitelugontspanningshulpbron, *South African Geographer*, **5**, 29–40.

Huttenback, R. A. (1976) *Racism and Empire: White settlers and colored immigrants in the British self-governing colonies, 1830–1910*, Cornell University Press, Ithaca.

Inskeep, R. R. (1978) *The Peopling of Southern Africa*, David Philip, Cape Town.

Jackson, S. P. and Tyson, P. D. (1971) *Aspects of Weather and Climate over Southern Africa*, Department of Geography and Environmental Studies, University of the Witwatersrand, Johannesburg.

Johnson, H. B. (1976) *Order Upon the Land. The US Rectangular Land Survey and the upper Mississippi country*, Oxford University Press, New York.

King, L. C. (1963) *South African Scenery*, Oliver and Boyd, Edinburgh.

Kokot, D. F. (1948) *An investigation into the evidence bearing on recent climatic changes over southern Africa*, Irrigation Department, Pretoria.

Lemon, A. (1976) *Apartheid: a geography of separation*, Saxon House, London.

Lenta, G. (1978) *Development or Stagnation?: agriculture in KwaZulu*, Department of Economics, University of Natal, Durban.

Lewcock, R. (1963) *Early Nineteenth Century Architecture in South Africa: a study of the interaction of two cultures 1795–1837*, Balkema, Cape Town.

Lewis, P. R. B. (1966) A 'city within a city' – the creation of Soweto, *South African Geographical Journal*, **48**, 45–85.

Liebenberg, E. C., Rootman, P. J. and van Huyssteen, M. K. R. (1976) *The South African Landscape: exercise manual for map and air photo interpretation*, Butterworths, Durban.

Lipton, M. (1977) South Africa: two agricultures? pp. 72–86 in Wilson, F., Kooy, A. and Hendril, D. (eds.) *Farm Labour in South Africa*, David Philip, Cape Town.

Mashile, G. G. and Pirie, G. H. (1977) Aspects of housing allocation in Soweto, *South African Geographical Journal*, **59**, 139–49.

Meinig, D. W. (ed.) (1979) *The Interpretation of Ordinary Landscapes: geographical essays*, Oxford University Press, New York.

Mills, M. E. and Wilson, M. (1952) *Keiskammahoek Rural Survey, 4 – Land Tenure*, Shuter and Shooter, Pietermaritzburg.

Moll, J. C. (1977) Dorpstigting in die Oranje-Vrystaat: 1854–1864, *Contree*, **2**, 23–8.

Moolman, H. J. (1977) The creation of living space and homeland consolidation with reference to Bophuthatswana, *South African Journal of African Affairs*, **7**, 149–63.

Morris, P. (1980) *Soweto: a review of existing conditions and some guidelines for change*, Urban Foundation, Johannesburg.

Mountain, E. D. (1968) *Geology of Southern Africa*, Books of Africa, Cape Town.

Natal (1904) *Report of the Zululand Lands Delimitation Commission*, Government Printer, Pietersmaritzburg.

Natal Town and Regional Planning Commission (1974) *Natal South Coast: draft regional plan*, The Commission, Pietermaritzburg.

O'Brien, R. (1979) *The Donkin Heritage Trail*, Historical Society, Port Elizabeth.

Olivier, J. J. (1976) Maatskappydorpe in Natal: Problematiek en Riglyne, *South African Geographer*, **5**, 198–204.

Pachai, B. (1979) *South Africa's Indians. The evolution of a minority*, University Press of America, Washington.

Palmer, R. and Parsons, N. (eds) (1977) *The Roots of Rural Poverty in Central and Southern Africa*, Heinemann, London.

Picton-Seymour, D. (1977) *Victorian Buildings in South Africa*, Balkema, Cape Town.

Pirie, G. H., Rogerson, C. M. and Beavon, K. S. O. (1980) Covert power in South Africa: the geography of the Afrikaner Broederbond, *Area*, **12**, 97–104.

Potgieter, F. J. (1977) *Developing Bophuthatswana: suggestions for a National Plan*, Institute for Regional Planning, Potchefstroom University, Potchefstroom.

Pretorius, D. A. (1979) *The Crustal Architecture of Southern Africa*, Geological Society of South Africa, Johannesburg.

Rogerson, C. M. (1975) *Government and the South African Industrial Space Economy*, Department of Geography and Environmental Studies, University of the Witwatersrand, Johannesburg.

Rogerson, C. M. and Franke, L. D. (1976) Geographers look at South Africa: a view from within, *South African Geographer*, **4**, 327–31.

Ross, R. (1976) *Adam Kok's Griquas: a study in the development of stratification in South Africa*, Cambridge University Press, Cambridge.

Sadie, J. L. (1973) *Projections of the South African Population, 1970–2020*, Industrial Development Corporation, Johannesburg.

Schoeman, B. M. (1977) *Parlementere Verkiesings in Suid-Afrika, 1910–1976*, Aktuele Publikasies, Johannesburg.

Scott, P. (1951) The Witwatersrand goldfield, *Geographical Review*, **41**, 561–89.

Scott, P. (1955) Cape Town: a multi-racial city, *Geographical Journal*, **121**, 149–57.

Smit, P. (1973) *Die Ontvolking van die Blanke Platteland – Onlangse Tendense*, University of Pretoria, Pretoria.

Smit, P. (1977) Basic features of the population of Bophuthatswana, *South African Journal of African Affairs*, **7**, 175–201.

Smit, P. (1979) Urbanisation in Africa: lessons for urbanisation in the homelands, *South African Geographical Journal*, **61**, 1–28.

Smit, P. and Booysen, J. J. (1977) *Urbanisation in the Homelands: a new dimension in the urbanisation process of the Black population of South Africa*, Institute for Plural Societies, University of Pretoria, Pretoria.

Smith, D. M. (1973) *An Introduction to Welfare Geography*, Department of Geography and Environmental Studies, University of the Witwatersrand, Johannesburg.

Smith, D. M. (ed.) (1976) *Separation in South Africa*, 2 vols: 1, *People and Policies*; 2, *Homelands and Cities*, Department of Geography, Queen Mary College, London.

Smith, D. M. (1977) *Human Geography: a welfare approach*, Edward Arnold, London.

Smuts, F. (ed.) (1979) *Stellenbosch: three hundred years*, Town Council, Stellenbosch.

South Africa (1955) *Summary of the Report of the Commission for the Socio-Economic Development of the Bantu Areas, within the Union of South Africa*, U.G. 61–'55, Government Printer, Pretoria.

South Africa (1960) *Report of the Commission of Inquiry into European Occupancy of the Rural Areas*, Government Printer, Pretoria.

South Africa (1970) *Second Report of the Commission of Enquiry into Agriculture*, R.P. 84/ 1970, Government Printer, Pretoria.

South Africa (1978) *Official Place Names in the Republic of South Africa and in South West Africa*, Government Printer, Pretoria.

South Africa (1980) *South Africa, 1979: Official Yearbook of the Republic of South Africa*, Chris van Rensburg, Johannesburg.

South Africa, Department of Agriculture (1978) *Agriculture in South Africa* (2nd edn), Chris van Rensburg, Johannesburg.

226

South Africa, Department of Community Development (1979) *Community Development: the South African scene*, Chris Van Rensburg, Johannesburg.

South Africa, Department of Planning and the Environment (1975) *National Physical Development Plan*, Government Printer, Pretoria.

South African Institute of Race Relations' (1979) *Survey of Race Relations in South Africa, 1978*, The Institute, Johannesburg.

Stander, E. (1970) South African geography – trends and prospects, *South African Geographical Journal*, **52**, 3–12.

Steyn, J. N. (1972) Die lokalisering van karavaanparke in Suid-Kaapland, *South African Geographer*, **4**, 19–24.

Steyn, J. N. (1974) 'n Evaluering van die Ontspanningshulpbronpotensiaal van die Suid-Kaapse Kus, *South African Geographer*, **4**, 297–307.

Steyn, J. N. (1975) Vakansiehuise: 'n nuwe komponent in die Suid-Afrikaanse geografiese spektrum, *Acta Geographica,* **2**, 148–72.

Streak, M. (1970) *Lord Milner's Immigration Policy for the Transvaal, 1897–1905*, Rand Afrikaans University, Johannesburg.

Taylor, V. (1975) The recreational business district: a component of the East London urban morphology, *South African Geographer*, **5**, 139–44.

Thom, H. B. (ed.) (1952) *Journal of Jan Van Riebeeck 1651–1662*, Volume 1, Balkema, Cape Town.

Thorrington-Smith, Rosenberg and McCrystal (1978) *Towards a Plan for KwaZulu: a preliminary development plan*, KwaZulu Government, Ulundi.

Tyrrell, B. H. (1968) *The Tribal Peoples of South Africa*, Books of Africa, Cape Town.

Tyson, P. D. and Dyer, T. G. J. (1978) The predicted above-normal rainfall of the seventies and the likelihood of drought in the eighties, *South African Journal of Science*, **74**, 372–77.

Tyson, P. D., Dyer, T. G. J. and Mametse, M. N. (1975) Secular changes in South African rainfall, 1880–1972, *Quarterly Journal of the Royal Meteorological Society*, **101**, 817–33.

Vance, J. E. (1970) *The Merchant's World: the geography of wholesaling*, Prentice Hall, Englewood Cliffs.

Van der Merwe, I. J. (1975) Die Evolusiebaan van die sentrale sakekern-die geval van Kimberley, *Acta Geographica*, **2**, 127–147.

Van der Merwe, I. J. and Nel, A. (1975) *Die Stad en sy Omgewing*, Universiteits-Uitgewers, Stellenbosch.

Van der Merwe, P. J. (1938) *Die Trekboer in die Geskiedenis van die Kaapkolonie*, Nasionale Pers, Cape Town.

Van Jaarsveld, F. A. (1975) *Van van Riebeeck tot Verwoerd 1652–1974: 'n inleiding tot die geskiedenis van die Republiek van Suid-Afrika*, Perskor, Johannesburg.

Van Reenen, T. H. (1962, with supplements) *Land: its ownership and occupation in South Africa*, Juta, Cape Town.

Van Zyl, J. A. (1967) Blanke vestigingspatrone in die Oranje Vrystaat, *Acta Geographica*, **1**, 155–90.

Venda (1979) *A framework for development planning in Venda*, Venda Government, Sibasa.

Walton, J. (1955) *Vroeë plase en nedersettings in die Oranje Vrystaat*, Balkema, Cape Town.

Walton, J. (1974) *Water mills, wind mills and horse mills of South Africa*, Stuik, Cape Town.

Wellington, J. H. (1955) *Southern Africa: a geographical study*, Cambridge University Press, Cambridge.

Western, J. (1978) Knowing one's place: 'The Coloured People' and the Group Areas Act in Cape Town, pp. 297–318 in Ley, D. and Samuels, M. S. (eds) *Humanistic Geography: Prospects and Problems*, Croom Helm, London.

Whittlesey, D. (1935) The impress of effective central authority upon the landscape, *Annals of the Association of American Geographers*, **25**, 85–97.

Williams, M. (1974) *The Making of the South Australian Landscape*, Academic Press, London.

Wilson, F. (1972) *Labour in the South African Gold Mines, 1911–1969*, Cambridge University Press, Cambridge.

Wilson, M. and Thompson, L. (1969) *The Oxford History of South Africa*, vol. 1, Clarendon Press, Oxford.

Wright, J. B. (1971) *Bushman Raiders of the Drakensberg, 1840–1870*, University of Natal Press, Pietermaritzburg.

Young, B. S. (1973) Two intra-metropolitan industrial models, *South African Geographer*, **4**, 131–8.

Index

Page numbers printed in italics refer to illustrations